DK
POCKET
ENCYCLOPEDIA

COOK'S
INGREDIENTS

Contributing editor
Adrian Bailey

DORLING KINDERSLEY • LONDON

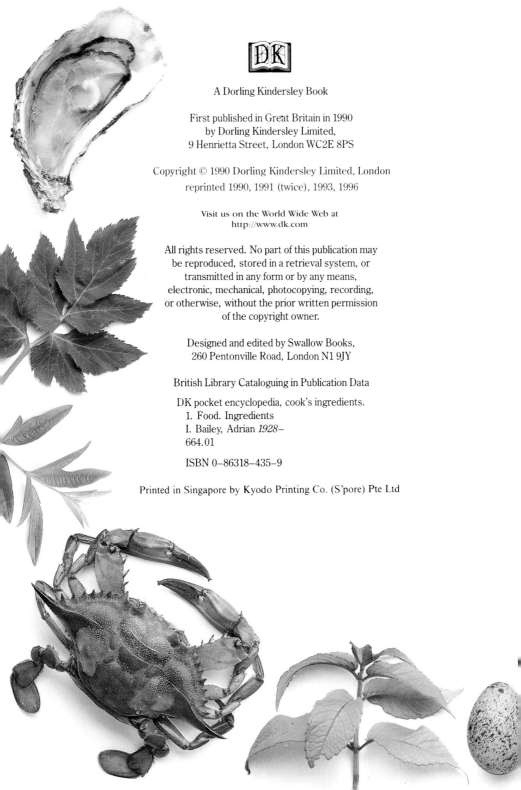

DK

A Dorling Kindersley Book

First published in Great Britain in 1990
by Dorling Kindersley Limited,
9 Henrietta Street, London WC2E 8PS

Designed and edited by Swallow Books,
260 Pentonville Road, London N1 9JY

British Library Cataloguing in Publication Data

DK pocket encyclopedia, cook's ingredients.
1. Food. Ingredients
I. Bailey, Adrian *1928–*
664.01

ISBN 0–86318–435–9

Printed in Singapore by Kyodo Printing Co. (S'pore) Pte Ltd

CONTENTS

Introduction 6

INTRODUCTION

Today's shopper is faced with a bewildering array of ingredients. Do you know what "vegetable spaghetti" is? Have you ever wondered why lobsters turn red when boiled? How do you think parmesan cheese is made? And do you really know your onions? There are, of course, thousands of recipe books that give instructions for assembling meals, but almost all of them neglect the most important thing of all – that good cooking and good eating depend on a knowledge of the ingredients and the best way to prepare them.

In recent years consumers have begun to scrutinize labels to see what they're *really* giving the family to eat – good wholesome food, or a plateful of preservatives. People are now demanding top-quality natural ingredients, and this has meant that the range of foodstuffs to be found in the shops has had to grow in response. Rice is no longer "just rice", it's basmati, patna or brown, and now a vast range of other cereals offers further alternatives: do you know what polenta, soy flour or matzoh meal are, or how to use them?

Recipes all too often ignore the breadth of the range of foods available. The delicatessen today is a feast for the eye, with mountains of cheeses and salamis. A look at the salad vegetables reveals many more types of lettuce and endive than were available just a few years ago – and nettles and thistles too. As for the fishmonger's slab, it offers us a taste of the seven seas as never before.

Written to help you through the maze of ingredients that can be found, this book is the ultimate armchair shopping guide, giving new breadth to your repertoire, whether you are a beginner or an experienced cook. It tells you where these primary foods originated, how they are produced, what nutritional values they have and how they are prepared for the table in different parts of the world.

The ingredients are grouped together with their near relatives, into a spectacular gallery of vegetables and pulses, herbs and spices, sauces and seasonings, fruit and nuts, cereals, dairy products and meats. There are hundreds of hints and tips on using each ingredient – is it best dried, flaked, sliced or peeled; how should it be cooked, or is it served raw; and what other foods does it complement?

Packed with mouth-watering photographs, this is both a fascinating read and an essential work of reference that will make your shopping and cooking more profitable – and eating a whole new pleasure.

VEGETABLES

VEGETABLES, LIKE FRUITS, ARE the edible products of certain plants. They share several characteristics: they are savoury rather than sweet, we add salt to them, and, in most countries, they are associated with poultry, meat or fish as part of a meal, or as an ingredient. Some vegetables are botanically classed as fruits: tomatoes are berries, and avocados are drupes, but both are commonly used as vegetables because they are not sweet. Some people would also add the distinction that vegetables are usually cooked, while fruits are eaten raw, but this is a very loose definition since we frequently eat vegetables raw in salads, and many dishes call for fruit that has been cooked.

The history of vegetable cultivation

All our cultivated vegetables have derived from primitive varieties whose origins are, in some cases, unknown, but we do know that many of our present-day vegetables have been cultivated since prehistoric times. We have evidence that peas were grown in Turkey by 6500 BC, from the wild pea (*Pisum elatus*) and that gourds, lima beans and perhaps maize were grown in Mexico before 5000 BC. It is also possible that the potato was then being harvested, and probably the tomato, too.

There was probably a spontaneous genesis of primitive vegetable farming in widely separate parts of the world – in China, the Middle East and South America. By 3000 BC the farmers in Mesopotamia were growing crops of turnips, onions, broad beans, peas and lentils, leeks, garlic and radishes.

From this early cultivation of food crops in western Asia, varieties began to spread towards Europe. The Greeks and Romans encouraged vegetable production on a fairly large scale and, in the wake of the Roman armies, local farmers began to grow the crops that the Romans had introduced: carrots, leeks, artichokes, cauliflower, garlic, onions and lettuces. The Islamic invaders of Spain, thrusting northwards towards France, paused long enough to plant rice, spinach, aubergines, carrots and citrus fruits.

By the Middle Ages, extensive vegetable farming was carried out in Europe, especially in the Low Countries, where market gardeners were able to export a proportion of their harvest. Following the Spanish conquest of South America in the late fifteenth century, there was an important exchange of crops between the Old World and the New. Throughout the sixteenth and seventeenth centuries crops were gradually established in both continents. From the Americas came sweetcorn, potatoes, sweet potatoes, tomatoes, peppers, kidney beans, pumpkins, Jerusalem artichokes and, despite their name, French beans. Settlers from Europe introduced to America broad beans, chick-peas, black-eyed peas, radishes, carrots, cabbages, okra and yams – black-eyed peas, okra and yams being brought on the slave ships from Africa.

The production of vegetables for the table became a well-developed industry, especially in France, when the chemist Nicolas Appert pioneered canned foods at the end of the eighteenth century. Appert's technique was soon to revolutionize the marketing of vegetables, and was not to be equalled in importance in this field until the American physicist, Clarence Birdseye, introduced a new process of freezing foods in 1929, which is widely used today.

Composition of vegetables

Flavour accounts for a very small percentage of a vegetable's composition. Most contain at least 80 per cent water, the remainder being carbohydrate, protein and fat. Squashes, in particular, contain a high percentage of water, while potatoes contain a great deal of starch, used by the vegetable as a reserve food supply. Invert sugars are also a food source, and sucrose is present in sweetcorn, carrots, parsnips, onions, and so on. When vegetables age, the woody lignin increases, water evaporates, and sugars become concentrated: old raw carrots appear to be sweeter than young ones. But sugars change as soon as the vegetable is separated from the plant (a good example is sweetcorn, which is often rushed straight from the stalk to the pot in order to preserve its taste).

Protein accounts for about 1 per cent of a vegetable's composition but can be as high as 4 per cent in sweetcorn and 8 per cent in legumes. Vegetables are also a useful source of vitamins, which can vary according to the time of day, the temperature, and when the vegetables were harvested. Sunshine increases the vitamin C in turnips, which also have more vitamin B if harvested in the morning; cabbages grown at 10–15°C (50–60°F) have a greater concentration of B vitamins, and a higher nutritive value when freshly harvested. These nutrients tend to concentrate in the outer leaves.

Each vegetable owes its unique character to the arrangement of cells and the various substances it contains. The cell walls are made of cellulose and lignin – a cell-building substance that produces such textures as fibrousness (globe artichokes), stringiness (celery) and crispness (carrots); crispness also depends on the water content. Cells are cemented together by pectin, a form of carbohydrate. Common factors in vegetables are water and starch; most contain a substantial amount of water, in particular squashes and vegetable marrows.

The familiar qualities of some vegetables are due to small amounts of chemical compounds, such as sulphur in brassicas – hence the far-reaching smell of boiled cabbage – while onions contain an enzyme that brings tears to the eyes. In addition, there are lipids or fats, organic acids, and pigments such as green chlorophyll, yellow and orange carotenoids, and purple or blue anthocyanins.

Vegetables in the kitchen
When choosing vegetables, you should obviously avoid those that are limp and wilting, discoloured or damaged by harvesting. Leaf vegetables need careful picking over to avoid serving garden pests on the plate. Vegetables should be prepared for the pot as simply as possible just before cooking. When peeled and cut, vegetables lose vitamins and nutrients if they are left in the air, or even more rapidly if they are left to soak in water. They should only be peeled thinly: vitamins are usually found just under the skin.

We cook vegetables in order to break down the starch and cellulose, and render them more digestible; heat achieves this, however we apply it. Ideally, most vegetables should be cooked as briefly as possible, to preserve their character, taste and freshness. Although boiled vegetables lose a quantity of their nutrients, the actual volume of cooking water makes no difference once the vegetable has been immersed. The cooking water of vegetables often contains valuable minerals and vitamins and is useful for soups. A good alternative to boiling or stir-frying is to cook vegetables in a steamer, while both pressure-cooking and microwave cooking preserve the maximum amount of nutritive elements present in vegetables.

On contact with air certain vegetables tend to discolour, regardless of whether they are cooked or raw. This is because certain enzymes cause oxidization. This activity can be halted by the addition of an acid, which is why cooks plunge celeriac and apples into acidulated water (water with a little lemon juice added) after peeling them. Blanching helps to preserve colour, especially in green vegetables, but some vegetable dyes are lost in the cooking process. Purple broccoli contains both chlorophyll (green) and anthocyanin (purple), the latter being water-soluble, so cooked broccoli always looks green. Red cabbage reacts like litmus paper – it turns blue in the presence of an alkali (the lime in tap water), so you need to add a dash of acid, such as vinegar, to preserve the colour.

Vegetables can be classified according to their botanical family, such as the brassica (cabbages) group, or by identifying the edible part: root, leaf, shoot and stem or bulb.

Leaf Vegetables

LETTUCE (*Lactuca sativa*)

Probably native to the Mediterranean region, but now cultivated worldwide, there are three main varieties of lettuce: crisphead, which has a tight solid head (the variety shown is 'iceberg'); cos or romaine, which has elongated, coarse leaves; and cabbage or round, which varies from the very soft-leaved to the robust. The little gem lettuce is a compact variety of dwarf cos. Although they may be braised or used in soups, lettuces are normally used raw in salads; lettuce hearts are an ingredient in *petits pois à la français*. Other varieties with red-tinged leaves have been developed over the past few years, such as feuille de chêne, lollo rosso and quattro stagioni. Lettuces are available all year round, but are not grown in midsummer in hot countries.

WATERCRESS (*Nasturtium officinale*)

High in vitamins, the clean, fresh, peppery taste of watercress greatly recommends it for salads. It is also used in soups, in oriental stir-fry dishes and as a garnish. Native to Europe, it is cultivated throughout the world and is available all year round.

SPINACH (*Spinacea oleracea*)

Thought to be of Persian origin, spinach has a pleasant acidic taste due to oxalic acid. It is an annual plant, but obtainable all year round. It is at its best eaten raw in salads or lightly cooked (usually boiled in a little water). The word "Florentine" denotes its use in recipes. New Zealand spinach (*Tetragonia expansa*), although not botanically related to spinach, looks and tastes similar and is prepared in the same way. It is a summer vegetable.

Cos or romaine lettuce

Watercress

Cabbage lettuce

Crisphead lettuce

Spinach

Dandelion

Lamb's lettuce

Mustard and cress

DANDELION
(*Taraxacum officinale*)

A wild meadow plant with a bright yellow flower and long tap root, dandelion leaves should be eaten young, before the plant flowers, as they become bitter. The blanched leaves are used for salads, especially in France and the American South. The roots make a coffee substitute, and are used in Japan as a vegetable.

LAMB'S LETTUCE
(*Valerianella olitoria*)

A wild plant indigenous to Europe, but now grown worldwide, this is also known as corn salad and in France as *mâche*. The leaves have a delicate, slightly bitter taste and are useful in winter salads.

MUSTARD (*Sinapis alba*) and CRESS (*Lepidium sativum*)

Mustard and cress are usually found in combination and are eaten at the seedling stage. They have a peppery taste and are used raw in salads and sandwiches. They are available all year round, and are easy to grow yourself.

ROCKET (*Eruca sativa*)

Native to the Mediterranean, this plant is grown for its leaves, which are slightly pungent and peppery in taste. They are used raw in salads or cooked like spinach.

Rocket

OTHER LEAF VEGETABLES

CALALOU
(*Colocasia esculenta*)
The West Indian and Creole name for the tops of the taro plant or Caribbean spinach is "callalloo greens". The leaves are used like cabbage.

CELTUCE (*Lactuca sativa*)
Originally from China, celtuce is a sort of hybrid lettuce with a celery texture and taste. It can be used raw in salads, or cooked and is available in the spring and summer.

LAND CRESS
(*Barbarea verna*)
Also known as American cress and winter cress, this is indigenous to Europe and America. It has a slightly peppery taste, is available in winter, and can be used in the same way as watercress, which it resembles.

SAMPHIRE
There are two unrelated samphires, both wild plants indigenous to Europe: rock samphire (*Crithmum maritinum*) and marsh samphire or glasswort (*Salicornia europaea*). Marsh samphire, a small, succulent plant, is used in summer salads or cooked as a vegetable; rock samphire, with fleshy, aromatic leaves, is cooked as a vegetable and can be pickled.

VINE LEAF (*Vitis vinifera*)

The vine, originally from the Mediterranean region, is now found worldwide. It is much used in Turkish, Greek and Middle Eastern cooking, and is best known in the form of *dolmades* (vine leaves stuffed with rice and minced meat). Sold fresh or packed in brine, they are also wrapped around game and used decoratively in fresh fruit dishes.

Vine leaf

SORREL (*Rumex acetosa*)

There are several varieties, but the main ones are common sorrel (shown here) and French sorrel (*Rumex scutatus*). A perennial plant native to Europe and Asia, and now also found in America and Australia, it has a refreshing, slightly sour taste (the name "*acetosa*" implies its acid character, mainly from oxalic acid). It is related to rhubarb. Sorrel can be used as a vegetable (raw, in salads, or cooked as a type of purée, like spinach) and as a herb (in soups and sauces and, with other herbs, as a stuffing for fish). It is available throughout the summer.

Sorrel

Radicchio

RADICCHIO
(*Cichorium endivia*)

This red-leafed member of the chicory family is from the Treviso area in northern Italy. The leaves are firm and crisp, with a slightly bitter, peppery taste. Its rich red colour makes it a dramatic addition to mixed salads and an excellent garnish. It is available all year round.

ENDIVE (*Cichorium endivia*)

This curly-leaved and slightly bitter-tasting plant is native to southern Asia and northern China. There are several varieties, including the curly endive or French frisée shown, and the more wavy Batavian endive or escarole. Used mainly in salads, they can also be braised, and are available winter and summer.

Endive

Swiss chard

Nettle

SWISS CHARD
(*Beta vulgaris*, var. *cicla*)

Also known as seakale beet, this is related to sugar beet, but the root is not used. There are other varieties, including ruby or rhubarb chard, which has red stems, and spinach beet, which tastes rather like spinach. The plants are valued for their firm stems, although the green leaves are also used. It is available from spring to midwinter.

NETTLE (*Urtica dioica*)

Available worldwide, nettle is a perennial plant that can be cooked in the same way as sorrel and spinach. The stinging hairs are destroyed by cooking. It is the basic ingredient of nettle soup, and is also used to make beer and tea.

Brassicas

SPRING GREENS
(*Brassica oleracea*, spp.)

All brassicas are native to Europe and western Asia. These greens – which are cabbages without hearts and are harvested when young cabbages are being thinned – are sold primarily in England. They are a good source of green vegetables when mature cabbages are scarce in early spring.

Spring greens

CAULIFLOWER
(*Brassica oleracea*, spp.)

Often referred to as the aristocrat of the cabbage family, cauliflowers were first cultivated in the Middle East, and known in Europe by the thirteenth century. Its flowers or "curds" are eaten raw or lightly cooked, and it is often served *au gratin* with a Béchamel sauce.

Cauliflower

Green kohlrabi

KOHLRABI (*Brassica oleracea*)

Kohlrabi, German for "cabbage-turnip", is a cabbage mutant that can be either purple or green. The thickened stem has a delicate turnip taste and may be boiled or grated raw into salads. The leaves can also be boiled and eaten.

Purple kohlrabi

BROCCOLI
(*Brassica oleracea*, spp.)

Related to the cauliflower, there are several varieties: white sprouting, purple sprouting, green or calabrese, purple hearting or purple cauliflower, and a perennial variety. They are eaten raw but are best steamed, and are excellent served with melted butter, Hollandaise or Béarnaise sauce. Broccoli is also used for hors d'œuvres and in soups. It is available all year round.

Green broccoli; calabrese

Purple hearting broccoli; purple cauliflower

KALE (*Brassica oleracea*, spp.)

There are many varieties of kale, both crinkly and smooth-leaved. It and its close relative collard probably originated in the eastern Mediterranean, where they have been cultivated for 2000 years. A winter vegetable, kale is rather coarse in texture but offers a good source of green vegetables in winter months. Kale is best poached, drained and served with butter.

Kale

BRUSSELS SPROUTS
(*Brassica oleracea*, spp.)

A type of miniature cabbage, Brussels sprouts are thought to have originated in Belgium. They grow from tall, woody stems, and should ideally be harvested as small buds, and cooked just long enough to retain some firmness and bite. They are available from late summer to mid spring. Recipes include cooking sprouts with chestnuts or walnuts. They can be cooked and creamed, sautéed, or made into soup. The leaves from the top of the main stalk can be used as a vegetable.

Brussels sprouts

Cabbages

Cabbages are classed according to season (spring, summer, autumn and winter varieties) and to type (semi-hearted, green-hearted, hard white and red). Spring cabbages are smooth-leaved, loose and small-hearted. Green-hearted may have round or conical hearts, and include the Savoy. Hard whites are the Dutch and winter white. Chinese cabbage has a more subtle taste than ordinary cabbage.

Savoy cabbage

SAVOY CABBAGE
(*Brassica oleracea*, spp.)

The Savoy is a type of green cabbage, probably of Italian origin. It is eaten both cooked and raw – it is very good sliced in salads – and its wrinkly leaves, which make a decorative alternative to the plain ones of the roundhead cabbage, are those used in recipes for stuffed cabbage leaves.

ROUNDHEAD CABBAGE
(*Brassica oleracea*, spp.)

Also known as the common cabbage, this is eaten raw or lightly cooked. Like the conical-shaped cabbage, it is available in summer and winter.

Roundhead cabbage

Pe-tsai

Pak-choi

Red cabbage (whole)

Red cabbage (cut)

White cabbage

PE-TSAI (*Brassica pekinensis*)

With its long shape, this variety of Chinese cabbage is similar to the cos lettuce. It is used a great deal stir-fried in Chinese cooking, but can also be eaten raw, and is interchangeable with ordinary cabbage. The midribs of the outer leaves can be cooked like asparagus. It is known in Japan as *hakusai*.

PAK-CHOI (*Brassica chinensis*)

At its best late in the year, the plant does not form a heart and the leaf is reminiscent of spinach or chard. It is usually eaten raw in salads, but can also be stir-fried with rice. It is used extensively in Chinese cooking.

RED CABBAGE
(*Brassica oleracea*, spp.)

Usually cooked with vinegar to preserve its colour, this is often served with game. In Britain, red cabbage is pickled, while the Dutch, Danes and Swiss stew it with apples and spices. It can also be eaten raw.

WHITE CABBAGE
(*Brassica oleracea*, spp.)

Also known as Dutch cabbage, this variety keeps well and is good for storing. Its crisp, tight head is particularly good for grating and is used for coleslaws and sauerkraut.

Shoot Vegetables

GLOBE ARTICHOKE
(*Cynara scolymus*)

Really a type of thistle, the globe artichoke is the flower head of a perennial plant native to north Africa, but now cultivated in Europe as a winter vegetable and in North America all year round. It can be pickled whole when small, and its tender base or heart is also sold canned and frozen. It can be baked, fried, boiled, stuffed and served with various sauces and dressings, such as vinaigrette, mayonnaise and Hollandaise sauce. The stalk of the head is often used blanched in soups and stews. Young, fresh artichokes may also be eaten raw.

BAMBOO (*Bambusa vulgaris*)

The white inner part of the young bamboo plant, bamboo shoots are conical and sold fresh in Asian markets, but cooked and canned everywhere else. Their crispness and slight acidity provide a good complement to pork in particular.

PALM HEARTS
(Family: *Palmaceae*)

A tropical delicacy, these are the tender terminal shoots of some varieties of palm trees. They may be eaten raw, but are sold pre-cooked and canned.

ASPARAGUS
(*Asparagus officinalis*)

The young shoot of a plant native to Europe, there are about 20 varieties, the most common being green (a weedier version is known in England as "sprue") and white, preferred by the French, Belgians, Italians and Germans. Asparagus is served hot with butter, or cooked and cold with vinaigrette. It is also used in soups, quiches, soufflés and other dishes, and is available fresh in spring and early summer.

Globe artichoke

White asparagus

Bamboo

Green asparagus

Palm hearts

FENNEL (*Foeniculum vulgare*)

A bulbous leafstalk native to Europe, Florence fennel tastes very much like aniseed. Available all year, it can be eaten raw, boiled, braised or grilled, used as a stuffing for rich meats, or sliced and served with cheese sauce.

Chicory

Celery

Fiddlehead fern

Fennel

CELERY (_Apium graveolens_)

Developed by Italian gardeners in the sixteenth century, there are several varieties of celery, some self-blanching, and some which need earth piled around the stems to blanch them. Available all year round, either fresh (in heads or loose sticks) or canned, celery is eaten raw or cooked.

CHICORY (_Cichorium intybus_)

Native to Europe and western Asia, but also grown in America, this is available from autumn to early summer. Slightly bitter, it is used raw in salads, braised or fried.

FIDDLEHEAD FERN
(_Pteridium aquilinium_)

Many varieties of this fern, also called bracken, grow wild in America and Europe. The young shoots can be served cooked, like broccoli, with Hollandaise sauce, or raw in salads. Available canned, or fresh in spring and summer.

OTHER SHOOT VEGETABLES

CARDOON
(_Cynara cardunculus_)
A thistle related to the globe artichoke, cardoon is indigenous to the Mediterranean region. Its blanched stalks are similar to celery, and are eaten raw or, alternatively, braised.

SEAKALE
(_Crambe maritima_)
A wild seashore plant indigenous to western Europe, seakale may also be grown as a cultivated crop. It is gathered for its white stems which are steamed and eaten in the same way as asparagus.

Fruit Vegetables

AUBERGINE
(Solanum melongena)

Also known as eggplants, aubergines are probably native to India. They can be various shapes and colours ranging from deep purple to white, although purple is the most common. Available all the year round, the mealy yellow-green flesh is eaten cooked, and may be sliced, hollowed and stuffed. Typical recipes include *ratatouille*, *moussaka* and *imam bayeldi*.

TOMATO
(Lycopersicum esculentum)

Originally from South America, and once known as the "love-apple", the tomato is in fact a berry and a relative of the potato. There are numerous varieties, shapes and sizes of this attractive fruit, including green, plum, beefsteak and cherry tomatoes. Available throughout the year, tomatoes can be bought fresh or canned and are eaten raw or cooked. Red tomatoes are available as juice, purée or ketchup, while green tomatoes are often used in pickles and chutneys.

Purple thick aubergine

Naples early purple aubergine

'Slim Jim' aubergine

Cherry tomato

Beefsteak tomato

Purple thick aubergine

PEPPERS (*Capsicum annuum*)

Native to tropical America and the West Indies, peppers are either sweet or hot (chillies) and come in many colours and sizes (the green sweet pepper is the unripe red or yellow pepper). Both varieties are available fresh or canned all year round. The sweet pepper is mild in taste and can be eaten raw or cooked. Chilli or hot pepper is used almost exclusively as a seasoning, especially in Indian curries and Mexican and Latin American dishes.

AVOCADO (*Persea americana*)

This nutritious buttery fruit is grown in many tropical countries, but originated in Central America. Also known as the alligator pear, there are two main varieties, one with dark green skin and one with warty black skin. A wild variety, *aguacate,* can be found in the American south-west. Available fresh all year, avocados are used in salads, sauces, dips and mousses or as an hors d'œuvre, and form the main ingredient in the Mexican dish *guacamole.*

Avocado

Sweet peppers

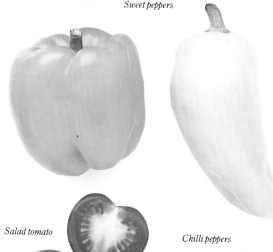

Salad tomato

Chilli peppers

OTHER FRUIT VEGETABLES

AKEE (*Blighia sapida*)
History maintains that akee fruits were introduced to the West Indies by Captain Bligh of the *Bounty,* hence the botanical dedication. The outer pink covering of the medium-sized fruit is poisonous, but benign portions are used as a vegetable with salt cod in Jamaica. It is mostly available canned.

BREADFRUIT
(*Artocarpus communis*)
Like the akee, this is also associated with Captain Bligh, who introduced it to the West Indies. The large fruits contain a pulp used as a vegetable, generally roasted.

Squashes and Gourds

Squashes and gourds share the distinction of being native to both the Old World and the New. They feature in American and West Indian cooking, in African and Middle Eastern dishes, and also in the Orient. There are many different varieties.

SPAGHETTI SQUASH
(*Cucurbita pepo*)

Also known as vegetable spaghetti, this melon-shaped squash is available in winter. Usually boiled in its skin, the white flesh, which resembles spaghetti, is then taken out, seasoned and eaten hot with butter, tomato sauce or other seasonings, or chilled and served with meats or salads. It can also be deep-fried in batter.

Acorn squash

Spaghetti squash

ACORN SQUASH
(*Cucurbita pepo*)

Harvested in autumn, this thick-skinned American variety keeps well for several days in a cool, airy place before it is used. Sold fresh, canned and frozen, it has sweet-tasting, yellowish flesh. It is usually cooked whole, because of its tough skin, but peeled it can also be cut into rings and steamed. It is particularly suitable for stuffing and baking.

CUSTARD SQUASH
(Cucurbita pepo)

Also known as pattypan squash and custard marrow, this is a summer squash with a somewhat floury taste which is at its best when very ripe. The skin, flesh and seeds can all be eaten, and it can be steamed, boiled or stuffed and baked.

GOLDEN NUGGET
(Cucurbita pepo)

Orange with greenish flesh, this native American summer squash is usually eaten when immature and tender and can be steamed, boiled or stuffed and baked like a vegetable marrow. It can also be left on the vine to ripen and develop a thicker skin that must be peeled before cooking, but that allows it to be stored for several days. When mature, it can be boiled and mashed with butter and seasoning, or baked.

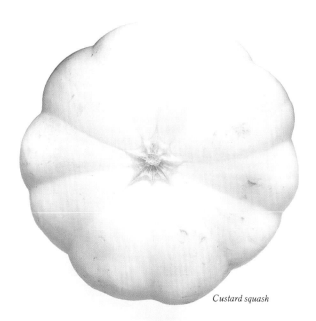

Custard squash

Golden nugget squash

OTHER SQUASHES

CHAYOTE *(Sechium edule)*
Also called christophene or chaci, the name chayote, from the Aztec *chayotl*, reveals the Central American origin of this squash. Varying widely in size, shape, shade and texture, it has a high water content: the bigger it grows, the more insipid it becomes. Chayote can be prepared in the same way as smaller squashes, used in chutneys, baked or stuffed.

CROOKNECK SQUASH
(Cucurbita moschata)
This bright yellow squash has a distinctive hooked shape, hence its name. It is a summer variety, with a thin skin. Younger squashes can be eaten seeds and all.

WEST INDIAN PUMPKIN
(Cucurbita pepo, spp.)

A close relative of the common pumpkin, the West Indian pumpkin (or calabaza or winter squash) is actually a giant squash. It lacks the dense texture and sweet taste necessary for pies, but otherwise can be used as any small squash.

Pumpkins are similar in shape, but usually have a bright orange skin and are particularly noted for their use in pies. They are often served as a fruit with fresh cream, but may also be used as a vegetable either lightly boiled or sliced and fried. They can also be puréed and used for soups; in France pumpkin jams are made and in Italy mashed pumpkin is used as a filling for sweet ravioli. Pumpkin seeds are rich in fats and proteins and an edible oil is produced from them.

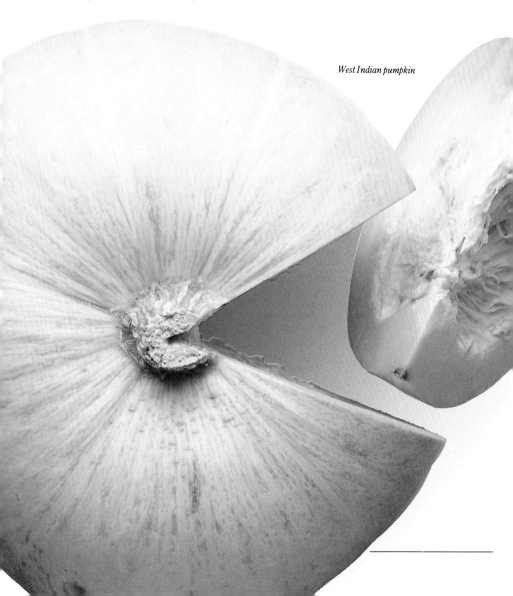

West Indian pumpkin

SNAKE SQUASH
(*Trichosanthes cucumeriana*)

This curled, eye-catching squash is native to south-east Asia and Australia, but it can be grown in Europe and America. Eaten in the summer when immature and thin-skinned, it is usually sliced in rounds and steamed, or boiled and served with butter, salt, pepper and herbs such as tarragon, dill or marjoram.

Snake squash

Butternut squash

BUTTERNUT SQUASH
(*Caryoka nuciferum*)

The fruit of a plant native to tropical America but now cultivated in North America and Europe, it is picked either in the summer, when tender and best sliced and stewed, boiled and served in a light sauce or baked in a pie, or later in the autumn, when the squash is split, parboiled and baked. It is also used to make jams, preserves and pickles.

MARROW (*Cucurbita pepo*)

An edible gourd indigenous to the
Americas, this summer vegetable
should be firm and heavy, and
about 30 cm (12 in) long. It can be
steamed, boiled, stuffed and
baked, cubed and served *au gratin*
or made into chutney or jam.
Marrow flowers can be served
Italian style, dipped in batter and
deep-fried.

COURGETTE (*Cucurbita pepo*)

Also known as zucchini and Italian
squash, the courgette is an
immature marrow, harvested
before it has a chance to grow into
the huge vegetable so loved by
English gardeners. Available all
summer, it does not need peeling,
but can be simply topped, tailed,
sliced and eaten raw, steamed,
baked, sliced and fried in batter,
made into soups and stews, or
used in *ratatouille*. As with
marrow, the flowers can be dipped
in flour and fried.

CUCUMBER (*Cucumis sativus*)

Although not generally thought of
as a squash, the cucumber belongs
to the same family. An ancient
cultivated fruit thought to be
indigenous to India, there are two
basic types: the long, thin, smooth
variety grown under glass and
known as the hot-house,
greenhouse or frame cucumber,
and the thick, rough-skinned
variety known as the ridge
cucumber because it is grown on
raised ridges of soil. Available all
year round, cucumbers can be
bought fresh or pickled, and may
be eaten raw or cooked. In India
cucumber is added to yoghurt to
make the refreshing *raita*,
used to temper curry dishes.
Northern Europeans combine it
with sour cream and the French
garnish cucumber salad with salted
whipped cream. Cucumbers may
be salted, used in soups, in a sauce
(especially with poached salmon)
and in salads. Slices should be
salted and pressed to remove
water before adding dressing.

Striped marrow

Plain marrow

Courgette

Ridge cucumber

Hot-house cucumber

Bulb Vegetables

LEEK (*Allium porrum*)

Not as pungent as onions or shallots, the leek is a winter plant native to Europe. Available from autumn to spring, leeks can be braised, served with sauces, *au gratin*, or in soups and stews. Welsh onions, native to Siberia, not Wales, are small leek-like bulbs with a delicate flavour which can be used to flavour stews.

PICKLING ONION
(*Allium cepa*)

Picked when the plant has just formed bulbs, the small size of these onions makes them ideal for pickling. They are also good boiled and served in sauce.

SPANISH ONION (*Allium cepa*)

Dubbed "The King of Vegetables" because of its dominant taste, long reign and widespread influence, the onion is extremely versatile. There are two general types, mild or pungent, and two shapes, globe and elongated. Available all year round, they are eaten raw, boiled, steamed, braised, fried and in many prepared dishes, stuffings and sauces. Like all varieties, the Spanish onion originated in central Asia and is today found worldwide. Unlike most white varieties, it is mild and keeps well. It is available all year round fresh, dehydrated or as reconstituted juice.

Leek

Pickling onions

Spanish onion

ITALIAN RED ONION
(*Allium cepa*)

Oblong, mild and sometimes sweet, this variety is grown in many places. It is attractive when sliced thinly in rings and used raw as a garnish, as cooking blanches red onions. Like all onions, leeks and shallots, this variety becomes bitter when its cut flesh is exposed to the air too long before use.

Italian red onion

GARLIC (*Allium sativum*)

Garlic is probably of central Asian origin, as both Chinese and Egyptians were using it early in their history. It is sold all year round in heads, but usually used in small amounts of one or two cloves at a time. It is not used simply as a vegetable, but compounds the taste of an infinite variety of savoury dishes (one of the most notorious is *lièvre à la royale,* a French dish that calls for some 30 cloves). Garlic cloves can be planted .

Shallot

SHALLOT (*Allium ascalonicum*)

Unknown in ancient times and of uncertain origin, this is a close relative of, but less pungent than, the onion. It is widely used in France, where there are grey, pink and golden-brown varieties, and is mostly available in summer and autumn. Mainly used in sauces, the elongated varieties tend to be stronger-tasting.

SPRING ONION (*Allium cepa*)

Picked when young and tender before the bulb forms, the spring onion is available from midwinter to midsummer and is used fresh in garnishes, relishes and salads.

Spring onion

Garlic

LARGE RED ONION
(*Allium cepa*)

This variety is mild and often has a fairly sweet taste. It can be eaten raw in salads, boiled or baked as a vegetable, or used to flavour soups, sauces and stews.

Large red onion

Root Vegetables

WHITE RADISH
(Raphanus sativus)

Grown since prehistory in the
Middle East, radishes were a
favourite in ancient Egypt. The
wild radish probably originated in
southern Asia. White cultivated
varieties are found in many
countries, and are usually at their
best in the spring. Available
throughout the year, the white
radish is primarily used as a
salad vegetable.

DAIKON RADISH
(Raphanus sativus)

This traditional Japanese radish is
often sold in oriental food shops.
Milder than other types, it can be
grated and used as a garnish, or
pickled. In Japan it is finely sliced
and cooked with other vegetables
or used in soups.

Daikon radish

Navette

White radish

NAVETTE *(Brassica rapa)*

A type of French turnip available in
winter and early spring, this can
be boiled or used in soups, stews
and casseroles. The flesh is
usually white, although there are
yellow and black varieties.

Scorzonera

SCORZONERA
(*Scorzonera hispanica*)

Scorzonera and its close relative
salsify (also called oyster plant
because of its delicate flavour)
have long tapering roots and are
members of the daisy family.
Native to Europe and the
Mediterranean, scorzonera has a
black skin and salsify a white skin.
Both plants can be used for soups,
salads, as a cooked vegetable,
puréed, in hors d'œuvres or
casseroles. Also known as black
salsify, scorzonera is at its best in
late autumn.

PARSNIP (*Pastinaca sativa*)

A sweet root vegetable native to
Europe but now also grown in
America, it is sold fresh all year
round but is at its best in winter. It
can be braised, boiled, roasted,
puréed, candied or even made
into wine.

Turnip

Parsnip

TURNIP (*Brassica rapa*)

The swollen root of a plant thought
to be native to Europe, this can
vary considerably in size, shape
and colour. Available all year
round, turnips are cooked whole
when young and small, and puréed
or used in stews and soups when
older. The green-leaved tops are
used as a spring vegetable.

SWEDE (*Brassica napobrassica*)

This heavy, coarse-skinned root vegetable originated in Europe but is also common in America, where it is called rutabaga. It is at its best in winter and resembles the turnip, but has yellow-orange flesh. It can be baked, roasted with meat, sliced and fried, boiled and mashed (as when served with haggis in Scotland) or cubed, blanched and added to stews. In Finland it is casseroled with cream and spices.

RED RADISH
(*Raphanus sativus*)

Native to southern Asia, cultivated varieties of red radish are sold all year round in Europe and America, but taste less peppery in spring. Usually eaten raw in salads or with bread and butter as an hors d'œuvre, its leaves add pungency to salads.

BEETROOT (*Beta vulgaris*)

Beetroot and its close relatives all developed from *Beta maritima*, a Mediterranean seashore plant whose root was cultivated in Germany in the Middle Ages. Widely grown around the world, it is sold throughout the year. Available fresh or canned, it can be boiled or baked and served hot, or cooled and pickled. Beetroot is an ingredient in the classic Russian soup *bortsch*, and is much used as a salad vegetable. In America, small beetroots are served in orange juice as Yale beets, and in a sweet-sour sauce as Harvard beets.

Red radish

Swede

Beetroot

CELERIAC
(*Apium graveolens,* var. *rapaceum*)

This special variety of celery, with a similar taste, is cultivated for its thick, tuberous root. A winter vegetable, it should be firm and must be peeled before cooking – this is easier if it is cut into slices first. It can be eaten raw, grated, or boiled until tender and served with sauce, blanched and dressed with vinaigrette sauce, or puréed and used in soups and stews. Celeriac tends to discolour when cut, so a few drops of lemon juice should be added to the cooking water or salad to prevent this.

Celeriac

Carrot

CARROT (*Daucus carota*)

Thought to be native to Europe, wild carrots were cultivated by the Dutch in the Middle Ages. Carrots are available all year round but are most tender in early summer when they are also smaller and sweeter. Sold fresh, canned and frozen, carrots are good steamed or boiled, or sautéed in butter and herbs, roasted with meat or used in stews and soups. They are also used to make carrot cake. Their fresh juice is nutritious and delicious.

OTHER ROOT VEGETABLES

APIO and ARRACACHA
(*Apios tuberosa*)
Members of the Legume family, these are native to North America and can be cooked like potatoes or used in desserts. They are very similar in flavour and are interchangeable.

A similar plant from South America, and also called Arracacha, is the Peruvian carrot (*Arracacia xanthorrhiza*). Cultivated in the Andes – and native to Columbia, not Peru, despite the name – the roots may be baked, fried or used in soups and stews, like potatoes. A flour from the roots is used to make breads and pancakes.

ARROWHEAD
(*Sagittaria sagittifolia*)
Tule potato or wappato are other names for this water plant with arrow-shaped leaves. Both leaves and root are used in Chinese cooking.

BITTERROOT
(*Lewisia rediviva*)
This plant of the purslane family is native to North America's north-west. The roots are fleshy, succulent and nutritious and, despite the name, are not bitter when peeled.

BLACK RADISH
(*Raphanus sativus*)
Unlike the more common radishes, the black winter variety is the size of a small turnip. It is used mostly as a winter salad vegetable.

BURDOCK (*Arctium lappa*)
This is a wild, thistle-like plant common to the northern hemisphere. Young leaf stems are used in salads; in Japan, where it is called *gobo*, the entire plant is used.

CHINESE ARTICHOKE
(*Stachys affinis*)
Native to China and developed in Europe by the French, this tuber can be grated raw into winter vegetable salads, used as an accompanying vegetable to meat dishes, and in Chinese mixed vegetable dishes. It is available in the late autumn.

HAMBURG PARSLEY
(*Petroselinum hortense*)
Also called turnip-rooted parsley, this plant is cultivated for its root, which is white, slender and closely resembles a parsnip. Its popularity in eastern and northern Europe may help to account for its name. Used in soups and stews, it can also be an accompanying vegetable like celeriac. It has a slightly nutty flavour.

HORSERADISH
(*Armoracia rusticana*)
Native to south-east Europe and western Asia, this root is usually crushed and made into a sauce. It has a pungent flavour and is a popular condiment with roast beef and cold meats (page 56).

LOTUS
(*Nelumbium nuciferum*)
This sacred plant of India and China is used extensively in the cooking of the Far East, where it is indigenous. The cut root is perforated with holes, a decorative quality exploited in Chinese and Japanese dishes. It is available fresh or canned, and can be made into a starch, pickled or steamed. The raw leaves are used in salads.

Tubers

YAM (*Dioscorea batatas*)

Native to Africa and Asia, yams are also grown in tropical America. There are many varieties of this mild, tuberous root, which is high in starch. In Africa, yams are mashed, peppered and spiced to make *foufou* and *kalajoum*. They may be cooked in the same way as potatoes and are a popular feature of West Indian cooking.

JERUSALEM ARTICHOKE (*Helianthus tuberosus*)

Indigenous to North America and introduced to Europe in the seventeenth century, there are several varieties, ranging from beige to brownish red. It has a nut-like taste, and can be eaten raw in salads, or cooked in sauces and casseroles. It is mainly a winter vegetable.

Jerusalem artichoke

SWEET POTATO (*Ipomœa batatas*)

Sweet potatoes are not related to ordinary potatoes, although both hail from Central America. Sweet or "Spanish" potatoes arrived in Europe before the common potato, and were highly regarded. Traditional in America at Thanksgiving, they are available from autumn to early summer. There are two main varieties, which may be interchanged: the red sweet potato, with its sweet orange flesh, is good with roasts, or mashed and used in cakes, soufflés and stuffings; the white sweet potato is smaller with drier yellow flesh. It can be fried, boiled or used in casseroles.

Yam

White sweet potato

Red sweet potato

OTHER TUBERS

CASSAVA (*Manihot utilissima*)

Also known as manioc, this starchy tuber from Central America is used to make tapioca (page 106). Fermented, it is used in an alcoholic drink and the leaves can be eaten as a vegetable. Cassava flour is used in cakes and pies.

TARO (*Colocasia antiquorum*)

This tuber contains fine-grained and digestible starch and is used as a vegetable in West Indian cookery, cooked like the potato. In the West Indies the leaves are eaten, like cabbage.

Potatoes

A member of the nightshade family, the potato is indigenous to South America, but is now cultivated worldwide. There are many varieties. Whites are best for boiling and frying, reds for roasting.

NEW POTATO
(Solanum tuberosum)

A modern variety, new potatoes grow quickly, have white flesh and are usually dug in the early summer when they are sold in most markets. They are best scraped and simply boiled in their skin and served with butter, salt and pepper.

CRAIG ROYAL RED POTATO
(Solanum tuberosum)

A maincrop potato variety ready in July, this is non-floury and white-fleshed with red or pinkish-white skin, and has a uniform size and shape. Its waxy texture is best for frying, boiling and using in salads.

DESIREE POTATO
(Solanum tuberosum)

This high-quality potato is floury and excellent for baking and frying, also for boiling and mashing.

CYPRUS NEW POTATO
(Solanum tuberosum)

New, or young, potatoes are mostly available from late winter to early spring. When tiny, they should be bought in small quantities as they quickly lose their earthy taste. They do not need peeling, but should merely be scrubbed before use. They are not good for mashing and are also available canned.

PENTLAND HAWK POTATO
(Solanum tuberosum)

Firm with pale yellow, creamy-textured flesh, this is a medium grade, all-purpose potato. It can be steamed or boiled, sliced with or without skin, and served with butter, herbs, salt and pepper or mayonnaise. It is also good for mashing and baking.

New potato

Craig Royal red potato

Desiree potato

Cyprus new potato

Pentland Squire potato

Pentland Hawk potato

Maris Piper potato

King Edward potato

Pentland Crown potato

PENTLAND SQUIRE POTATO
(Solanum tuberosum)

Firm and white-fleshed, this is a medium grade all-purpose potato. Like many other varieties, it is commercially frozen for frying, or sold dehydrated or canned.

PENTLAND CROWN POTATO
(Solanum tuberosum)

A thin-skinned, creamy-white variety that is best just before Christmas when the tuber is mature. It has a floury texture and is excellent for baking, though, like all floury varieties, it becomes less mealy as it cools.

KING EDWARD POTATO
(Solanum tuberosum)

One of the best-quality potatoes, the King Edward has creamy-white, sometimes yellowed flesh, and is good for all cooking.

MARIS PIPER POTATO
(Solanum tuberosum)

This variety's medium-firm, creamy-white flesh is prized for boiling as it rarely blackens. It can be used in salads, sautéed or fried.

Pods and Seeds

PEA (*Pisum sativum*)

Possibly the earliest of all cultivars, the pea was first grown in the Middle East. Garden peas are sold fresh (from early summer to autumn), frozen, canned and dried (page 39), and may be puréed, used in soups, stews and as a cooked vegetable. The pods are usually discarded, but may be used to make pea soup.

MANGETOUT (*Pisum sativum*)

Also called the snow pea or sugar pea, this is an early variety of pea (usually available in spring) that has very tender pods. They are topped and tailed before cooking and are eaten pod and all. Asparagus peas (*Lotus tetragonolobus*), although not of the pea family, are eaten in the same way.

PETITS POIS (*Pisum sativum*)

These are garden peas picked very young while they are sweet and tender. Particularly popular in France, they are often considered to be the finest of all varieties.

Petits pois

Mangetout

Garden pea

OKRA (*Hibiscus esculenta*)

Also known as lady's finger or gumbo, this pod is the fruit of an annual plant of the cotton family, native to tropical Africa. Widely used in the southern states of America, in okra soup and dishes with rice, it appears in Indian cooking as *bindi,* and as *bamia* in the Middle East, cooked in a lamb stew. Available fresh, canned or dried, it may be used to thicken soups and stews, or alternatively eaten as a vegetable.

SWEETCORN (*Zea mays*)

Also named corn, maize and Indian corn, this variety is indigenous to America, but now grown throughout the world. Available in its immature state, it may be fresh, frozen or canned, and is used as a vegetable, boiled or roasted and eaten with butter. Also used in soups, it may be puréed, made into fritters, cornmeal, corn bread, corn pone and hominy.

Okra

Sweetcorn

BEAN SPROUTS
(Phaseolus aureus)

Virtually any grain or large seed can be sprouted, but the one most frequently sprouted commercially is the mung bean (page 41). Alfalfa beans are also commonly sprouted. Used as a vegetable in oriental cooked dishes, bean sprouts may also be eaten raw in salads.

Sprouting mung beans

Alfalfa sprouts

Bean sprouts

Broad bean

Mature runner bean

BROAD BEAN *(Vicia faba)*

The only bean native to the Old World, this seed has been grown and eaten throughout Europe and the Middle East since prehistoric times (pages 38 and 42). A brown Egyptian variety provides the staple *ful*. They may be creamed, served with a sauce or puréed, and are the traditional complement to ham or bacon. Broad beans are available frozen or canned, and fresh in the summer months. Normally shelled, very young pods may also be cooked and eaten.

GREEN BEAN
(Phaseolus vulgaris)

Native to Central America and grown for their pods, there are many varieties, including runner, lima and French or haricot beans. French beans need only be topped and tailed before cooking; runner beans must have their tough strings stripped off even when they are very young. There is also a yellow variety, known as wax bean, which is popular in North America. Monguete is a Spanish variety of French bean.

French bean

Monguete

DRIED PULSES

PULSES ARE THE EDIBLE seeds of certain plants of the Legume family and include beans, peas and lentils. Some, like green beans, broad beans, lima beans and green peas are eaten fresh; others are eaten dried and in this form have been a staple food in many parts of the world for thousands of years.

Archaeological research into plant origins has shown that beans were among the first plants cultivated when agriculture began. The "common bean" (which includes kidney and its many varieties such as pinto and black) was first cultivated in Mexico; lima beans in Peru; broad beans and chick-peas in the Middle East; soy and aduki beans in China, and black-eyed peas and pigeon peas in Africa. Pulses have become widely naturalized outside their native regions, however, so that today most of them are available worldwide.

Pulses remain as popular as ever in the cooking of the Middle East, Asia, the Caribbean, Mexico and Central and South America, while in North America and Europe there is an ever-growing interest in them due in part to the high cost of meats and to the increasing popularity of vegetarian cooking.

Methods of processing
Beans are dried as quickly as possible after picking to preserve their flavour, plumpness and texture. They are then graded and any stones removed before packing. Most pulses are now artificially dried and graded by machine. Mung beans and soybeans may also be sprouted for their shoots, which are eaten as a fresh vegetable.

Dried beans, peas and lentils are in some cases also available cooked and canned and a few types are fermented or processed into some other form, such as flour, oil, fresh pressed bean curd or dried bean curd sheets. The fermentation processes that are used vary considerably. In China black beans are fermented in salt, and in Africa in wood ash. The process may continue for months, as for the soybeans used to make soy sauce.

Dried pulses in the kitchen
Most pulses are widely available and the lesser-known varieties can usually be found in shops specializing in oriental and health foods. They keep well and are easily reconstituted but should be stored in a cool, dry place and used within 6 to 9 months.

Beans, peas and lentils may be used whole in casseroles, salads and vegetable dishes, puréed in soups or ground and used for croquettes and dips. All types of beans and lentils are high in protein and 30 per cent more is released if they are eaten with a cereal; this is why there are many dishes around the world in which pulses are served with rice or bread.

In many recipes, one pulse can be successfully substituted for another, but variation in flavour and texture should be taken into account since this makes some pulses much more suitable than others for certain dishes. Those beans, peas or lentils that become very tender with cooking will absorb other flavours well and are particularly good in spicy or herby casseroles, while those with a firmer texture are the best to serve whole as a vegetable or used in salads.

Remember that most pulses need soaking and cooking, the exact times depending on the particular type and quality of the bean. Pick over the beans before washing and soaking them to remove any stones or pieces of grit, and add salt towards the end of cooking time, as this will make the beans soften more quickly.

Peas

BLUE PEA (*Pisum sativum*)

Dried peas were an important vegetable before frozen peas appeared, but they have now lost much of their popularity. In Germany, whole dried peas are still baked with sauerkraut and soured cream. The blue pea is one of the most tasty of several varieties of dried peas. Its texture is floury, but it retains its shape when it is cooked.

Blue pea

SPLIT GREEN PEA
(*Pisum sativum*)

This is sweeter than the blue pea. It cooks to a purée to make the traditional English pease pudding served with salt pork, a complementary combination that is also successful in split pea soups made with a ham bone, and may be used in vegetable dishes.

Split green pea

SPLIT YELLOW PEA
(*Pisum sativum*)

Like the split green pea, these make excellent purées for soup and for vegetable dishes served with ham.

Split yellow pea

Mediterranean chick-pea

CHICK-PEA (*Cicer arietinum*)

Also known as garbanzo, ceci (Italy) and chana dal (India), there are several varieties of this large pea, native to western Asia. Available whole or split, they can be served in casseroles, soups and stews and are the main ingredient of *humus*, a savoury dip, or *felafel*, deep-fried patties. A staple food of the Middle East, chick-peas also appear in many European and oriental dishes.

Middle Eastern chick-pea

Split skinless chick-pea

Lentils and Beans

GREEN LENTIL
(Lens esculenta)

Lentils are particularly rich in protein. This variety, also known as the continental lentil, is popular in European cooking. It retains its shape after cooking and may be served as a vegetable. There are large and small varieties.

Large green lentil

Small green lentil

Puy lentil

YELLOW LENTIL
(Lens esculenta)

Because of their Asian origin, many lentils are often referred to by their Indian names as various types of dal. Also known as yellow dal, this lentil is often served as a main or side dish with curry.

Yellow lentil

Orange lentil

Indian brown lentil

ORANGE LENTIL
(Lens esculenta)

There are many different varieties of lentil, usually identified by and named after their colour. They all have the same flattish round shape, but vary in size and may be sold split or whole. Lentils play an important part in Indian cookery, where they are usually served as a main or side dish with curry, and the split red variety is a staple food throughout the Middle East, where it is often served with rice. The lentil is the only pulse that may not need soaking before cooking. This familiar orange lentil quickly cooks to a purée.

FLAGEOLET
(Phaseolus vulgaris)

A small green variety of common bean (haricot) native to the Americas, this can be eaten fresh or dried and is also available pre-cooked and canned. Its fresh texture and delicate taste make it especially good as a vegetable or in salads. In France it is traditionally eaten with roast lamb.

Flageolet

PUY LENTIL
(Lens esculenta)

These dark French lentils, which vary in size, are highly regarded and considered the best of their type. They retain their shape when they are cooked.

INDIAN BROWN LENTIL
(Lens esculenta)

Also known as masoor dal, these are red lentils with their seedcoats. They become a purée when they are cooked.

OTHER BEANS
PINTO BEAN *(Phaseolus vulgaris)* These beans are kidney-shaped and beige dappled with brown flecks. They lose their colour but not their flavour when cooked.

MUNG BEAN (*Phaseolus aureus*)

Also known as moong dal or green gram, these are widely cultivated in India and China. They have a good flavour and very high vitamin content, and are available whole, split or skinless. Probably best-known in the form of bean sprouts (page 37), mung beans are widely used in China, where the sweet tender shoots are processed to make *fen tiao* noodles, and in India where they are curried. They are used in stews.

Whole mung bean

Skinless mung bean

Split mung bean

LARGE WHITE BEAN
(*Phaseolus vulgaris*)

A large, creamy-white, flat variety of the common bean, this is also known as white haricot. It is used in stews and casseroles, and is generally interchangeable with other types of beans.

Large white bean

BOSTON BEAN
(*Phaseolus vulgaris*)

This small white variety of common bean is also known as pearl haricot, navy bean and pea bean. It is used to make the French dish *cassoulet* and the traditional Boston baked beans, the forerunners of modern canned baked beans.

Boston bean

URD BEAN (*Phaseolus mungo*)

Also known as urd dal or black gram, this bean is sold in several forms. It is thought to be native to India and is widely grown in both India and the Far East.

Whole urd bean

Skinless urd bean

Split urd bean

BROAD BEAN (*Vicia faba*)

Native to north Africa, this was cultivated by the ancient Egyptians and Greeks. It is available fresh (page 37) or dried. The dried beans have a fine texture and can be eaten on their own or in stews and salads.

Broad bean

BLACK BEAN
(*Phaseolus vulgaris*)

This shiny black variety of common bean, tender and sweet-tasting, is a staple food in the Caribbean, Mexico and Central and South America. Fried black beans and rice *(gallo pinto)* is the national breakfast dish of Costa Rica, while *feijoada completa,* a dish of mixed meats and black beans served with cassava meal *(farofa),* diced oranges, hot fresh pepper sauce and collard greens is the national dish of Brazil.

Black bean

BORLOTTO BEAN
(*Phaseolus vulgaris*)

Also known as saligia beans, borlotti beans come from Italy. They cook to a creamy consistency and are baked in spicy casseroles or may be used in dips and salads.

Borlotto bean

RED KIDNEY BEAN
(*Phaseolus vulgaris*)

This sweet-tasting bean with a floury texture comes in many varieties ranging from dark pink to maroon. It is most readily identified with Mexican cooking, particularly for its use in the hot, spicy dish *chilli con carne.*

Red kidney bean

CANNELLINO BEAN
(*Phaseolus vulgaris*)

A creamy-white kidney bean, this is slightly larger than the Boston bean and with a fluffier texture. Used mostly in Italian cooking, cannellini beans (or fagiola beans) are often used with tuna fish to make *tonno e fagioli.*

Cannellino bean

BLACK FERMENTED CHINESE BEAN (*Glycine max*)

These are smallish black beans – usually soy – which, in China, are fermented in salt and added to meat and vegetable dishes.

Black fermented Chinese bean

LIMA BEAN (*Phaseolus lunatus*)

There are two sizes and several varieties of these kidney-shaped beans which are eaten both fresh and dried. Available fresh, dried and frozen, they are usually pale green or cream, which accounts for the fact that they are sometimes referred to as butter beans. They are also known as Madagascar beans because they are grown there so extensively, although they were originally found in South America. Dried limas retain their shape well and are often served by themselves as a hot vegetable, or in salads.

Lima bean

FUL MEDAMES
(*Lathyrus sativus*)

A small variety of broad bean widely eaten in the Middle East, where it originated, its white counterpart is called ful nabed. Dried broad bean patties or *taamiya* are eaten throughout the Middle East and ful medames have given their name to one of Egypt's national dishes, in which they are baked with eggs, cumin and garlic. They are also good when cooked and served as a vegetable.

Ful medames

ADUKI BEAN
(Phaseolus angularis)

Also called adzuki beans, these small dark red or black beans are very tender when cooked and have an unusually sweet, quite strong flavour. The seeds of a bushy annual native to China, they are valued in the Far East for their medicinal properties and have been eaten in rice dishes and soups for thousands of years. Their sweetness has also made them a common ingredient in oriental confectionery.

Aduki bean

BLACK-EYED BEAN
(Vigna sinensis)

Native to China, this bean has come to be identified with the "soul food" of the southern states of America, where it has given its name to a classic dish of salt pork and beans cooked with tabasco. Also known as cowpeas and black-eyed peas, in China they are stir-fried and mixed with meat or fish to make *chiang ton chia*.

Black-eyed bean

RICE BEAN
(Phaseolus calcaratus)

Native to south-east Asia, rice beans are grown in limited amounts in China, India and the Philippines. They are named because of their rice-like taste.

Rice bean

LABLAB BEAN
(Dolichos lablab)

Hard-skinned beans from the hyacinth plant, also known as hyacinth beans, these originated in India but are now eaten throughout Asia and the Middle East, particularly in Egypt. They must be shelled before cooking.

Lablab bean

PIGEON PEA *(Cajanus cajan)*

Also known as gunga peas and toor dal, these beige beans take their name "pea" from their shape and size and have a sweetish flavour. Native to Africa, they are a staple food in the Caribbean, used in dishes such as *jugjug* from Barbados and pigeon pea soup from Trinidad.

Pigeon pea

SOYBEAN *(Glycine max)*

Soybeans range in colour from yellow, green and red to black. They are very high in nutrients, especially protein, and have been an important part of oriental diets for many years. They are used for making bean curd (known in Japan as *tofu*), delicate noodles called *harusame* and a sweet confectionery paste. The beans are also fermented and used to make flavouring pastes and condiments, notably soy sauce (called *shoyu* in Japan), *tempeh* from Indonesia and *miso* from Japan. More recently, soybeans are used for making a variety of basic western foodstuffs, as well as for industrial purposes such as the manufacture of plastics. They provide an important oil (page 75), can be ground to make a flour (page 107) and are the basis of most meat-substitute chunks and granules. Soybeans are also often used for their milk.

One of the "five sacred grains" of ancient China, soybeans are very hard and require lengthy preparation for cooking, but a pre-cooked variety known as soy splits is also available. The beans may be sprouted for their long, crisp shoots, which are best raw.

Black soybean

Yellow soybean

MUSHROOMS AND TRUFFLES

CONFUSION EXISTS OVER THE terms "mushrooms" and "fungi". Here we use the term "mushroom" to describe all forms of edible fungi. Mushrooms can be wild, domesticated, fresh, canned, pickled and dried. They are made into sauces and ketchups and are used in a great variety of dishes in most countries throughout the world. Mushrooms contain about 80 per cent water, 8 per cent carbohydrate and 1 per cent fat. They are also a good source of protein, and other vitamins and minerals, such as riboflavin and thiamine, iron and copper, potassium and phosphates.

Mushrooming is a favourite pastime in many countries, though the mushrooms sought are different. In America alone there are about fifty edible wild species. However, not all mushrooms are edible. Certain mushrooms of the Amanita family are deadly, indeed *Amanita phalloides* is known as death cap, or, more picturesquely, death angel. Mushrooms of the *Psilocybe* species found mostly in Mexico are hallucinogenic and were once regarded as sacred. Amateur mushroom hunters are urged to gather only those easy to identify, among them the morel, held to be the finest of all mushrooms, the shaggymane and the puffballs. In America, membership of one of the many mycology societies takes care of the problem with expert identification; in France local pharmacists give the same kind of expert help.

Cultivating mushrooms

Ignorance about the growth and life-cycle of mushrooms was widespread until in 1678 the French botanist Marchant demonstrated that mushrooms grew from spawn, appearing on a lace-like structure, the mycelium, just beneath the surface of the soil. Market gardeners in Paris swiftly put theory into practice and transplanted the "roots" of the wild mushroom to a bed of horse manure, and thus bred the ancestors of a remarkably successful commercial product.

In the 1890s, French scientists finally consolidated their long monopoly by developing a pasteurized spawn, and therefore more dependable crops. American growers, who had first raised mushrooms in New York City, adopted the French technique in the late nineteenth century. Today the mushroom industry is a thriving one, with centres in Europe, America, Australia and South America.

Elsewhere the cultivation of mushrooms remains a local industry on a limited scale, mainly in China and Japan, although wild mushrooms have a ready market in Europe. Russia's *Lactarius deliciosus* is gathered in conifer forests and sold in dried form, likewise the boletus, and chanterelles in France, Italy, Poland and Germany, where over 300 species of edible mushrooms are sold. Five types of mushroom are now cultivated: the common mushroom, the French and Italian truffle, China's padi-straw mushroom and cloud ear fungus, and Japan's shiitake. The matsutake, from Japan, while not cultivated, is extensively gathered and canned for export.

Mushrooms in the kitchen

Some mushrooms may need parboiling first, especially chanterelles. Large varieties can be sliced, dipped in egg and breadcrumbs, and fried in bacon fat, while young mushrooms are excellent sliced raw in salads. Dried mushrooms are a useful standby ingredient, and they keep for over a year. They are dried on wire trays in a current of air maintained at 54°C (130°F). Unless their skin is tough and discoloured, mushrooms need not be peeled. Wipe the caps with a damp cloth or paper towel. If they are very dirty or sandy and must be washed, do it quickly without letting them soak. Wild specimens should be carefully sorted and checked for insects and grit. Cook as soon as possible after gathering. Dried mushrooms will need soaking in warm water until soft – about 15 minutes. To store fresh mushrooms, put them in an open plastic bag in the refrigerator, where they will keep for four or five days; dried mushrooms keep for at least a year. Roughly 85g (3oz) of dried mushrooms when reconstituted are equal to 450g (1lb) of fresh mushrooms.

TRUFFLES
(Tuber magnatum, melanosporum)

These are tubers that grow near the roots of oak or beech trees – they are "cultivated" to the extent that oak groves are planted to encourage them. The two main varieties, and the most highly prized in cuisine, are the black Périgord truffle *(Tuber melanosporum)* and the white Piedmontese truffle *(T. magnatum)* of Alba, Italy, both expensive luxuries. There is also the red-grained black truffle *(T. æstivum)*, which grows in England but is largely ignored, and the violet truffle of Europe *(T. brumale)*. Fresh truffles are gathered in the autumn, and are only marketed locally, so most of us are obliged to buy them cooked and canned, when they have lost some of their characteristic taste and aroma.

White truffles have a powerful taste and aroma. They are usually grated, raw, on pasta, risotto or egg dishes, although one classic recipe suggests cooking them with Parmesan cheese. Black truffles can be used as a decorative garnish, in *pâté de foie gras,* aspic dishes, or cooked with scrambled eggs, as in *brouillade de truffe.*

Périgord black truffle

Piedmontese white truffle

WOOD EAR
(Auricularia polytricha)

A distant cousin of the European Jew's ear, this Chinese mushroom is cultivated on wood, or gathered wild from tree trunks on which it grows. It is also known as cloud ear and Chinese black fungus. Dried, it forms a gelatinous, tough product that needs reconstituting in several changes of warm water for about 30 minutes.

Boletus

Morel

Shiitake

Wood ear

Chanterelle

Rubber brush

RUBBER BRUSH
(Hydnum repandum)

Commonly found in all types of woodland in the autumn and early winter, the rubber brush or wood hedgehog is unique in having spines instead of gills, hence its names. A good cooking mushroom, it is useful for fricassées.

BOLETUS *(Boletus granulatus)*

Also known as the yellow mushroom, this is a fruity-smelling mushroom found in conifer woods in the summer and autumn. The dried version is shown here.

MOREL *(Morchella esculenta)*

Not a true mushroom, the morel is easily recognizable by its brown, sponge-like cap, pitted with hollows in which the spores are produced, and which gives rise to its other common name of sponge mushroom. It can be found in woodland clearings during spring and early summer and can also be bought, dried or canned, in speciality food shops. This is a dried version.

SHIITAKE *(Lentinus edodes)*

Also known as Chinese mushrooms, these are the most widely used mushrooms in oriental cooking and are grown in China and Japan on the wood of dead deciduous trees. *Lentinus edodes* takes its name from the *shii* tree *(Pasania)*, but also grows on the oak and hornbeam. The spawn is planted into holes or wedges cut in the logs, and crops last for 3–6 years. Shiitake are dried by sun or artificial heat. Dried ones should be soaked in warm water for 20 minutes before using.

CHANTERELLE
(Cantharellus cibarius)

Commonly found in woods, especially beech, from summer to midwinter, the chanterelle (also called girolle or egg mushroom) is extremely popular throughout Europe. It smells faintly of apricots and, when cooked, tastes slightly peppery with a delicate ·perfume. Its firm flesh requires longer cooking than other fungi. Chanterelles cannot be artificially cultivated but are available dried or canned.

Mushrooms

CULTIVATED MUSHROOM
(*Agaricus bisporus*)

The cultivated mushroom is traditionally grown from spawn on stable manure. It comes in three sizes, the smallest or button, the medium-sized or cup and the largest or open (flat) mushroom.

FIELD MUSHROOM
(*Agaricus campestris*)

A "wild" version of the cultivated mushroom, this is found in meadows from late summer to the end of autumn.

CUP MUSHROOM
(*Agaricus bisporus*)

The medium-sized version of the cultivated mushroom.

FLAT MUSHROOM
(*Agaricus bisporus*)

Also called the open mushroom, this is the largest and most strongly flavoured form of the cultivated mushroom.

BUTTON MUSHROOM
(*Agaricus bisporus*)

The smallest, most immature form of the cultivated mushroom.

BLEWIT (*Lepista*, spp.)

Named for their bluish-violet cast, blewits are found under deciduous trees or conifers as well as on grassy pastures and in woods. They appear from October to December, and are best fried or baked.

FIELD MUSHROOM
(*Agaricus vaporarius*)

One of the many varieties of wild mushroom found in meadows and pastures in summer and autumn.

Field mushroom
(Agaricus campestris)

Cultivated mushroom

Cup mushroom

Blewit

Button mushroom

Flat mushroom

Field mushroom
(Agaricus vaporarius)

BEEFSTEAK FUNGUS
(Fistulina hepatica)
Named after the beef-like appearance of its flesh, this is found occasionally on living trees, especially oaks.

PARASOL MUSHROOM
(Macrolepiota procera)
A summer and autumn fungus found standing tall on grassy hillsides, often near trees, its size makes it easy to find. The parasol or umbrella mushroom gets its name from the way in which its cap opens out from its stem on maturing. It should be picked young. Although this is an excellent tasting mushroom, the stalk should not be eaten as it is tough and fibrous.

CEP *(Boletus edulis)*
Also known as the cèpe or boletus (but not to be confused with *Boletus granulatus*), this is a superior-tasting wild mushroom widely eaten in Europe. The Greeks and Romans used the term *bolites* to describe the best edible mushrooms, but this term has since been applied only to the boletus. Found in woodland clearings in late summer and autumn, usually under beech or coniferous trees, they are distinguished by their stout stalks with delicately raised white veins running towards the top, and by the vertical tubes underneath the cap in which the brown spores are produced.

OTHER MUSHROOMS

FAIRY RING MUSHROOM
(Marasmius oreades)
These small mushrooms with pink-brown caps are best eaten when young and tender, and keep their flavour well when dried. The fairy ring mushroom can be eaten with steak, in soups, sauces and stews, or be pickled and used to make a ketchup.

GIANT PUFFBALL
(Lycoperdon giganteum)
All true puffballs are edible, but can only be eaten when they are young, firm and white. The giant puffball can be found in woods and meadows from August to October.

HORSE MUSHROOM
(Agaricus arvensis)
Similar to the field mushroom in habitat and taste, the horse mushroom has a yellow-tinted cap and greyish gills.

MATSUTAKE
(Tricholoma matsutake)
This type of wild mushroom grows on the *matsu* (pine) tree. A cousin of the European blewit, matsutake is a delicate, fine-tasting mushroom which is collected wild, and sold canned or fresh (in Japan). It is used in several Japanese dishes, including *tori mushiyaki*.

OYSTER MUSHROOM
(Pleurotus ostreatus)
A wild mushroom with a bluish-grey cap, this is eaten fried or grilled.

PADI-STRAW MUSHROOM
(Volvariella volvacea)
These small, conical mushrooms are grown on wet rice straw beds, and sold fresh, canned or dried. The local industry, in Canton, is probably quite old. They feature in such recipes as the vegetarian dish *sushi-chin,* and steamed or fried chicken dishes.

Beefsteak fungus

Cep

Parasol mushroom

Herbs, Spices and Seeds

HERBS ARE NON-WOODY PLANTS – usually annual and mostly grown from seed – of which the flowers, leaves, seeds, stems and roots are used as flavourings in cooking, or for medicinal purposes. The name "herb" comes from the Latin word *herba,* meaning grass or herbage. They are plants of great antiquity going back to earliest civilizations, with records from ancient Persia, Egypt, Arabia, Greece, India and China giving details of their cultivation and use. The names of many are a reminder of the medieval period after the fall of Rome when the monasteries of Europe were centres of agriculture, each having its own herb or "physic" garden.

Herbs gathered for the medicine chest have an alchemistic ring to them, with names like skullcap, St John's wort, wormwood, woodruff, balm and self-heal. All herbs do, in fact, have medicinal qualities and some – rue, for example – still provide a source for a substantial number of vital drugs used in pharmacy. Many have a dual purpose as they are used both in cooking and in medicine and, although the original purpose is unknown, the general consensus is that their primary use was culinary. Centuries before the birth of Christ it was suggested that medicine was a by-product of cooking. One use must have followed the other rapidly since the Sumerians were using thyme and laurel medicinally by 5000 BC and in 2700 BC the Chinese had a herbal listing 365 plants.

Herbs are also credited with magical and religious significance. The Romans, for example, believed that a wreath of bay leaves would protect the wearer from lightning during a storm. Nicholas Culpeper's herbal of 1653 was extremely popular and influential, mixing herbs with magic, medicine and astrology.

Herbs in the kitchen

The use of herbs in the kitchen is ruled by culinary traditions which vary from country to country. Every cuisine has its favourite herbs: oregano, mint and dill are used a great deal in lamb dishes in the Middle East and Greece; in Thailand, coriander leaves garnish almost every dish on the table, and lemon grass flavours fish and chicken dishes. In Britain, sage is a favourite with pork and gives its green colour to Sage Derby cheese, while roast lamb is often served with mint sauce.

Dill is an important flavouring: for fish in Scandinavia, soups in Russia and Denmark, and for pickling cucumbers in America. Italians acknowledge the happy union of basil with tomatoes and rosemary with lamb, the Germans of savory with beans, and the French of tarragon with chicken and fennel with fish. The herbs of Provence are justly famous for their pungency and aroma: thyme, marjoram, tarragon, juniper, lavender, bay, rosemary and fennel owe much to the soil of the region and to the long hours of sunshine. The amount used in cooking depends partly on individual taste, and partly on the type of herb. Strongly flavoured herbs should be used only sparingly.

Fresh herbs are always preferred to dried ones, and many, such as parsley, basil, fennel, marjoram or thyme, can be grown in pots on a window sill. Dried herbs are much more concentrated than fresh because the water content has been removed. For every teaspoon of dried herbs, use 3 teaspoons or 1 tablespoon of fresh.

Bouquet garni, much used in French cooking, is a bouquet of herbs tied with a piece of string or in a small square of muslin and put into sauces, stews or *court bouillon.* Strictly, the herbs are parsley sprigs, thyme sprigs and bay leaf but other seasonings may be added such as celery, garlic, rosemary, marjoram, savory and so on. The bouquet is always removed at the end of the cooking time. Bay leaves put directly into a dish are also removed at the end of cooking, and so are dried sprigs of herbs like thyme or marjoram, as they would be unattractive in a finished dish.

Storing and drying herbs

To store fresh herbs, wrap them separately in paper towels, then put them into plastic bags and keep in the vegetable compartment of the refrigerator. To dry herbs, pick them just as they begin to flower when their flavour will be at its strongest. Gather them on a dry day, tie them in bunches and hang in a warm room away from strong light, or dry them in a very slow oven. Rub the dried leaves and flowers on to paper towels, then sift them into airtight containers and store away from the light in a cool place. Dried herbs will gradually lose their flavour.

SPICES AND SEEDS

Spices – most of which come from the tropics – are dried parts of aromatic plants and include flowers, seeds, leaves, bark and roots. Their use is of great antiquity and they have played a large and important role in human history. Their great value ensured that governments in countries with a big spice trade became rich on the taxes they levied.

Although there are no exact dates, it is believed that the trade in spices that came along the hazardous caravan routes from China, Indonesia, India and Ceylon to the eastern Mediterranean lasted about 5000 years. A favourite route went through Peshawar, over the Khyber Pass, through Afghanistan and Persia, eventually to reach Europe. The Phoenicians were great spice traders, so were the Arabs and the Romans, and later the Venetians and Genoese. After the fall of the Roman Empire there was a long, stagnant period until the Portuguese found a sea route to the East via the Cape of Good Hope, which led to competition between the Portuguese, Dutch, French and English.

During the centuries of struggle to control the trade, wars raged and empires rose and fell, but the spices that cooks have needed and used since early times – nutmeg, cloves, cinnamon, pepper, ginger, saffron and, from the New World, allspice, annatto, vanilla and chocolate – continued to arrive. Though once as costly as gold, they are today reasonably priced, neatly packaged items on the spice shelves of every supermarket. No longer do they come from a few precious sources; there is now hardly a country that does not produce at least one spice of its own.

The use of spices grew out of the natural cooking techniques of India, China and south-east Asia, where herbs and spices are still widely employed. The spices indigenous to these areas, such as ginger and nutmeg, provide a lively and enjoyable accent to the blandness of rice and bring out latent flavours in vegetable, fish, poultry and meat dishes; in south-east Asia spices complement the fiery sambals and fermented fish sauces and are essential in the variety of curries prepared throughout the sub-continent.

Spices in the kitchen

Today, spices still have a wide range of uses. Some, like pepper, are used exclusively in savoury dishes. Others, such as ginger, can also be used for baking or pickling. Ginger should be bought fresh, as ginger root; alternatively, the dried root can be bought, which will need to be soaked before grinding.

Roasting or dry-frying dried seeds, bark or roots helps to release their aromatic essential oils, and thus increases the flavour. Heat must be gently applied, then the spices can be pulverized – it's rather like first roasting then grinding coffee beans for maximum flavour. Spices can be used in whole pieces – in *birianis* and *pilaus* you can add pieces of cinnamon, or whole cloves or cardamoms to perfume the rice. They can also be used singly, as in China, where star anise is used to flavour pork and beef, ginger to add piquancy to fish and chicken, or in combination, as when using five-spice powder, in such dishes as Szechwan duck. In Japan a favourite condiment is *shichimitogarashi*, seven-flavour spice, a seasoning powder which is made from ground hot red peppers, ground Japanese pepper leaf (*sansho*, the leaf of the prickly ash), sesame, mustard, rape and poppy seeds and dried tangerine peel.

The French *quatre épices* is another popular combination of spices consisting of ground peppercorns, nutmeg, cloves and cinnamon. Ginger is sometimes substituted for the cinnamon. Many modern cooks combine allspice berries and black and white peppercorns in pepper mills for on-the-table use. The art of blending spices is as subtle as that of blending teas, perfumes, or liqueurs; cooks usually vary ingredients according to individual preference.

Herbs

TANSY (*Chrysanthemum vulgare*)

Native to Europe, tansy is now also common in other parts of the world. The leaves are chopped and used fresh. Once widely used to flavour egg and fish dishes, tansy now features as an ingredient in drisheen sausage.

TARRAGON
(*Artemesia dracunculus*)

Tarragon is a very aromatic, distinctive herb, related to wormwood. There are two main species, French tarragon and Russian tarragon, the latter being inferior in flavour, with a coarser leaf. French tarragon, native to Europe, is used for Béarnaise and Hollandaise sauce, *poulet à l'estragon*, savoury butters, soups, fish dishes and salads. It is available fresh, as dried leaves, or in powdered form.

MARIGOLD
(*Calendula officinalis*)

An annual plant native to southern Europe and Asia, the petals of this golden flower were used in medieval cookery, both as a flavouring and a dye to colour cheese, in custards and cakes. Today they are used to colour and flavour rice, meat and fish dishes, or in soups and salads. The petals are sold dried.

LEMON BALM
(*Melissa officinalis*)

So-called because of its lemony scent (but also known simply as balm), the leaves of this plant native to Europe are used in vegetable and fruit salads, drinks – especially punch and cordials – soups and sauces, as a tisane, or wherever a faint lemon flavour is required. Fresh or dried leaves are available.

Tansy

Tarragon

Dried tarragon

Dried marigold

Marigold

Woodruff

Dried woodruff

Lemon balm

Dried lemon balm

CORIANDER
(*Coriandrum sativum*)

A member of the carrot family, this ancient herb is indigenous to the Mediterranean and the Caucasus, and is often sold as cilantro or Chinese parsley in Latin American and Chinese markets. It has a fresh taste, similar to orange, and is greatly used in India, Asia, Mexico, South America and the Middle East in its fresh, leafy form. The seeds (page 59) are used as an ingredient in curry and to flavour alcoholic drinks such as gin. In Thailand, the roots are used in curries.

Coriander

Hop

HOP (*Humulus lupulus*)

Well-known as a flavouring for beer, hops are the flowers of a vine-like plant native to Europe. The young shoots are used as a vegetable, and can also be made into a salad. Pillows stuffed with hops are said to aid insomnia, as is hop tea.

WOODRUFF (*Asperula odorata*)

Also known as sweet woodruff, this perennial herb is native to Europe and Asia. It has a distinctive scented taste, and the leaves can be used fresh or dried. It is used dried in "May Cup" – a traditional English drink – and in tisanes; also infused in champagne, Benedictine and punch.

BORAGE (*Borago officinalis*)

An annual plant native to the Middle East, this is now common in southern Europe and southern England. The flowers and the leaves are used, fresh or dried, in vinegar, sauces and salads. The taste is reminiscent of cucumber, and may be used in Pimm's wine cups. Finely chopped leaves can be used to flavour cream cheese and yoghurt.

BASIL (*Ocimum basilicum*)

A strong and pungent herb, this annual plant is native to India. Also known as sweet basil, its use in the West is relatively recent. The leaves are used, fresh or dried: the fresh leaves have a taste similar to cloves, but when dried they taste more like curry. It has many uses, notably in the Italian pesto sauce.

Borage

Dried borage

Winter savory

Burnet

MINT (*Mentha,* spp.)

There are many varieties, but from the cook's point of view, spearmint (*Mentha spicata; M. viridis*) and applemint (*M. rotundifolia*) are the two most important. Spearmint is native to southern Europe and is the common or garden mint, used for mint sauce, mint jelly, stuffings, salads and to flavour drinks such as Moroccan mint tea. Applemint, or round-leaved mint, has a fine flavour. The leaves are covered with a fine down, and such varieties as Bowles mint (*M. villosa alopecuroides*) are recommended for all culinary uses. Eau de cologne mint (*M. citrata*), or orange mint, has a pleasant perfume, and can be used chopped in salads, or to flavour iced summer drinks. Other mints include peppermint (*M. piperita*), used for flavouring sweets and in crème de menthe, and horsemint (*M. longifolia*), used in curries.

BURNET (*Poterium sanguisorba*)

Native to Europe, today burnet (or salad burnet) is used mainly in French and Italian cooking. The leaves are similar to borage in flavour and are used, fresh or dried, in salads, soups, cordials and casseroles, and also in cocktails.

WINTER SAVORY
(*Satureia montana*)

Both this and summer savory (*S. hortensis*) are very similar and seasonal according to their names, although winter savory is considered by some cooks to possess a coarser flavour than its warm-weather relative. They are fairly strong, aromatic herbs, which can have the same applications as thyme.

SAGE (*Salvia officinalis*)

Native to the northern Mediterranean, sage is a well-known plant with downy leaves and a strongly aromatic flavour. There is much variation in the colour of the leaves and the flavour. Garden sage (shown here) is used for stuffings, particularly with pork or duck, and may be used with discretion in meat stews and casseroles, though it tends to overpower subtle flavours.

Basil

Dried basil

Applemint
(Mentha rotundifolia)

Spearmint
(Mentha viridis)

Dried spearmint

Dried sage

Sage

BAY (*Laurus nobilis*)

Also called sweet bay or laurel, but not to be confused with varieties of laurel that are poisonous, this refers to a leaf of the sweet bay tree native to the Mediterranean, which is usually used dried, although powdered bay is available. Used to flavour meat dishes, milk puddings, soups, stews and sweet white sauces, bay is one of the ingredients in bouquet garni.

THYME (*Thymus* spp.)

There are many varieties of this perennial herb, which is native to southern Europe and the Mediterranean. The leaves (fresh or dried) have many uses and form the basic part of bouquet garni. Thyme has a strong, sharp taste so lemon thyme, which is less strong with a lemon tang, is often used instead. Thyme can be used to flavour soups, stews, roast meat and poultry stuffings.

LOVAGE (*Levisticum officinale*)

This is a large, celery-like plant native to the Mediterranean that yields an essential oil and has a strong aromatic flavour. The entire plant is used: stems and root can be cooked in the manner of celery or candied as for angelica, leaves, roots and seeds are used in salads, soups and sauces, and seeds can be used in baking. Lovage is available dried, as whole seeds or in root form.

Bay

Common thyme
(Thymus vulgaris)

Dried lovage

Dried bay

Lemon thyme
(Thymus citriodorus)

Dried thyme

Lovage

LEMON VERBENA (*Lippia citriodora*)

Also known as verbena, this herb is a native of South America, and was introduced to Europe by the Spanish. It can be used to impart a lemon flavour to drinks and salads and as a herb. It is available fresh or dried.

Lemon verbena

PARSLEY (*Petroselinum crispum*)

Native to the Mediterranean area, there are several varieties of parsley, including broad-leaved parsley, curly-leaved parsley, Hamburg parsley (page 31), grown for its roots, and Neapolitan or Italian parsley, grown for its celery-like stems. Parsley has many uses, not the least of which is as a garnish. It is used in bouquet garni, in *fines herbes*, added to sauces and stuffings or fried as an accompaniment to fish. It is available fresh and dried.

Parsley

Dried parsley

OREGANO (*Origanum vulgare*)

This aromatic herb has been used for centuries in Asia and Europe and is now especially popular in Italy, where it is used in pizzas. Oregano or wild marjoram is also used with tomatoes, cheese, beans and aubergines. There are many Greek varieties, collectively called rigani, the flowers of which are used to garnish meat dishes. The leaves are usually used dried.

Oregano

Dried oregano

CHIVE (*Allium schoenoprasum*)

A native of Europe, the chive is a member of the onion family. The fine, hollow stems are used fresh and chopped finely in cream soups, scrambled eggs, omelettes, salads and hors d'œuvres. Chinese chives (*Allium odoratum*) have larger leaves, flowers that smell of roses, and taste of garlic.

Chive

Rosemary

Dried chives

MARJORAM
(*Origanum majorana*)

Although the name "marjoram" covers numerous plants, including wild marjoram (see oregano, opposite) and pot marjoram (*Origanum onites*), the name is normally used to refer to sweet, or cultivated, marjoram. It can be used fresh or dried in omelettes, stuffings, sausages, bouquets garnis, meat sauces, potato dishes, soups and stews.

Marjoram

Dried marjoram

Dried rosemary

ROSEMARY
(*Rosmarinus officinalis*)

A plant of Mediterranean origin, rosemary is found growing wild over most of Europe, and in America. Its hard, spiky leaves contain oil of camphor, and are widely used for flavouring meat dishes, most notably lamb, and chicken and fish. Rosemary is seldom used in salads or soups except in powder form, when some of its qualities become muted. It is available fresh, as dried leaves or in powder form.

MIXED HERBS

A ready-prepared mixture of dried herbs, usually consisting of thyme, marjoram, parsley, rosemary and basil. It can be used in most savoury dishes.

Mixed herbs

UNUSUAL HERBS

COSTMARY
(*Chrysanthemum balsamita, Tanacetum balsamita*)
Costmary is similar to tansy, being spicy but less bitter. Native to the Far East, the leaves were traditionally used in Britain and America as flavouring for beer, hence its other name "alecost". It is used with game and veal and in soups, and is available dried.

EPAZOTE
(*Chenopodium ambrosiodes*)
Also known as Mexican tea, wormseed, goosefoot and Jerusalem oak, epazote grows wild in the Americas and in parts of Europe. It is used as a green herb in Mexican cooking and as a tisane in Europe.

LEMON GRASS
(*Cymbopogon citratus, flexuesus, nardus*)
This includes several species of grass, all possessing the flavour of lemon due to the presence of citric oils. It is native to south-east Asia, where in some places the lemon tree is absent, and is available as sereh powder. It is useful in flavouring salads, fish dishes and soups. In Thailand, and other parts of south-east Asia, the leaves of the Kaffir lime (*Citrus hystrix*) are also used for fish dishes.

ROSELLA
(*Hibiscus sabdariffa*)
A native of tropical Asia, also known as sorrel and flor de Jamaica, rosella is grown for its fleshy red sepals, which are commonly used to make drinks and preserves.

VERVAIN
(*Verbena officinalis*)
Often confused with lemon verbena, this ancient European herb is mainly used to make herb tea. It is available as dried leaves.

BERGAMOT (*Monarda didyma*)

There are many varieties of this strongly flavoured herb, native to America and now also available in Europe. Related to the mint family, it is also known as oswego and bee balm. The flowers and leaves are used, fresh or dried, in tisanes and teas. The leaves can also be used in salads.

DILL (*Anethum graveolens*)

A plant of the parsley family native to Europe and western Asia, dill is now grown throughout the world. Dill weed (as it is sometimes called) is best known for its affinity with fish and its use in flavouring dill pickles. Also used in soups, egg dishes and sauces, dill is available as seeds or as dried leaves. The seeds have a more pungent, arresting flavour.

NASTURTIUM (*Tropaeolum majus*)

Native to Peru, this annual plant is now available worldwide. The leaves (usually fresh), petals and seeds are all used; their peppery taste makes them useful for salads and sandwiches. The seed pods can be pickled and used like capers.

Dill weed

Nasturtium

Bergamot

COMFREY (*Symphytum officinale*)

Native to Europe and Asia, comfrey is related to borage. Its leaves are used either fresh (in salads) or dried and powdered (in tea). The dried root is also used, mainly as a flavouring for wine.

Dried dill

Dill seeds

FENUGREEK (*Trigonella foenum-graecum*)

Native to western Asia, fenugreek or methi also grows in the Mediterranean. The leaves, which have a faintly bitter taste, are used, fresh or dried; also the rock-hard seeds (page 61). It is an important ingredient in curries.

Dried fenugreek leaves

Comfrey root

Dried comfrey

CURRY (*Chalcas koenigii*)

Dried curry leaves

A relative of the lemon tree, and a native of south-east Asia, the leaves bestow a curry-like flavour to certain commercial curry powders. They are also used throughout southern India in vegetarian dishes. The curry leaf is available in fresh or dried form, although the fresh leaves are usually preferred.

BOUQUET GARNI

A combination of dried herbs such as thyme, parsley and bay used in soups, stews and sauces. Usually wrapped in muslin, they are removed before serving.

Bouquet garni

Comfrey

CAMOMILE
(*Chamaemelum nobile*)

There are many varieties of this daisy-like plant found growing wild throughout Europe and parts of America. The leaves and flowers are used to make a refreshing tisane, camomile tea. It is available fresh or dried.

Camomile

Dried camomile

HYSSOP (*Hysoppus officinalis*)

The leaves have a pungent and slightly bitter, minty taste and are used for flavouring liqueurs such as Benedictine and Chartreuse, and may also be used fresh in salads and fresh or dried in soups, stuffings and stews.

Hyssop

Dried hyssop

CHERVIL
(*Anthriscus cerefolium*)

A native of southern Russia and the Middle East, this parsley-like plant with feathery leaves is considered one of the *fines herbes* in French cuisine. It is used to flavour soups, salads and stuffings and is also employed as a garnish. Available dried, it is best when used fresh.

Dried chervil

YARROW (*Achillea millefolium*)

A perennial plant native to southern England, yarrow or milfoil is now grown in many countries, including America. The leaves (fresh or dried), seeds and roots are used.

Yarrow

Dried yarrow

Fennel

ANGELICA
(*Angelica officinalis, archangelica*)

A member of the parsley family, angelica is a native of northern Europe. The entire plant can be used, as even the root provides a drug, but its more familiar form is as a candied stem used in baking (page 125).

Angelica

FENNEL (*Foeniculum vulgare*)

A tall plant with feathery leaves and yellow seeds, fennel is a native of southern Europe. Like dill, it has long been used as a fish herb, and now grows wild throughout the world, although it is produced commercially. The leaves can be used in salads and stuffings, and the stems are cooked as a vegetable (page 18). In Provence, grey mullet and bream are often *flambéed* on a bed of dried fennel stalks. The seeds have a slight liquorice taste.

Dried fennel

Fennel seeds

Spices and Seeds

CURRY POWDER

This is a blend of any number of spices, bought ready-prepared. It can vary from mild to hot depending on the spices included, and its use in curries is confined mainly to the West.

Curry powder

PICKLING SPICE

A mixture of spices, consisting basically of black peppercorns, red chillies and varying proportions of mustard seed, allspice, cloves, ginger, mace and coriander seed. It is used in pickles, chutneys and vinegars.

Pickling spice

GARAM MASALA

The name means, literally, "hot mixture", and is applied to a combination of roasted spices (such as coriander seed, chilli and black pepper) ground into a powder. Although freshly blended and ground in India and the East, in the West it is bought ready-prepared. It is used as a basic flavouring for many Indian dishes.

CHINESE FIVE-SPICE POWDER

This is a Chinese spice mixture consisting of equal parts of finely ground anise pepper, star anise, cassia or cinnamon, cloves and fennel seed. It has a subtle taste and, apart from its wide use in oriental cookery, can be used in any pork or beef dish.

Chinese five-spice powder

ANNATTO (*Bixa orellana*)

Also known as achiote, bija, bijoul and roucou, this is the fruit and seeds of a tree native to tropical America. The dye from the fruit is orange and used for colouring foods. Seeds are ground and used as a spice in Latin America, and in south-east Asia, where they feature in *ukoy*, or shrimp and potato cakes.

Annatto

Garam masala

GALANGAL

Both greater (*Alpinia galanga*) and lesser (*Alpinia officinarum* – shown here) galangal are root spices related to ginger but with a faint flavour of camphor. Available in root or powder form, they are used in the Far East in curries and in Malay dishes, and also in liqueurs and bitters.

Galangal

HORSERADISH

(*Armoracia rusticana*)

The pungent root of the plant may be grated, and is sometimes sold dried. Its most important use is as the basis for a sauce traditionally eaten with roast beef. It is most pungent when fresh.

Fresh grated horseradish

Dried ground horseradish

CASSIA (*Cinnamomum cassia*)

Similar to cinnamon and often confused with it, cassia spice (or Chinese cinnamon) is the dried bark of an evergreen tree native to Burma. Also used in powder form, it is popular in oriental cookery.

Cassia bark

Ground cassia

NIGELLA (*Nigella sativa*)

These black seeds have a peppery taste and are sprinkled on bread and cakes. Nigella, or wild onion seed, is often confused with the black variety of cumin.

Nigella

CELERY SEED
(*Apium graveolens*)

The dried seeds of the celery plant, native to Italy, have a rather bitter taste and are used in soups and stews.

Celery seed

FENNEL SEED
(*Foeniculum vulgare*)

The aromatic dried seeds of the fennel plant, native to the Mediterranean area, have a slight aniseed taste and can be used in a wide range of dishes, including apple pie, curries and fish dishes.

Fennel seed

SUNFLOWER SEED
(*Helianthus annuus*)

These are the dried seeds of the sunflower plant native to Peru. Their main use is as a source of oil (page 75), but they can also be eaten roasted in their husks. There are many varieties.

Sunflower seed

TAMARIND (*Tamarindus indica*)

The fruit pods and pulp of an African tree, now grown throughout India. The pods contain a very sour juice used as a flavouring for some Indian curries. Sold as sticky, broken pods minus the seeds, and dried.

Tamarind

SESAME SEED
(*Sesamum indicum*)

The dried fruits of the sesame plant (an annual native to India), the seeds are best known as a source of oil (page 75). In the Middle East they are ground to produce tahini (page 69) and halva. They are sometimes used to decorate cakes and breads in the West.

Black sesame seeds

White sesame seeds

PUMPKIN SEED
(*Cucurbita maxima*)

The seeds of the native American plant are used as a source of oil, but can also be eaten roasted.

Pumpkin seed

DILL SEED
(*Anethum graveolens*)

The dried fruits of the dill plant, native to southern Europe; the seeds taste like caraway and are used with fish.

Dill seed

CAYENNE PEPPER
(Capsicum frutescens)

Made from a type of red chilli pepper said to be native to Cayenne in French Guyana, other seeds, salt and spices are often added to the powder in its commercial form. It is very pungent and thus should be used sparingly. It is used in curries, white sauces, soups, stews, with smoked fish, oysters, shrimps, whitebait and cooked cheese.

Cayenne pepper

PEPPER *(Piper nigrum)*

A type of vine pepper not to be confused with the capsicum varieties, this is native to Asia, but used in most cuisines. Black peppercorns are the sun-dried berries of the pepper vine, picked while still green. White peppercorns are from the same plant, but the berries are picked when ripe and the skin is removed. Both are used as a seasoning, though white pepper is much less aromatic.

Mignonette pepper is a coarse-grained pepper made by grinding and sieving black or white peppercorns. It is used a great deal in French cookery. Szechwan peppercorns, from China, are red and have a slightly numbing effect when roasted.

White peppercorns

Black peppercorns

ANISE-PEPPER
(Zanthoxylum piperitum)

The dried berries of a tree native to China, this is also called Szechuan pepper. It has a hot aromatic flavour and is used in Chinese five-spice powder and oriental cooking.

Anise-pepper

NUTMEG *(Myristica fragrans)*

The dried kernel or "nut" of an evergreen of the myrtle family, native to Indonesia, this is encased in a fleshy apricot-like fruit which splits open when ripe, and is thought to be addictive. Small quantities are soporific and digestive. It can be used whole or ground.

Ground nutmeg

Whole nutmeg

Green peppercorns in brine

CLOVE *(Eugenia aromatica)*

The dried, aromatic flower buds of an evergreen of the myrtle family native to south-east Asia, cloves are normally used whole, but the central "head" of the bud can also be ground into a powder. They contain an essential oil used for relieving toothache, but are mainly used in sweet and savoury dishes, spiced wines and liqueurs.

Whole cloves

Ground cloves

GARLIC *(Allium sativum)*

The bulb of a perennial plant (page 29), garlic can be dried and used as flakes or ground into a powder. It has a pungent taste and smell.

Garlic flakes

Ground garlic

MACE (*Myristica fragans*)

Mace, in blade form, is the outer net-like covering of nutmeg. The blades are pressed flat and dried before use, and can be ground.

Ground mace

Blades of mace

CINNAMON
(*Cinnamomum zeylanicum*)

A member of the laurel family and native to India, cinnamon is used for its aromatic bark. Available in sticks, quills or as a powder, cinnamon is used for baking and desserts, also to flavour rice dishes and fish, chicken or ham. It keeps well.

Cinnamon stick

Cinnamon quills

Ground cinnamon

PAPRIKA
(*Capsicum tetragonum*)

Made from a type of pepper native to South America, paprika varies in taste from mildly hot to mild and sweet and in appearance from rosy brown to scarlet. The national spice of Hungary – there is also a Spanish version called *pimentón* – it is used in goulashes, white sauces, meat and chicken dishes, cream soups and cream cheese.

Paprika

POPPY (*Papaver somniferum*)

The seed of the opium poppy flower native to the Middle East, there are two types: white and grey-blue. They are used in Indian, Jewish and Middle Eastern cooking.

White poppy seeds

Blue poppy seeds

CUMIN (*Cuminum cyminum*)

The dried fruit of an annual plant related to parsley and indigenous to the Upper Nile, cumin has a pungent, hot and somewhat bitter taste and is a very popular culinary spice in the East, Mexico and North Africa. It can be used whole or ground.

CORIANDER
(*Coriandrum sativum*)

The leaves are used as a herb (page 50), the seeds as a spice; they are quite different in flavour. Coriander is a leading item in curry pastes and powder. It is used with lamb and pork, in pickles, marinades and *à la grecque* recipes and dishes.

Ground coriander

Coriander seeds

SAFFRON (*Crocus sativus*)

The dried stigmas of a crocus flower native to Greece, saffron is one of the world's most expensive spices. Aromatic, pungent and slightly bitter, it yields a brilliant yellow dye. It is used for colouring and flavouring rice dishes, cakes, breads and soups, particularly in *bouillabaisse* and *paella*. It is available as stigmas or powder.

Saffron

Ground cumin

Whole cumin

CARDAMOM
(Elettaria cardamomum)

The pods are the aromatic dried fruits of a perennial plant of the ginger family native to India. They can vary from green to black; the white pods are sun-bleached and not as aromatic as the green pods. They contain small seeds, which may be ground up and used. Cardomom pods and seeds are used in many Indian recipes, and to flavour rice.

Black cardamom pods

White cardamom pods

Green cardamom pods

Cardamom seeds

ALLSPICE (Pimenta officinalis)

The berries are the dried fruit of the evergreen pimento tree, native to the West Indies. Called allspice for its versatile nature (but also known as pimento and Jamaica pepper), it tastes like nutmeg, cinnamon and cloves. It is used in baking, pickling and savoury dishes, and is available whole or powdered.

Ground allspice

Allspice berries

TURMERIC (Curcuma longa)

A bright yellow spice obtained from the rhizomes of a plant of the lily family, native to south-east Asia. It is an inexpensive spice, used in curries, curry powder and pickles. It is available as a powder and a dried root.

Ground turmeric

Turmeric root

CARAWAY (Carum carvi)

Well-known in Europe, where the sickle-shaped seeds are used in baking, cheese-making and many savoury dishes, caraway is native to Europe and Asia. Related to anise, it has a pungent, characteristic taste and is also used to flavour liqueurs.

Caraway

OTHER SPICES AND SEEDS

GRAINS OF PARADISE
(Amomum melegueta)
Piquant, strongly flavoured brown seeds of a plant related to allspice, used as a substitute for pepper. Known as Guinea pepper and malegueta pepper, it is indigenous to west Africa.

MUSTARD (Brassica, spp.)

The seeds come from three plants of the cabbage family. The black are hotter than the white; the powder is a mixture of both.

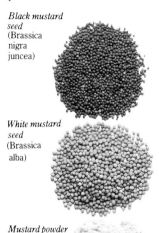

Black mustard seed (Brassica nigra juncea)

White mustard seed (Brassica alba)

Mustard powder

STAR ANISE (Illicium verum)

The small star-shaped seed of a tree native to China, and related to the magnolia, this contains the same essential oils as anise. It is used in oriental cooking, especially with braised beef, chicken and lamb, and is an ingredient in Chinese five-spice powder.

Star anise pods

Star anise seeds

GINGER (*Zingiber officinale*)

The rhizome or root stem of this plant native to south-east Asia can be bought whole, sliced or ground. Refreshingly pungent in flavour and slightly hot, it is used in oriental and Indian dishes, baking, confectionery and also in certain liqueurs.

Chilli powder

Chilli flakes

Ground ginger

Ginger root

Dried ginger slice

CHILLI (*Capsicum frutescens*)

A type of red pepper made from dried ground or flaked chilli peppers. Not to be confused with paprika, it can vary from mild to very hot. Nepal pepper is a mild yellow variety of ground chilli pepper used a great deal in India.

FENUGREEK
(*Trigonella foenum-graecum*)

The pods of a flowering plant native to western Asia contains seeds which are dried and then ground into powder. The leaves are used as a herb (page 54).

Ground fenugreek

Fenugreek seeds

ANISE (*Pimpinella anisum*)

Grown for the seed which yields a sweet-scented anise flavour, it is used mainly in confectionery and baking; it also features in pastis, Ricard and other anise-flavoured alcoholic drinks. Both the seeds and fresh leaves are used.

JUNIPER (*Juniperus communis*)

Native to the northern hemisphere, juniper is used to flavour gin, game and pork. In Germany it is used in sauerkraut and in preserves. The berries are usually sold dried.

Ground anise

AJOWAN (*Carum ajowan*)

The seed of a plant native to India, this has a strong taste of thyme and is used extensively in Indian and Middle Eastern cookery.

Juniper

Anise seeds

Ajowan

Flavourings

PEOPLE HAVE NEVER BEEN content merely to accept nourishment for its own sake: the pursuit of taste to enliven a staple diet has always been an important part of eating habits, and as new and interesting flavours were discovered so were they adapted and incorporated. In Central America the staple ingredients of maize and potatoes were heightened by the use of chillies. Chillies were eventually to make an enduring impact on the curries of India and the sambals of south-east Asia. In the same way two plants originally enjoyed only by the Aztecs – chocolate and vanilla – were destined to contribute enormously to international cooking.

Many synthetic flavourings have been developed which are by and large preferred by some sections of the industry because they are concentrated, stable at high temperatures, and have a reduced moisture content.

There is, however, still a demand for the real thing. Extracts, mainly essential oils, are produced from the plant by processes which soften and break down the oil-bearing cells. Essences are extracted from various parts of the plant according to its nature: from crushed seeds or stones, from flowers and leaves, or the dried bark and roots.

Flavourings in the kitchen

Flavouring extracts will keep indefinitely stored in tightly sealed bottles, and in a cool, dark place. If a recipe demands "a few drops" of some essence, add the essence drop by drop until the desired strength is reached. Ice cream needs stronger flavouring than temperate foods, because mixtures lose their flavour as they get progressively colder – also, cold numbs the taste buds.

Vanilla pods are preferable to vanilla essence. Whole pods can be cooked in sweet sauces to flavour them, after which the pods can be washed, dried, and used again. Vanilla sugar is a useful form of flavouring, and a pod of vanilla can be kept in a jar of fine sugar for adding to cakes and confectionery.

DRIED PEPPERS
(*Capsicum frutescens*)

Many varieties of pungent chilli peppers are dried and used to flavour savoury dishes, particularly in Latin American cooking. They include ancho, jalapeño, mulato, pasilla, and the traditional red chilli.

VANILLA (*Vanilla planifolia*)

The cured pod of a climbing orchid native to Central America, vanilla is used as a flavouring in sweet sauces, cakes, chocolate, puddings and ice creams.

LIQUORICE (*Glycyrrhiza glabra*)

One of the most ancient of flavourings, liquorice is the root of a small perennial plant grown in southern Europe and the Middle East. It has a bitter-sweet taste and is used in confectionery, desserts, cakes and drinks. The root can be sliced or ground.

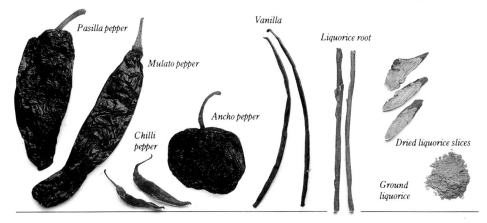

Pasilla pepper

Mulato pepper

Chilli pepper

Ancho pepper

Vanilla

Liquorice root

Dried liquorice slices

Ground liquorice

DRIED MANGO
(Mangifera indica)

The mango fruit (page 92), native to India, is often dried and sliced as shown and used as a flavouring for curries. It is also used to make mango chutney (page 67), or may be pickled (page 68).

Dried mango

ANGOSTURA BITTERS

These bitters, named after an old Venezuelan town, are made in Trinidad. They consist of cloves, cinnamon, mace, nutmeg, prunes, quinine, rum and gentian. Their most popular use is in cocktails, but they are also used in ice cream, fruit juices, preserved fruits and puddings.

GRENADINE

A popular term for the extract of pulp from the pomegranate *(Punica granatum)* native to Kurdistan. It is used in soft drinks, cocktails, ice cream and confectionery.

Angostura bitters

Grenadine

OTHER FLAVOURINGS

BITTER ALMOND ESSENCE

This commercial almond essence, much stronger than oil of sweet almond, is derived from the bitter *Prunus amygdalus* and from the kernels of peaches and apricots. It is used in baking, confectionery and desserts.

CAROB

A flavouring from the pulp of the carob or locust bean *(Ceratonia siliqua)* originating in the Middle East, this is used in soft drinks manufacture and in the baking and confectionery industry.

CHOCOLATE

Chocolate and cocoa come from the fruit of the Mexican *Theobroma cacao,* in beans containing 20–30 white seeds which, when fermented, dried, then roasted are a source of cocoa butter, cocoa powder, drinking chocolate and baking chocolate (page 125). Milk chocolate contains dried full cream milk powder. Apart from the familiar use of chocolate in baking and confectionery, it is also used, unsweetened, to flavour some Mexican meat dishes.

COLA

Extract from the nuts of *Cola nitida,* native to west Africa, and a main ingredient of cola drinks. The nuts are macerated to obtain an extract, then mixed with syrup.

NEROLI BIGARADE

The fruit and flowers of the bitter orange tree (*Citrus aurantium* var. *bergamia,* the Bergamot orange), yield a powerful, aromatic oil, called neroli oil, which is used in soft drinks, ice cream, confectionery and baked goods.

ORRIS

The peeled rhizomes, "orris root", of *Iris germanica,* native to the Far East, yield orris extract which is used in ice cream, confectionery and baked goods.

PEPPERMINT OIL

Steam distillation of the flowering plant *Mentha piperata* gives peppermint oil, which is used in soft drinks, beverages, confectionery, ice cream and also in icings.

SANDALWOOD OIL

The dried bark of a tree native to southern India is distilled to yield an essential oil, containing aromatic sanatol. It is used in ice cream, confectionery and various baked goods.

SARSAPARILLA

The roots from the Mexican tree *Smilax aristolochiaefolia* yield an extract with a bitterish, liquorice taste. It is used in soft drinks, ice cream, confectionery and baked goods, and also in medicine.

SASSAFRAS ESSENCE
(Sassafras albidum)

The roots, bark and leaves of this tree native to North America are used and steam-distilled to produce a lemon-scented oil with a spicy flavour. It is used in soft drinks, confectionery and ice cream.

YLANG-YLANG OIL

The flowers of a large tree *(Cananga odorata)* native to the Philippines are steam-distilled to obtain their oil, which has a strong, flower-like odour and a bitter aromatic taste. Used in soft drinks, ice cream, confectionery and baked goods.

Seasonings and Extracts

THE PURPOSE OF SEASONINGS is to enhance and accentuate flavours, especially flavours dormant in food, or to create a dominant taste in bland foods. In the West salt is the principal seasoning, and in the East soy, either in the form of soy sauce or as a paste.

SALT

Salt is the mineral sodium chloride; when obtained from the evaporation of sea water it is sea or bay salt; when mined from deposits left by primeval seas, it is rock salt. Although salt contains no calories, proteins or carbohydrates, traces of other minerals are present in unrefined salt, including calcium, magnesium, sulphur and phosphorus; magnesium in salt gives it a bitter aftertaste.

The mineral elements in unrefined sodium chloride can affect foods cooked with salt. For example, rock salt contains calcium, which will toughen the skin of beans and pulses – for this reason we are advised not to boil sweetcorn in salted water. Calcium also increases the moisture retention of salt, so that anti-caking agents are needed; the hygroscopic properties of salt cause it to solidify or to become heavy with moisture in damp conditions. Manufacturers have now improved their techniques by treating salt with YPS (sodium ferrocyanide), a chemical that causes small tentacles to form on each grain, preventing them from sticking together.

A measure or a "pinch" of salt is an essential ingredient in a limitless variety of recipes, savoury and sweet. Salt enhances the taste of foods, and actually reduces the sourness of acid, and increases the sweetness of sugar – or appears to increase it – when added to sweet dishes. Salt and sugar react together as balancing agents: sugar will reduce saltiness, while over-sweet foods can be moderated by adding a touch of salt.

You will need salt in the majority of bread recipes, for it strengthens the gluten – the building fibre of wheat – and helps to form a crisp crust on bread. Yet too much salt will inhibit the action of yeast, so bakers must measure carefully, according to the recipe. The best salt to use in the kitchen is the fine, free-flowing table salt, or the larger crystals of pure sea salt, crushed in the fingers or in a mill.

FOOD EXTRACTS

Meat and vegetable extracts further fulfil the purpose of seasoning, since they are concentrates and have excellent keeping properties. Although commercial extracts are a fairly recent invention – the German chemist Justus von Liebig developed a concentrated beef paste at Fray Bentos, Uruguay, in 1847 – the usefulness of food concentrates must have been evident to the first cooks who used meat gravy, and to the Chinese who, many thousands of years ago, made a paste from fermented soybeans, an early type of yeast extract. In the late nineteenth century, German chemists found that autolysis of brewer's yeast with salt created a vegetarian equivalent of beef extract.

Food extracts have a long shelf life, though stock cubes may absorb moisture if stored in a damp place. Soy pastes have a shelf life of over six months, and once opened tend to slowly dry out; they can be moistened with a little oil.

STOCK CUBES

These contain monosodium glutamate, herbs and spices, yeast extract, starch, caramel, lactic acid, sugar, salt, fat, onion, celery and pepper. Stock cubes are available in beef, chicken, lamb and vegetarian flavours.

Stock cubes

Stock powder

STOCK POWDER

This is powdered dehydrated meat extract containing herbs. As its name implies, it is used for stocks, gravies and soups and occasionally in sauces.

SALT

Bay salt is obtained by the evaporation of sea water in pits by the natural heat from the sun. Kitchen (or block, lump or common) salt is a refined rock salt without additives most commonly used for pickling or curing meat. Flavoured salts, including garlic salt and celery salt, and the spiced seasoned salt, or *sel épice*, are a mixture of salt and other ingredients and are useful seasonings. Freezing salt is a rough, coarse version of salt in crystals, not considered fit for human consumption. Pretzel salt is currently mined on the Gulf of Mexico, where there is a rare deposit of salt that forms large, regular, flat flakes that are perfectly suited to coating pretzels. Rock salt is purified by a similar process to sea salt – boiling down and crystallizing the saline to varying degrees of fineness, to produce cooking or kitchen salt, and table salt. Sea salt is produced from tidal pools of concentrated saline, filtered and heated in shallow pans, left to crystallize and artificially evaporated.

Seasoned salt

Garlic salt

Table salt

Crystal rock salt

Kitchen salt

Sea salt

Celery salt

BENTOO NO TOMO

A Japanese seasoning compound consisting of dried fish, salt, soy sauce, seaweed and monosodium glutamate, this is also used in oriental cooking.

Bentoo no tomo

MONOSODIUM GLUTAMATE

The salt of glutamic acid, one of the amino acid food proteins, this is flavourless in itself but enhances other foods. Also known as MSG and Ve-tsin, monosodium glutamate may be used as a salt substitute.

Monosodium glutamate

ASAFOETIDA

A resin from the plant *Ferula asafoetida*, this is sold as shown or as a powder, and only minute quantities are needed. It is particularly useful in fish recipes and is often used in Indian cooking as a salt substitute.

GRAVY THICKENER

This is a dehydrated meat extract with added thickening agents, such as corn starch or wheat flour. It can be used in stews and casseroles.

Gravy thickener

Asafoetida

SETO FUUMI

A Japanese seasoning compound consisting of dried seaweed, tuna, sesame seed and monosodium glutamate, this is widely used in oriental cooking.

Seto fuumi

SOY PASTES

There are two types of paste made from soy, the fermented and the unfermented. The Japanese *miso* shown here is a fermented type, made by cooking the beans, mixing them with *koji* (steamed rice treated with a growth of the fungus *Aspergillus oryzae*), salt and water, then inoculating the mass with yeast. It is then left to ferment for several months. Extracts from the red, yellow and black varieties of soybean are shown. *Natto* is a similar preparation. *Tempeh* is fermented bean cake from Indonesia. Unfermented bean pastes are prepared as *tofu* or Chinese bean curd, and the sweet red bean paste used in confectionery.

Yellow

Red miso

Black miso

GRAVY BROWNING

This is basically a colouring agent which enhances the appearance of brown sauces and gravies. It should be used with caution. The usual composition of gravy browning is simply caramel, salt and water. Sometimes flavours are added, such as hydrolized vegetable protein and MSG.

Gravy browning

MALT EXTRACT

Malt extract is made by soaking powdered malt in water, heating, and then reducing the mixture to a syrup or paste. It is used in brewing and distilling, in the manufacture of breakfast cereals, as a coffee substitute, and in baking. It gives a moist texture to brown bread, helps the dough to rise, and imparts a sweet flavour.

YEAST EXTRACT

The liquid from fresh yeast is separated, evaporated and added to vegetable extract. It has similar characteristics to meat extracts and is used as a seasoning.

Yeast extract

Malt extract

Beef extract

BEEF EXTRACT

A concentrated meat soup reduced by evaporation to a thick dark-brown salty paste.

OTHER EXTRACTS

MALTED MILK

Malted beverages arose from the pioneer work done during the mid-nineteenth century on invalid diets and infant foods. In 1869, an English immigrant to America, William Horlick, developed a maltose-dextrin-milk powder that found favour with the medical profession, and was marketed as Horlicks in 1887. Malted milk, one of the drinks originally sold in America's drugstores and soda fountains, is itself an ingredient, used to make biscuits, cake mixes, icings, and ice cream.

PICKLES, CHUTNEYS AND PASTES

PICKLES, CHUTNEYS AND PASTES are flavourings designed to enliven or to provide a contrast to their accompanying foods. Most are products of preserving techniques using oil or vinegar, sugar and salt.

Pickles are vegetables or fruits (either whole or coarsely chopped) which are preserved in brine or vinegar. The word "pickle" also describes a brine or spiced vinegar solution for preserving meat, fish, fruit or vegetables.

Chutneys are mixtures of fruits or vegetables, either fresh or cooked in a thick sauce. They are sweet-tasting, thick and spicy, and are, in fact, similar to sweet mixed pickles, though these are generally darker in colour and sharper in flavour. Fresh chutneys, as made in the East, need no preservative, but the chutneys made in the West are cooked preparations, and so include vinegar.

Pastes are finely-ground products based on a main ingredient such as nuts, meat or salted fish. Their keeping qualities are due to the presence of oil or salt.

The word "relish" is often used to describe any chutney or sweet pickle preserved in a sweet-sour foundation. Certain foods are traditionally connected with certain types of relishes. Indian curries, for example, are linked with many such accompaniments, including mango, tamarind and coriander chutneys, pickled limes and cauliflower. Indonesian pickles, or *sambals*, also vary in taste.

HORSERADISH RELISH

The grated root of the horseradish is mixed with cream, agar-agar, vinegar and salt in this relish, which is used with hot or cold meats and fresh or smoked fish.

Horseradish relish

TOMATO CHUTNEY

A rich and tangy blend of tomatoes, gherkins, chillies and spices, this can be eaten with cold meats and cheese.

Tomato chutney

CUCUMBER CHUTNEY

A sweet-tasting mixture of cucumbers, mustard seed, sugar, vinegar, onions, peppers and spices, which goes well with cold meats, cheeses and grills.

Cucumber chutney

MANGO CHUTNEY

Perhaps the best-known Indian chutney, this can be hot or mild. It is usually eaten with curries.

Mango chutney

OTHER CHUTNEYS

APPLE CHUTNEY
Made with cooking apples, this relish can be sweet or savoury. Similar chutneys can be made with green tomatoes or pears. They are all best served with cold meats.

APRICOT CHUTNEY
An excellent blend of apricots, raisins, chillies and spices, this is a hot chutney with a very good flavour. It can be eaten with cold meats and curries, or used for canapés and other savoury fillings.

CORIANDER CHUTNEY
Fresh coriander leaves pounded with green chillies, yoghurt, and spices make this slightly sour chutney that is eaten with cooked fish, meat or vegetables.

MINT CHUTNEY
Made using mint leaves, tomatoes, apples, onions and raisins, this is excellent with cold meats and curries.

Pickles and Pastes

SWEET PICKLE

Despite its name, this is more like a sweet chutney. It contains a wide range of fruits and vegetables and is best eaten with cheese and most cold meats.

Sweet pickle

CAPER
(Capparis spinosa, var. rupestris)

Members of the *Capparidaceae* family, capers are the unopened buds of a shrub native to the Mediterranean region. They are used only in their pickled form, as a flavouring and a garnish, in salade Niçoise and black butter sauce. French capers are reputed to be the best and include capucines and nonpareilles.

Capers

MANGO PICKLE

A spicy mixture of mangoes, chillies, spices and vinegar, this can be eaten with any bland foods.

Mango pickle

MIXED PICKLES

A mixture of cauliflower, onions and gherkins in a vinegar solution, these can be eaten as an accompaniment to cheese and cold meats.

Mixed pickles

PICKLED WALNUTS

The nuts are picked while still green, retained in their shells, steamed and packed in a solution of vinegar, caramel, black pepper and other spices. They are eaten with cold meats and cheese.

Pickled walnuts

PICKLED ONIONS

Onion pickling is one of the most ancient forms of pickling – evidence of it was found in the ruins of Pompeii. They are best eaten with cheese and cold meats.

Pickled onions

PICCALILLI

There are two main types: American and English. The American is made with green tomatoes, onion and sweet pickles in spices and sweet vinegar. The English (shown here) is a mustard pickle with mixed vegetables. Piccalilli is used mainly as an accompaniment to cheese.

Piccalilli

INDONESIAN RELISH

Really a pickle containing a variety of vegetables such as cabbage, onions, leeks, carrots and cucumbers, this is mild in taste and is eaten with smoked fish.

Indonesian relish

PICKLED RED CABBAGE

The cabbage is machine-shredded, packed in brine, then drained and repacked in spiced vinegar. Pickled cabbage is used in salads.

Pickled red cabbage

PICKLED GHERKINS

These small cucumbers, grown exclusively for pickling, can be eaten with cold meats, sausages and in salads.

Pickled gherkins

PATUM PEPERIUM

A preparation based on anchovies, butter, herbs and spices, this was invented in 1828 by an Englishman living in Paris. Advertisements in *The Times* attracted the nobility, hence the name 'Gentleman's Relish'. It is used for canapés and as a spread.

Patum peperium

OLIVE (*Olea europea*)

A member of the Oleaceae family, this is the fruit of a tree native to Mediterranean coasts. The difference between green and black olives is simply that the black ones are fully ripened. There are several varieties, as shown here, and they are used only in their pickled form in recipes and as finger food. Some olives are stoned, then stuffed and used for canapés and hors d'œuvres.

JAPANESE PICKLED RADISH

The Japanese daikon radish (page 30) is pickled in a solution of soy sauce and sugar, and is often eaten with fish.

Japanese pickled radish

PEANUT BUTTER

A paste made from crushed peanut seeds, this is used mainly as a spread. In Indonesian cooking it is used to thicken sauces.

Peanut butter

TAHINI PASTE

A paste made from crushed sesame seeds, this is widely used as a flavouring in Middle Eastern and Latin American cookery.

PICKLED DILL

There are four main types: fermented (usually in brine); unfermented (packed in brine with vinegar); sour (prepared in fermented salt stock, then packed in a vinegar solution); and sweet (packed in brine, then drained and packed in a sugar syrup with vinegar). Dill pickles are often eaten with cold meats and hamburgers.

SAUERKRAUT

Finely shredded green or white cabbage, fermented in brine and flavoured with juniper berries, sauerkraut or choucroute is sold canned or in plastic packs in supermarkets, and loose (from the barrel) in speciality food shops. It is often eaten with cold meats.

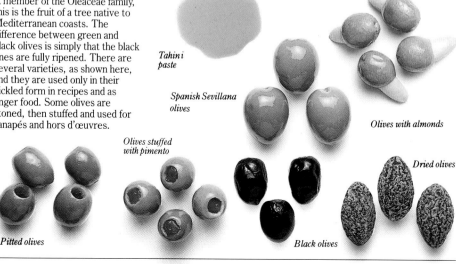

Tahini paste

Spanish Sevillana olives

Olives with almonds

Olives stuffed with pimento

Dried olives

Pitted olives

Black olives

MUSTARDS, VINEGARS AND OILS

MUSTARD IS A CONDIMENT PRODUCED from three different plants of the Cruciferae family, the colour of the seeds giving the name of the mustard type: *Sinapis alba* is white mustard (sometimes called yellow mustard), *Brassica nigra* is black mustard and *Brassica juncea* brown mustard (sometimes also called black mustard). In fact, when black mustard is used, it is normally the *B. juncea* variety rather than *B. nigra,* which is now considered unsuitable for modern farming. Although mustards are probably thought of as hot – as their name would imply – the majority are mild, and only freshly prepared English, Chinese and Japanese mustards are really fiery.

Types of mustard
The pungency of mustard is due to an essential oil that is only formed by the action of water on pulverized seeds. Only *B. nigra* and *B. juncea* contribute the familiar "hot" or pungent flavour of mustard, the black being the stronger of the two. White mustard contributes its own, characteristic flavour, and commercial mustard powders – basically the dry residue after oil has been extracted from the seeds – are a combination of the two types.

Mustards are made in a wonderful variety of flavours, derived from the addition of herbs and liquids such as verjuice, wine, vinegar, lime or lemon juice. They may be prepared with whole mustard seeds, or with tarragon, allspice, peppercorns, mint, chillies and garlic. The French, among others, also produce green mustards, which are mild and flavoured with a mixture of herbs.

Mustard in the kitchen
Mustard can be used in the form of whole seeds (page 60), but is more usually found in its prepared form, or as a powder. Mustard powder should be prepared with cold water to make a smooth paste. Hot water or vinegar will inhibit the action of the enzyme, and result in a mild mustard. The pungency is fully developed after about ten minutes. After a while the pungency deteriorates, although the typical mustard flavour may be retained.

In the preparation of sauces, mustard should be made into a paste (or used straight from the jar) and added only after the sauce has completed cooking. Mustard powder alone makes a sauce lumpy, and excess heat destroys pungency. Prepared mustard may be used in mayonnaise, and the French Dijon mustard is an ingredient for many sauces.

All types of mustard can be used in the kitchen. Although the black mustard is stronger, white mustard also has its advantages; its enzymes are not so easily damaged, and it is strongly preservative, discouraging moulds and bacteria, which is why it is often included in pickles (page 67). It also helps prevent mayonnaise from separating.

VINEGAR

Vinegar is a by-product of fermentation and should, strictly speaking, be made from wine (the word "vinegar" comes from the French *vin aigre,* meaning "sour wine").

Vinegar develops through a completely natural process involving two fermentations, the alcoholic and the acetous. The first occurs when natural yeasts present in the air or on fruit turn the sugar content into alcohol. Vinegar yeasts, also natural but usually added by the manufacturer, are then introduced. These acetobacters multiply to form the vinegar plant, a floating raft of yeast cells called the vinegar mother, which converts the alcohol into acetic acid (the main component of vinegar), thus completing the second stage of the process, acetous fermentation. (Anyone can, in fact, make their own vinegar by obtaining a vinegar mother.)

Strengths and types
The strength of acetic acid varies considerably with each type of vinegar: wine vinegar is stronger than malt or cider vinegars, while distilled or fortified vinegars are the strongest of all. The minimum level of acetic acid required by law in Britain and America is 6 per cent and above for wine vinegars and 4 per cent and above for other types.

Regional and national varieties depend on the raw materials available. In the Far East vinegar is made from rice wine and from fruit.

Vinegar in the kitchen

Vinegar was originally used as a preservative. Over the years, however, it has also become a valued aromatic condiment.

Wine vinegars particularly lend themselves to herb, spice and fruit flavourings; these include rosemary, tarragon, dill, garlic, chilli peppers, peppercorns, lemons, raspberries, rose petals and violets. Cooks should keep a selection of these vinegars, as different types suit different recipes. As a general rule, the choice of vinegar depends upon the country of origin of the recipe: rice vinegar should be used in Chinese and Japanese recipes, wine vinegar in Mediterranean recipes, cider vinegar in traditional American recipes, and malt vinegar in English recipes.

Other points worth bearing in mind are that cider or wine vinegar can be used for general cooking purposes; wine, rice, sherry or any herb vinegar for salads, and distilled, spirit or malt vinegar for pickling.

OILS

Oil is the vehicle that moves mayonnaise so smoothly over vegetables, salads and eggs. Italians pour it into soup, over pasta, over salads and practically everything else. Its lubricity makes salads palatable, when mixed with vinegar or lemon juice to make a vinaigrette dressing. Bakers use oil to encourage the expansion of bread dough, and to coat their baking tins. Cooks brush oil over meat prior to roasting or grilling, and fry potatoes in one of the many oils on the market. Sources of oil include sesame seeds in the Middle East, poppies in Europe, and olives in Crete and Palestine.

Modern agriculture has substantially added to the primitive and unrefined oils used by our ancestors. The sunflower, first cultivated by the American Indian, was introduced to Europe during the sixteenth century and first became established as an oil crop in Russia, where it was produced commercially in the 1830s. Also, corn, cottonseed, soybean, colza and peanut oil

have all substantially overtaken poppy, olive and almond oil in productivity.

Types of oil

Each oil has its specific character, colour and culinary purpose. Some are naturally darker than others, and darken with age, but because consumers prefer light-coloured oils, colour is bleached out – except for olive oil, which is often green or deep yellow.

The majority of oils possess two main characteristics: they tend to collapse or revert during cooking, and they may solidify in cold weather or in the refrigerator. You may have noticed how, in cold weather, oil has a tendency to go opaque in the bottle. The first manufacturers of commercial mayonnaise found that their products were inclined to "de-emulsify" in low temperatures as the oil gradually hardened. It was for this reason that winterized oils were developed. "Winterizing" means artificially freezing the oil until the solids can be separated off. The remaining oil can then be marketed as "salad oil".

Several types of oil are unstable, and break down during increases in temperature to give strong or unpleasant flavours. Safflower, sunflower and soy-bean oil can develop a fishy taste, and this is why most oils are now stabilized during processing, by a hardening technique known as hydrogenation.

There are basically three types of fat: saturated, unsaturated and polyunsaturated. Saturated fats are considered to increase levels of cholesterol in the blood, and oils containing polyunsaturated fatty acids, such as safflower, sunflower and corn oil, are thought by some to be beneficial to the diet-conscious. Compounds such as emulsifiers may be added – a chemical, lecithin, is important to cooking oils, since it is a natural emulsifier, and helps to prevent food from sticking to the pan and water droplets from splattering.

When frying food in oil, you need to maintain a constant correct temperature to prevent the oil from entering the food and making it greasy. The temperatures should not be too high – from 162°C (325°F) to 195°C (385°F), depending on the type of food. If the oil gets too hot it darkens and burns the outside of the food, leaving the inside undercooked.

Mustards

MUSTARD WITH GREEN PEPPERCORNS

This mustard, containing crushed green peppercorns, is one of the Dijon varieties from Burgundy. It is fairly hot and therefore goes best with bland foods, such as grilled steaks and chops.

DIJON MUSTARD WITH WHITE WINE

This is a hot mustard, best used with bland foods. Its additional wine flavouring makes it suitable for many sauces and dressings.

MOUTARDE DE MEAUX

Whole seed mustard, known as moutarde de meaux, is Dijon mustard containing the seeds of brown mustard, so that biting into the seed releases a quantity of the pungent oil. There are many varieties, and some may contain coarse mustard seeds and include white wine, spices, vinegar and salt. Like the Dijon and English mustards, these mustards are fairly hot and therefore should be reserved for use with bland foods which need to be enhanced.

ORIENTAL MUSTARD

CHINESE MUSTARD
Usually prepared from dry mustard and water or flat beer, this is an extremely hot preparation. It is traditionally served with egg rolls.

GREEN HERB MUSTARD

A very mild mustard, delicately combined with a mixture of herbs, this should be eaten with cold meats and sausages.

FRENCH MUSTARD WITH TARRAGON

One of the darker Bordeaux mustards, this variety containing tarragon is mild and therefore good with cold meats and spicy food.

Green herb mustard

Mustard with green peppercorns

Dijon mustard with white wine

French mustard with tarragon

Moutarde de meaux

Coarse-grain mustard

COARSE-GRAIN MUSTARD

This is a coarse-grained variety of moutarde de meaux and contains white wine. It is excellent with different types of bland food.

DUSSELDORF MUSTARD

The most popular type of German mustard, this is similar to the Bordeaux mustards. It is mild, and is eaten with spicy food.

ENGLISH WHOLE-GRAIN MUSTARD

This is a hot, pungent mustard made from whole mustard seeds, white wine, allspice and black pepper. It goes with bland foods.

English whole-grain mustard

AMERICAN MUSTARD

This mustard, made from *Sinapis alba* seeds, is mild and an excellent accompaniment to hot dogs and hamburgers.

Plain Dijon mustard

ENGLISH MUSTARD

English mustard is made of *Brassica nigra* seeds blended with *Sinapis alba* seeds, plus a quantity of wheat flour and, sometimes, a very small amount of turmeric. It is used as an accompaniment to boiled and roast beef, boiled ham, hamburgers, grilled herrings, chops and steaks, sausages and meat pies. As an ingredient, it features in toasted cheese dishes (Welsh rarebit) and in mustard sauce. Bear in mind that English mustard, if freshly made, is quite hot. It *should* be hot, for that is its true character.

PLAIN DIJON MUSTARD

There are four traditional types of French mustard: Dijon, whole seed, Bordeaux and Florida. Dijon mustard, from Burgundy, is the best known outside France. It is usually paler than its Bordeaux counterpart because it is made from *Brassica nigra* without the seed husk (the husk darkens the mustard). It is also the hotter of the two, and should be used with foods where the flavour needs enhancing, such as steaks, hamburgers and beef, and is also used in sauces such as ravigote, rémoulade, Dijonnaise and Russian sauce.

BORDEAUX MUSTARD

This is a plain mild French mustard. Bordeaux mustards contain the seed husk and are, therefore, dark, though they can vary slightly in colour. They may contain a variety of herbs, particularly tarragon, vinegar and sugar. They are mild, with a sweet-sour taste, and as such are best used with cold meats and spicy sausages. Bordeaux mustard can also be used in salad dressings, and makes a delicious sauce when mixed with honey or brown sugar and lemon juice.

American mustard

English mustard

Bordeaux mustard

German mustard

Dusseldorf mustard

Florida mustard

GERMAN MUSTARD

This sweet-sour mustard contains herbs, spices and caramel. It is lighter than the usual Dusseldorf mustard (left), is mild-tasting and is best eaten with cold meats and, of course, German sausage.

FLORIDA MUSTARD

This mild mustard is made with wine from the Champagne region. Like Bordeaux mustards, it is best with spicy food.

Vinegars and Oils

WINE VINEGAR

The finest wine vinegars are made in oak vats by a slow process which encourages a higher concentration of aromatic qualities. There are several kinds: red, white, rosé and sherry. White wine vinegar is best for mayonnaise, Hollandaise and similar sauces. Red wine vinegar should be used in a *sauce hachée* and *sauce à la diable*.

DISTILLED MALT VINEGAR

Although any vinegar can be distilled, malt vinegar is usually used. Distilled vinegars are colourless and very strong – simply because the distillation process has increased the percentage of acetic acid which they contain. It is because of their strength and their extreme slowness to deteriorate that they are used extensively for pickling (particularly onions). Manufacturers also use them in bottled sauces.

FLAVOURED VINEGARS

These usually consist of herbs steeped in wine vinegar, and may include tarragon, basil, lemons, savory, thyme, shallots, sugar, salt, horseradish, bay leaves and rosemary. Tarragon vinegar, particularly suitable for Béarnaise sauce and salad dressing, is the most popular.

RICE VINEGAR

Chinese vinegar can be red, white or black. There is also a Japanese variety called *su*. As a general rule, the white is most used, especially as a flavouring in soups, and in sweet-and-sour dishes. Cider or wine vinegar are the best substitutes.

SPIRIT VINEGAR

The liquid (often molasses or sugar beet alcohol) is distilled before all the alcohol has been converted to acetic acid. It is colourless, and is used mainly for pickling purposes.

MALT VINEGAR

Malted barley is mashed, heated with water and fermented into a crude type of beer, which is then fed into steel or plastic vats filled with beech shavings. The acetobacters are introduced and left for several weeks until acetic acid is formed. The vinegar is then filtered, matured and coloured with caramel. Malt vinegar is used for pickling (particularly walnuts) and is an ingredient in the well-known Worcestershire sauce.

CIDER VINEGAR

The sugar in apple pulp is converted to alcohol and then to acetic acid in the usual way. Home-produced cider vinegar is cloudy, while commercial types are crystal clear, due to filtering. It is used a great deal for general cooking purposes, and also makes an excellent substitute for rice vinegar in Chinese and Japanese cooking. It also makes good salad dressings.

Garlic vinegar

White wine vinegar with rosemary

White wine vinegar with green peppercorns

Dill vinegar

Distilled malt vinegar

Chilli vinegar

Red wine vinegar

White wine vinegar with tarragon

White wine vinegar

Spirit vinegar with lemon

Malt vinegar

Cider vinegar

WALNUT OIL

The kernels of the walnut, native to south-eastern Europe and Asia, contain oil with a pleasant nutty taste which is used mainly for salads. France and Italy are the main producers.

OLIVE OIL WITH FENNEL

This oil has been extracted from black olives; the fennel it contains makes it suitable for use with fish.

AVOCADO OIL

The pulp of the avocado fruit contains an oil which is used mainly for cooking. The oil is probably extracted only from damaged fruit because of the popularity of avocados as a fruit.

SESAME SEED OIL

Probably of African origin, the sesame plant *(Sesamum indicum)* yields an oil that is used for cooking and in salads. It is also popular in Chinese cooking.

SUNFLOWER OIL

The seed of the sunflower, native to North America, contains a tasteless oil excellent as both a cooking and a salad oil. It is also used for making margarine.

OLIVE OIL

This popular oil is produced mainly in Greece, France, Italy and Spain. Two types are sold: virgin oil and pure olive oil. Virgin oil is obtained only from the pulp of high-grade fruit; pure olive oil has been pressed from the pulp and kernels of lower-grade olives. Good olive oil (pressed cold from fresh ripe fruit) is a clear green and odourless; pale yellow oil (from secondary pressings under heat) is not usually of such good quality. Olive oil can be used in salads or for cooking.

GRAPE SEED OIL

Grape seeds contain an oil used for salads and making margarine.

SWEET CORN OIL

This oil, from the sweetcorn or maize plant, is a favourite with dieters. It is a good frying oil, and is used to make margarine.

PEANUT OIL

Peanuts contain about 50 per cent oil, which is excellent for salads and for frying. It is also used in margarine and canned fish.

OTHER OILS

ALMOND OIL
Sweet almond nuts contain oil used in baking and confectionery.

COCONUT OIL
An oil from the dried copra which is excellent for frying.

PALM OIL
Oil from the palm fruit seed used in margarine and cooking.

POPPYSEED OIL
The seeds contain an oil used in salads or for cooking.

RAPE OIL
Produced from the seeds of the rape plant *(Brassica napus)*, this is used for cooking.

SAFFLOWER OIL
This is used in special diet mayonnaise and salad dressings.

SOYBEAN OIL
The seeds of the soybean contain an oil used in salads, for cooking, and in margarine.

Walnut oil

Sesame seed oil

Avocado oil

Olive oil with fennel

Grape seed oil

Sunflower oil

Corn oil

Peanut oil

Olive oil

FRUIT

ATTEMPTS AT THE cultivation of fruit date back over 8000 years. Evidence of carbonized apples was found by archaeologists in ancient dwellings in Turkey; and neolithic sites in Denmark and Switzerland have yielded the fossilized remains of fruits such as sloes, blackberries, raspberries, strawberries, bilberries and crab apples. These apples were larger than the wild types found today, and assumed to be at an early stage of cultivation.

Apricots and peaches were grown in China some 3000 years ago. Their cultivation gradually spread westwards, the apricot becoming so well established in Armenia that the Romans called it *armeniacum*, "the Armenian apple".

Armenia, northern Persia and the foothills of the Caucasus contained the finest orchards of the ancient world. Here was the home of the vine, the quince, the medlar, pomegranate, and probably also the plum and the bullace. It is thought that the Phoenicians took the vine from Armenia to Greece and Rome, and that the Romans in turn planted vines in southern France and along the steep banks of the Rhine. The cultivation of fruit also spread southwards to the "fertile crescent" of Mesopotamia, where farmers grew crops of pomegranates, apples, cherries, peaches, mulberries and figs.

Oranges, native to China, are thought to have appeared in India during the first century AD, and from there went first to the east coast of Africa, then to the Levant. Roman horticulturists planted orange groves in Italy and may have introduced the orange to Spain, although the Spanish orange is also ascribed to the Moslem invaders who introduced the lemon. Oranges made their way to the New World in the sixteenth century, and were finally established in California in 1769. Bananas followed a similar route, though somewhat earlier; they reached India in about 500 BC, and from there migrated to the Canary Isles and the West Indies via Africa.

By the seventeenth and eighteenth centuries there was considerable exchange of fruits between Europe and America. The American cultivated strawberry was first introduced in 1660, and American apples were being sold in London's markets in the 1770s, along with bananas from the West Indies and a new, bright pink plant that nobody knew how to cook. It had come from Central Asia, probably Uzbekistan, where it was, and still is, eaten raw. This sour and acid-flavoured fruit was called rhubarb, and eventually became popular in Britain, where it is eaten stewed with sugar.

The pineapple was the only fruit from Central America to gain international status, until the modern trend for the avocado. The pineapple had been cultivated in Brazil and Peru at least a thousand years earlier, sharing its domestication with the guava, papaya, avocado, star apple and sour sop. All these fruits spread to the Caribbean islands, to mingle with those that were indigenous.

South-east Asia has a bounty of interesting and succulent fruits such as the banana, mango, carambola, durian, rambutan and mangosteen. The rambutan is unlikely to be found outside its native Malaysia, but the mango, which was transported to the Caribbean in the seventeenth century, has since become known throughout the world.

Varieties and hybrids

The willingness of some fruits to "marry" with others and to respond to selective crossbreeding has inspired horticulturists ever since the Romans first tried grafting plum trees. The development of fruits has come about by way of two botanical systems: variation and hybridization. Variations are produced by two parent plants of the same species that have different characteristics or qualities. Crossing two varieties of apple such as Worcester and McIntosh Red produces a third – "Tydeman's Early Worcester", which combines the best qualities of both parents.

Crossbreeding between parents that are genetically unalike, or distinctly different, results in a hybrid. Crossing a grapefruit with a tangerine produces a fruit which bears some of the characteristics of both species, in this case the tangelo. Of all fruits, the citrus family has responded best to hybridization. A few examples are the ugli fruit, also a cross between a tangerine and a grapefruit; the clementine, a hybrid of the tangerine and the sweet orange; and the citrange, resulting from a cross between a citron and and an orange.

Many of these hybrids may turn out to be mere botanical curiosities with little commercial application, but some are becoming popular in the world market. The Jamaican ortanique, a cross between the orange and one of the tangerine varieties, probably the satsuma, is an example of this.

Some seasonal varieties of fruit have an attractive quality or unusual appeal; examples are blood oranges, pink grapefruit and red bananas with pink flesh.

Commercial uses of fruit

All citrus fruits have aromatic oils in their skins – oils which are used in cooking, in liqueur-making and which are also essential to the perfume industry. Lemon oil is widely used as a flavouring agent, and the skin of bitter oranges, such as the bergamot orange and the Seville or bigarade, produces oil of neroli and oil of bergamot for use in scents. Countless fruits are used as a flavouring for liqueurs and brandies, some of the more famous being curaçao, based on the orange, and kirsch, based on the cherry.

Citric acid, found mainly in the pulp of the fruit, is a useful by-product of lemons. Prepared in crystalline form it is used for flavouring cordial drinks and confectionery. Enzymes of papaya and pineapple are used in meat tenderizers because they help to break down protein.

Many fruit flavours, such as bananas, pears and pineapples, have been synthesized for the food industry. They are particularly useful in the manufacture of ice cream and soft drinks.

Buying and storing fruit

When buying fruit, watch out for soft spots or bruises. If possible, buy produce that is displayed openly, rather than depending on prepackaged fruit; also, buy in season for reasons of both flavour and economy. Methods of testing for ripeness, however, vary with each individual fruit.

Unless you plan on eating the fruit immediately, it is best to buy produce that is slightly under-ripe and let it ripen at home over a two- to three-day period. Most ripe fruit should be stored in the refrigerator, while under-ripe fruit can be stored at room temperature. All fruits have individual characteristics and it is impossible to give an overall rule on when fruit is ready to be eaten.

Fruit in the kitchen

Fresh, canned or dried fruit can be put to a variety of uses in the kitchen. It can be eaten raw in salads, as a dessert or with cheese, or can be cooked with meat or on its own.

The sugars and acids in fruit contribute greatly to the flavour and ultimate purpose to which the fruit will be put – whether for cooking or as fresh, dessert fruit. The plantain, for example, contains a lot of starch and is less sweet than its close relative, the banana, so is used mainly as a vegetable. Cooking apples are also lacking in sugar, but are high in malic acid; they pulp easily when cooked, while dessert apples remain firm.

Citrus fruits as part of a salad or compote should be peeled with a knife to remove the white "pith". Ideally, the inner core, seeds and segment membranes – the rag – should also be removed. When shaving off the zest from the skin of citrus fruits, use a potato peeler and take off the top layer only. If you need a large amount to flavour a dessert, take off the whole peel, string the pieces together and blanch them several times. Then dry them and leave them in syrup to sweeten. If you want to use citrus peel as a sweetner, rub a sugar lump over the peel.

Don't sugar strawberries in advance, as the sugar absorbs the water content and the fruit goes mushy. Red currants, blackcurrants and the rarer white variety will need to be destalked, a tedious job but less so if a fork is used to strip the fruit from the stems. Most berries yield a fair amount of water; add sugar and cook briefly to keep them whole.

Melons, especially Charentais, should be prepared just before serving; otherwise they lose some of their fine aroma and flavour. Bananas, apples and pears all darken on exposure to air when peeled, and should be dipped in acidulated water (water with a squeeze of lemon juice, or a teaspoonful of tartaric acid or ascorbic acid). It is best to use slightly under-ripe fresh fruit for preserving, as the pectin content will be at its highest.

Stoned Fruit

PEACH (*Prunus*, spp.)

Probably of Chinese origin, this fruit has over 2000 varieties. The velvety soft skin encloses firm, juicy flesh with one large stone. Peaches are normally classified as being either freestone or clingstone, and can be eaten fresh, canned or dried in desserts, or used in preserves and liqueurs.

CHERRY (*Prunus*, spp.)

Popular varieties of sweet cherries are Napoleon Bigarreau, Frogmore Early, Merton Heart and White Heart. The best variety for cooking is the Morello, which is excellent for pies and jams. Cherries are also available canned and may be used in various types of liqueurs and brandies.

DATE (*Phoenix*, spp.)

Principally cultivated in the desert oases of southern Algeria and Tunisia, dates are also grown in South Carolina and Arizona. The most popular date varieties now cultivated – Medjool and Deglet Noor, among others – are all, as their names imply, of Arab origin. Dates can be bought fresh or dried all year round, and may be served as a garnish for a fruit tray or may be stuffed with cream cheese. Dates also freeze well and so may be kept for an extended period.

Peach

Cherries

Dates

NECTARINE (*Prunus*, spp.)

A smooth-skinned member of the peach family, nectarines have sweet, juicy flesh and are usually served as a dessert fruit. They are normally sold ripe and therefore should be eaten on the day of purchase. Nectarines can also be made into preserves.

Nectarine

Californian nectarine

APRICOT (*Prunus armeniaca*)

Native to China, apricots are in season through late spring and summer. The sweet flesh encloses a single stone and is covered by a tender skin. Available fresh, dried or canned, apricots can be eaten raw or used in desserts, or to make wines, brandies, preserves and confectionery.

Apricot

PLUM (*Prunus,* spp.)

A late summer to early autumn fruit, plums are normally classified as being used for desserts or for cooking. Both types can be eaten raw, although cooking plums are more acidic and rather dry in comparison to the juicy, richer-tasting dessert plum. Many different varieties are available. The damson is a European plum which, unlike other varieties, is not suitable for eating raw. It is very dark and tart with a thick skin and makes excellent preserves. The greengage (known as the Reine Claude) is a plum with a yellowish-green skin. It is one of the sweetest and best-flavoured plum varieties. The mirabelle is a small golden-yellow plum; it is eaten stewed, made into jam, and is also made into a liqueur of the same name. Small and dark blue, the sloe is a very sour variety of plum used to make sloe gin and jam. Most plums can be eaten fresh and all can be used in jam-making and for compotes to be served as desserts. They are available fresh, dried and canned.

UNUSUAL STONED FRUIT

LOQUAT
(*Eriobotrya japonica*)
The loquat or Japanese medlar belongs to the same botanical family as the apple. A native of China and Japan, it has been quite widely cultivated in Mediterranean countries. The yellow pear-shaped fruit is the size of a crab apple. It can be eaten fresh or stewed and is also made into jam.

LYCHEE (*Litchi chinensis*)
Although normally considered a fruit, lychees can be used as nuts. They are eaten fresh, canned or preserved in syrup, or the fruit may be dried, in which case the pulp acquires a nutty, raisin-like taste.

MEDLAR
(*Mespilus germanica*)
A fruit the size of a small apple with a brown skin and firm flesh, it is thought to be native to oriental countries and often grows wild in Britain and Europe. It is generally eaten fresh but can also be used to make preserves.

Red Ace plum

Greengage

Damson; prune plum

Switzen plum

Burbank plum

Californian Santa Rosa plum

Berries

BLACKCURRANT
(Ribes nigrum)

Usually sold stripped from their stalks, these summer fruits are always served cooked, as a filling for pies and puddings. They also make excellent preserves, and form the basis of the famous French liqueur, *cassis*. They are thought to have therapeutic properties in cases of arthritis.

Blackcurrant

CRANBERRY
(Vaccinium oxycoccus)

Grown almost exclusively in America, but also harvested in Finland, cranberries are too acid to be eaten raw, but are usually used as cranberry sauce, a traditional accompaniment to turkey. They are also used in pies, ices, liqueurs and jellies. Available fresh in winter, they can also be bought frozen.

Cranberry

RED CURRANT *(Ribes rubrum)*

Rather tart for eating raw, these summer fruits have many other uses: they make a sparkling jelly, excellent with roast lamb, poultry and game; a delicious summer salad tossed with grated raw vegetables; and, dipped by the bunch in lightly beaten egg white, then "frosted" with fine sugar, they make a simple but dramatic table decoration. They are also used in jams, syrups and wine.

Red currant

BLUEBERRY
(Vaccinium corymbosum)

Originally wild, this somewhat tart fruit is now grown commercially. Blueberries are eaten raw with sugar and cream, stewed, made into soups, preserves, and jams or used in pies. They are in season in midsummer.

Blueberry

WILD STRAWBERRY
(Fragaria, spp.)

The wild strawberry or *fraise du bois* is smaller and more aromatic than the ordinary cultivated variety. It is usually eaten fresh and does not need to be hulled before eating.

Wild strawberry

GOOSEBERRY
(Ribes grossularia)

Enjoyed in Europe since the Middle Ages, these are summer fruits with a very short season. Sweet varieties are delicious eaten raw; tart ones make excellent preserves and desserts and can be made into wine.

Gooseberry

LOGANBERRY
(Rubus loganobaccus)

A cross between the raspberry and the blackberry, the loganberry embodies the best of each. It is available fresh in the midsummer months, or canned.

Loganberry

RASPBERRY *(Rubus idaeus)*

Raspberries often appear in two crops, one summer, one autumn; the latter are often smaller but juicier. Raspberries can be eaten on their own with cream and sugar or made into drinks, soups, fine preserves, sorbets and other desserts. Available fresh or frozen, they are considered to have excellent diuretic properties.

Raspberry

BLACKBERRY
(Rubus fruticosus)

This nutritious black fruit decorates country hedgerows in late summer and early autumn, and has also been cultivated commercially for over a hundred years in America. Eaten fresh, blackberries make a refreshing dessert, or they can be made into preserves, pies and syrups, often combined with apples. Blackberries are also thought to aid infections of the mouth and throat.

Blackberry

STRAWBERRY
(Fragaria × ananassa)

A native of America, strawberries are available fresh and frozen and are delicious eaten alone or with cream. They can also be made into preserves, fruit soups, pies and many desserts. Their peak season is in late spring and early summer, though they are available all year.

Strawberry

OTHER BERRIES

ARBUTUS (*Arbutus unedo*)
This rather tasteless berry is the fruit of the strawberry tree. It is mainly used in prèserves, for the extraction of alcohol, and in a drink similar to cider.

BILBERRY
(*Vaccinium myrtillus*)
Acid-tasting when raw, this berry (also known as whortleberry and huckleberry) is used mainly in desserts, preserves and confectionery. It is also made into a wine in central Europe, used both for drinking and for medicinal purposes. Bilberries are available in summer.

BOYSENBERRY
(*Rubus*, spp.)
Similar in appearance to the loganberry, this fruit can be eaten fresh or are frequently used to make preserves.

BUFFALO BERRY
(*Shepherdia argentea*)
A tart yellow fruit the size of a currant and containing one seed, the buffalo berry or buffalo currant is used in making pies and preserves. It is native to North America.

CAPE GOOSEBERRY
(*Physalis peruviana*)
Similar in appearance to a ground cherry, this yellow berry can be eaten raw or made into preserves.

CLOUDBERRY
(*Rubus chamaemorus*)
A small golden fruit which grows in large areas of open moorland, the cloudberry can be used in desserts or jams.

GROUND CHERRY
(*Physalis pruinosa*)
Also known as the strawberry tomato and dwarf Cape gooseberry, this is a sweet, but slightly-acid tasting, fruit enclosed in a lantern-shaped husk. It is usually made into

preserves, but can also be eaten raw when ripe.

HAWTHORN
(*Crataegus*, spp.)
The haws (berries) of this plant are used in the making of jams and jellies. A wine can be made using the haws and flowers of the plant.

HONEY BERRY
(*Rubus*, spp.)
A relative of the raspberry, the honey berry can be eaten raw or can be cooked for use in desserts and preserves.

MULBERRY (*Morus*, spp.)
These are various species of this fruit, but the white mulberry (*Morus alba*) and the black mulberry (*Morus nigra*) are the most common. They are mostly eaten fresh or used in jams and wines, but can also be used to make a mildly astringent syrup.

NASEBERRY
(*Achras sapota*)
The pulp of this brown fruit is embedded with inedible black seeds and is palatable only when ripe. The flavour, however, is delicious, resembling the taste of brown sugar. It is also called sapodilla or chickoo.

PHENOMENAL BERRY
(*Rubus*, spp.)
Similar to the loganberry in both parentage and appearance, this fruit is usually cooked in jams and preserves, but can also be eaten raw.

SALMONBERRY
(*Ribes spectabilis*)
The salmonberry is an American wild raspberry or bramble. The name derives from the large berries that are salmon-red or wine-red when fully ripe. They can be eaten fresh or cooked in pies and desserts, and are sometimes made into preserves.

TANGLEBERRY
(*Gaylusacia frondosa*)
This is a type of bilberry that grows wild in some parts of America. The sweet-tasting berry may be eaten fresh or cooked in pies and desserts.

VEITCHBERRY
(*Rubus*, spp.)
A close relative of the loganberry, this fruit can be used in similar ways.

WHITE CURRANT
(*Ribes sativum*)
Less acid-tasting than the red currant, this berry can be eaten on its own or used in preserves or desserts.

WORCESTERBERRY
(*Ribes divaricatum*)
This is actually an American species of the gooseberry. The small black fruit was first sold in Worcester, USA when it was thought to be a hybrid of a gooseberry and a blackcurrant. It can be used in similar ways to the gooseberry.

Citrus Fruit

ORANGE (*Citrus,* spp.)

The best known of the citrus fruits, this, like other members of the citrus family, is native to China and south-east Asia. There are both bitter and sweet oranges. The two main varieties of bitter orange are the Bergamot (*Citrus bergamia*), used mainly for perfumery and essential oils, and the Seville orange (*C. aurantium*), which bears bitter-tasting fruits unsuitable for eating raw. The fruit itself is used in marmalades, though the rind is used for its oil which is extracted and used in liqueurs such as curaçao, or in orange flower water. Seville oranges are sometimes added to meat and fish dishes for piquancy.

Sweet oranges (*Citrus sinensis*) are available all year round and may be used in a multitude of ways: the fruit is served plain, cut up in salads or sliced for drinks or as a garnish; its juice is drunk plain or used in sauces and batters; its rind is grated for baking and used whole as a shell for salads and ices, or sliced and candied. They are extensively grown in Spain, Israel, South Africa and in the southern states of America, and are usually classified as normal, blood and navel. Common types of normal orange are Valencias and Jaffas – good for juicing and slicing for use in salads and fruit salads. Navel oranges, so-called because they have a circular mark at the stem end resembling a navel, are also good in salads. Blood oranges are small, with slightly rough skin, and have sweet, juicy flesh with flecks of red. They are usually eaten on their own, though they too can be used in salads. The Ortanique is another variety of orange, but flatter in shape.

TANGERINE (*Citrus reticulata*)

Native to southern China and Laos, the tangerine is a small, sweet orange containing numerous pips. Generally thought of as being the same thing as a mandarin orange (although biologists are still confused by their nomenclature), these fruits have very loose skin which is easy to remove. They are available fresh or canned, and can be eaten on their own or used in fruit salads. They are also sometimes candied and glazed, or used to make liqueurs and marmalades.

Tangerine

Navel orange

Spanish orange

Seville orange

Jaffa orange

KUMQUAT (*Fortunella japonica*)

Of Chinese origin and no bigger than a large olive, the kumquat has sweet skin and juicy, slightly bitter flesh. It can be served fresh and eaten with the skin, but is also available bottled in syrups. Kumquats may be included in mixed fruit salads, or used in marmalades and other preserves.

Kumquat

CLEMENTINE (*Citrus,* spp.)

This is regarded by some as a variety of tangerine, and by others as a cross between the tangerine and sweet orange. Mainly produced in northern Africa, it is practically seedless. The skin is easily removed.

GRAPEFRUIT (*Citrus paradiis*)

A popular species of the citrus family, it is native to the West Indies, but is now grown in many hot climates. Often served as a breakfast appetizer, it is thought to contain an enzyme which stimulates the metabolism, hence its frequent use in slimming diets. Available all year round, there are two basic varieties: white, which is particularly good for juicing, and pink, so sweet that it can be eaten without additional sugar. Often available in the form of canned segments, grapefruit can be eaten raw or grilled with brown sugar. It is also used in fruit drinks, juices and marmalades.

OTHER CITRUS FRUIT

POMELO (*Citrus glandis*)
The largest of the citrus fruits, the pomelo or shaddock has a thick skin and a bitter fibrous pulp similar to the grapefruit. It is usually eaten on its own.

TANGELO (*Citrus,* spp.)
A cross between the tangerine and the grapefruit, this tapers slightly at the stem end. It is good for juicing, eating as a fresh fruit, or in salads.

Florida Duncan (white) grapefruit

Clementine

SATSUMA (*Citrus,* spp.)

The satsuma is similar to the tangerine in taste and appearance, with loose, smooth skin and pale orange flesh. It contains no pips. It is normally eaten fresh, but can be used in preserves.

Satsuma

Texan Pink (pink) grapefruit

LIME (*Citrus aurantifolia*)

This small, thin-skinned fruit of Indian origin is closely related to the lemon and is, in fact, often used as a lemon substitute. It is used in juices, cocktails, pickles, preserves and curries. Its grated zest or peel is often used in sherbets and ice cream.

LEMON (*Citrus limon*)

Of Indian origin, and widely grown in Mediterranean countries, the lemon is easily the most versatile of all the citrus fruits. Its acid taste makes it unpleasant to eat as a fruit, but it has many culinary uses, particularly in baking and confectionery and in the preparation of lemon juice and sugar for lemonade. A few drops of lemon juice will enhance delicate fish or poultry dishes, creams and pies. The acid can also be used to prevent cut fruit from turning brown when exposed to the air.

CITRON (*Citrus medica*)

Native to China, the citron, unlike other members of the citrus family, is not cultivated for its flesh or juice but for its thick, fragrant rind, which is candied and used in cakes and confections, and in the preparation of candied fruits and liqueurs. It is an important part of the Jewish festival of Succoth.

Citron

Lemon

Lime

UGLI (*Citrus,* spp.)

Native to the East Indies, the ugli is a hybrid between the tangerine and the grapefruit. It is similar in appearance to the latter, but is slightly smaller with thick, knobbly skin, sweeter-tasting flesh and few pips. Uglis have the same uses as grapefruit, and are often substituted for them.

Ugli fruit

Pears

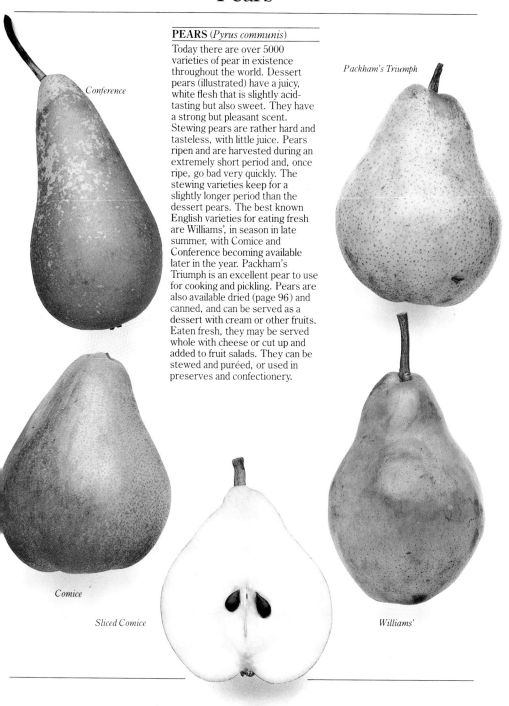

PEARS (*Pyrus communis*)

Today there are over 5000 varieties of pear in existence throughout the world. Dessert pears (illustrated) have a juicy, white flesh that is slightly acid-tasting but also sweet. They have a strong but pleasant scent. Stewing pears are rather hard and tasteless, with little juice. Pears ripen and are harvested during an extremely short period and, once ripe, go bad very quickly. The stewing varieties keep for a slightly longer period than the dessert pears. The best known English varieties for eating fresh are Williams', in season in late summer, with Comice and Conference becoming available later in the year. Packham's Triumph is an excellent pear to use for cooking and pickling. Pears are also available dried (page 96) and canned, and can be served as a dessert with cream or other fruits. Eaten fresh, they may be served whole with cheese or cut up and added to fruit salads. They can be stewed and puréed, or used in preserves and confectionery.

Conference

Packham's Triumph

Comice

Sliced Comice

Williams'

Apples

The many varieties of apple can be divided into two groups: dessert and cooking. Dessert apples (those that are eaten fresh) include Cox's Orange Pippin, Worcester Pearmain, Laxton's Superb and Egremont Russett. Some varieties which are good for eating raw and also for most cooking purposes (in purées, pies, or baked whole) are Grenadier, Lord Derby, Bramley's Seedlings, Newton Wonder and McIntosh.

GRANNY SMITH

Originally grown from a pip in nineteenth-century Australia, this apple's crunchy hard flesh, sharp distinctive taste and bright green skin have made it popular and easily recognizable. A worldwide choice both for cooking and eating.

Granny Smith

BRAMLEY

This is the foremost British cooking apple. Large and green, sometimes flushed with red, its flesh is sharp and juicy and is not usually eaten raw. It can be used in desserts such as apple pies or baked apples, for making apple chutney, or cored, peeled and sautéed in butter to serve with bacon and sausage.

GOLDEN DELICIOUS

One of the major varieties of dessert apples in America, South Africa and England, the Golden Delicious or Yellow Delicious is firm and crisp when the skin is greenish, or less crisp but sweeter when completely golden. It is a good contrast, both in flavour and texture, to blue cheese.

Golden Delicious

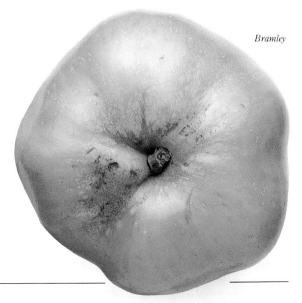

Bramley

STARKING

From France, a crisp dessert apple with red-streaked skin and very white, sweet flesh. Also called Starking Delicious, it is best served early in the season on its own at the end of a meal, with cheese, or made into a dessert by being cored, sliced in rounds and fried in a sweet batter as fritters.

CRAB APPLE

Available briefly in autumn, this small, acidic, apple-like fruit can be red or yellow. High in pectin, it is widely used in making jellies and preserves, and for other food accompaniments.

RED DELICIOUS

An American variety, this is one of the world's best eating apples. Firm, sweet and long-lasting, its red skin makes it look attractive in a fruit bowl as well as served baked with roast meat.

Red Delicious

Starking

Crab apple

SPARTAN

The Danes developed this firm apple with a custard-like taste that is popular for eating and cooking. It goes well in a cold salad with onions and cured meats.

McINTOSH

Slightly tart, best freshly picked, this all-purpose Canadian apple is good on its own, in salads, or with meat, and takes less cooking time than other varieties.

COX'S ORANGE PIPPIN

Crisp, firm and juicy, this is Britain's most popular eating apple. It is also good to cook.

McIntosh

Spartan

Cox's Orange Pippin

Grapes

Cyprus Gold

GRAPES (*Vitis vinifera*)

There are either white or black grapes available, and different varieties of both are grown in many parts of the world for eating fresh, for wine-making and for drying. Most likely originating in western Asia, they are one of the oldest cultivated plants. Grapes are a vinous fruit, growing in clusters, and have digestive and therapeutic properties which are rare in other types of fruit. They are normally classified as being either table grapes, which would include all the varieties shown here, or wine-making grapes (such as Pinot Noir, Chardonnay, Riesling and Cabernet Sauvignon), both of which are good for eating raw. They are available all year long. They can be eaten on their own or in fruit salads, and are often used as a garnish in desserts. Dried grapes, known as currants, raisins and sultanas (page 98), are produced mainly in America. Most grapes eaten in Britain are imported, but excellent dessert grapes can be grown under glass.

Superior

Emperor

Thompson

Benhanna

Melons

There are several types of melon, but broadly speaking there are three groups defined by form and colour. There are musk or netted melons, with a "network" pattern on the skin, winter melons, which are quite smooth-skinned, and cantaloupe melons, which have a warty exterior. There is also the watermelon (*Cucumis citrullus*), with a dark green skin and bright red flesh. Musk melons have flesh of a yellowish-green colour; the flesh of winter melons is greenish-tinged – the best-known types are Casaba and Honeydew. The flesh of the cantaloupe is orange-coloured. A new melon in this category is the Ogen (developed in Israel), which has greenish flesh.

Melon is eaten in its natural state either at the beginning of a meal as an hors d'œuvre or at the end as a dessert.

OGEN (*Cucumis melo*)

A small, round hybrid variety named after the kibbutz in Israel where it was first cultivated, this is widely sought after for the sweet succulence of its flesh. Available from spring to midwinter, one melon should be allowed per person.

WATERMELON
(*Cucumis citrullus*)

Indigenous to Africa, the rich red, occasionally yellow, flesh of the watermelon is especially refreshing as it is 91 per cent water. Grown in tropical countries and in warmer parts of America and Europe, it is available from summer to early autumn. Round or oblong, when ripe the skin should be a rich deep green or green variegated with dark grey, sometimes with a yellow underside, and its thin surface should come away easily when scraped with a fingernail. For vine-ripened sweetness, the stem end should be slightly sunken and calloused. Mostly eaten as a thirst-quencher in very hot weather, it can also be eaten in fruit salads or, sliced, with vinaigrette dressing.

Ogen

Watermelon

CHARENTAIS (*Cucumis melo*)

The Charentais's orange, sugary and fragrant flesh make this fruit popular both as a dessert or first course. Available all year round in many places, it keeps well when stored in a cool, dry place and ripens after several days in a warm room. When ripe, it is fragrant even before being cut. Although at its best when freshly cut, it can be stored in the refrigerator for up to two days if covered in plastic wrap.

Charantais

CANTALOUPE (*Cucumis melo*)

Thought to have originated in Asia, this melon is widely available during summer. When ripe, it is extremely fragrant and its flesh sweet. It can be served with ice cream.

Cantaloupe

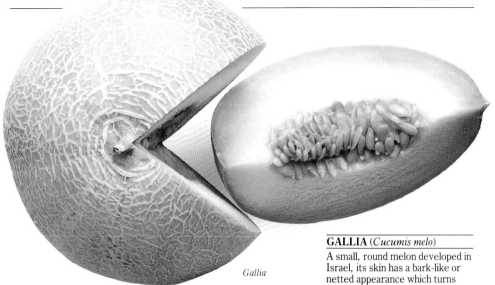

Gallia

GALLIA (*Cucumis melo*)

A small, round melon developed in Israel, its skin has a bark-like or netted appearance which turns from green to golden-yellow when ripe and sweet. To serve chilled, refrigerate briefly to preserve its taste.

HONEYDEW (*Cucumis melo*)

An oval melon available all year round in most places, its delicate taste and pale green flesh contrasts well with a thin slice of raw, cured ham or sweet wine such as muscatel or port.

Honeydew

Tropical Fruit

GUAVA (*Psidium guajava*)

This fruit of the guayaba tree is probably native to Haiti, but is now found in most tropical and subtropical countries. It varies in size from that of a walnut to an apple, and is one of the most commonly planted tropical fruits. When ripe, the skins are light yellow in colour, the pulp is juicy and contains small seeds. The flesh varies in colour from white to yellow to pale pink. Available in the spring and summer, the fruit has a sharp taste, and is therefore usually used for stewing and making tarts and preserves. It can be bought fresh (as shown) or canned (in slices). Guavas are noted for their high vitamin C content; in some varieties it is higher than that of citrus fruits.

Papaya

PAPAYA (*Carica papaya*)

Native to Central America, but widely cultivated in all tropical countries, the papaya or pawpaw is a large berry with a yellowish rind and yellow to salmon-coloured flesh with a large central cavity containing many seeds. It has a fairly sweet taste when ripe (similar to apricots and ginger) and, like melon, makes a good dessert or breakfast fruit. It can also be cooked as a vegetable before it is ripe, and is often used to make preserves and pickles. When served raw, papayas should be chilled and sprinkled with lemon or lime juice. They are most readily available in the spring and summer months.

MANGO (*Mangifera indica*)

This fruit, native to India, can be green or yellow-red (as shown), and contains a stone surrounded by a sweet and sticky pulp, tasting like nectar and peaches, which can be eaten on its own or used in preserves and chutneys. It is an important source of vitamin A. Available from midwinter to autumn, it can be bought fresh or canned. India is the biggest producer, although mangoes are grown in many tropical climates.

Guava

Kiwifruit

Passionfruit

Mango

PASSIONFRUIT
(*Passiflora edulis*)

The fruit of a perennial climbing plant native to Brazil, passionfruit (or purple granadilla) can be eaten fresh when the skins are deeply wrinkled and the fruit is juicy, or used to make preserves and ice cream. It is most readily available in the summer.

KIWIFRUIT (*Actinidia sinensis*)

A native of China, the kiwifruit or Chinese gooseberry is now grown in many countries, especially New Zealand. It has a slightly sour taste and a hairy skin, which should be removed before eating. It may be poached and sprinkled with lemon juice, but more commonly is eaten fresh, either on its own or in fruit salads. It is available from midsummer to winter.

Feijoa

Pineapple

FEIJOA (*Feijoa sellowiana*)
Now grown mainly in New Zealand, the feijoa is native to Brazil and Uruguay. The white flesh tastes like a combination of pineapple and strawberry and is delicious in fruit salads, but is principally used for jams and other preserves. It is available in late spring and summer.

PINEAPPLE (*Ananas comosus*)
The pineapple is really a cluster of fruits of the ananas tree, which all combine to form one "multiple fruit". Native to South America, it is now grown in most tropical and subtropical countries. It has a high sugar content and is one of the finest table fruits. Attractive and tasty, they are available all year round and make an excellent dessert fruit. Pineapples can be bought fresh (as shown), canned (in chunks, slices and rings), or crystallized (page 125).

OTHER TROPICAL FRUIT

BABACO (*Carica pentagona*)
Native to Central and South America, but now grown extensively in New Zealand, this is a five-sided relative of the papaya, and resembles it and the pineapple in its delicate flavour. It may be eaten raw or stewed, used in salads, pickles and chutneys.

CUSTARD APPLE
(*Annona,* spp.)
A term covering a group of fruits which includes the cherimoya (also known as sherbet fruit), sweet sop, sour sop and bullock's heart. They are tropical fruits which rarely appear in temperate zone markets. The cherimoya has a pineapple flavour while the sweet sop, or sugar apple, has a sweet, custard-like flesh. The flesh of the sour sop is white and more acid than the others. The flesh of the

bullock's heart is more solid and sweet; it gets its name from its shape and dark brown colour.

DURIAN (*Durio zibethinus*)
A fruit native to south-east Asia and much enjoyed there. Its main characteristic is a highly unpleasant smell which probably accounts for the fact that it has never attained a wider popularity. It has a dull yellow skin when ripe and its pulp, eaten raw, is creamy.

MANGOSTEEN
(*Garcinia mangostana*)
Similar in appearance to the lychee (page 79), but not related to it or the mango, despite the name, this slow-growing tree fruit is originally from south-east Asia. The thick rind and deep pink pith should be removed to reveal the delicately scented and

flavoured white flesh. Mangosteens may be eaten on their own or in fruit salads.

STAR FRUIT
(*Averrhoa carambola*)
Native to south-east Asia, but also grown in South America, the star fruit or carambola gets its name from the five-pointed star shape of the slices when the fruit is cut across. With its sour-sweet taste, it is refreshing in fruit salads or as a drink, and may also be used as a garnish.

TAMARILLO
(*Cyphomandra betacea*)
Indigenous to Peru, the tamarillo or tree tomato is related to the tomato. Rich in vitamin C, it has a strong sweet flavour and may be eaten raw, stewed, baked or grilled, or used in savoury dishes and preserves.

Other Fruit

QUINCE
(*Cydonia vulgaris/oblonga*)

There are many varieties of this hard and acid Asiatic fruit which, although one of the earliest known fruits, is not one that has a widely popular appeal. Rarely eaten uncooked, it is used principally in preserves and confectionery and turns pink when cooked. Japonicas are closely related and have the same uses.

PRICKLY PEAR
(*Opuntia ficus indica*)

Native to America, and now found in all temperate regions, the prickly pear or Indian fig is available from midsummer to midwinter. A member of the cactus family, it has a thorny skin which must be removed before eating. It can be eaten raw or stewed and is used in preserves.

FIG (*Ficus carica*)

There are several varieties of white, purple and red figs and their cultivation today is extensive, particularly in the Mediterranean countries. They are very good eaten fresh, some are canned or used in relishes and many are dried (page 96). Figs are excellent in baking and desserts and are also good when stewed.

Japonica

Quince

Prickly pear

Fig

PERSIMMON (*Diospyros kaki*)

There are several varieties of the persimmon – also called kaki fruit or Sharon fruit – which is native to China and Japan. It can be eaten fresh or cooked and is often candied. It is available from midsummer to midwinter.

BANANA (*Musa nana*)

Native to tropical countries, bananas are sweet-tasting and are usually eaten raw – often on their own or incorporated in fruit salads – although they can also be gently baked or flambéed with brown sugar, brandy or rum. The skin of the fruit is green when unripe changing to yellow when ready for eating. Available all year round, they are nutritious and rich in vitamin A.

Persimmon

Banana

POMEGRANATE
(*Punica granatum*)

The pomegranate, indigenous to Persia, is among the most ancient of fruits. It is available in the autumn months, and usually eaten as a raw fruit, though its juice is often extracted and used in drinks. In parts of the Middle East it is included in soups, and in the West Indies it is used widely in cooking and in preserves. Pomegranate seeds are used to make grenadine syrup (page 63).

PLANTAIN (*Musa paradisiaca*)

Native to the tropics, the plantain is a type of cooking banana, larger than dessert bananas and with a lower sugar content. Unsuitable for eating raw, it is cooked in a wide range of savoury dishes and is popular in West Indian and African cooking. It is available all year round.

RHUBARB
(*Rheum rhaponticum*)

The stem of a large perennial plant thought to be native to Tibet, rhubarb is, technically, a vegetable, though it is used as a fruit. Available from midwinter to midsummer, it can be bought fresh or canned, and is used in sauces, pies, preserves and wines.

Rhubarb

Pomegranate

Plantain

DRIED FRUIT

IF A RIPE FRUIT IS dried it loses most of its moisture, accumulates natural sugars, and keeps almost indefinitely. This fact has been known to Middle Eastern people for over 5000 years. They have always preserved dates, figs and apricots by sun-drying, which is still the most favoured technique, although some fruits are now artificially dried. Medieval Europeans put their apples into warm ovens, then peeled, cored and threaded them onto strings, and suspended them from the kitchen ceiling. In the monasteries, however, monks dried their plums, grapes and apples on straw-covered stone floors.

Dried fruit was introduced to America by the settlers, who also brought with them apples, nectarines, grapes, peaches, quinces and apricots, to add to the indigenous plums, cherries and persimmons. Today, California is the main producer of dried fruit.

Methods of processing
Approximately 2.5kg (6lb) of fresh fruit produce only 0.5kg (1lb) of dried fruit. The fruits are harvested by hand, the stalks and pits removed. They are then fumigated and graded before being spread out in the sun to dry. While sun-drying gives fruit a golden,

translucent appearance which cannot be achieved mechanically, it has many disadvantages, principally that of cost, which makes mechanical driers more popular. Most fruits are picked when ripe (except pears, which are picked while still green and left to ripen on trays). They are then chemically treated with either sulphur smoke or an alkali dip, depending on the fruit. Both methods accelerate drying, but the latter is preferred for whole fruits, such as prunes or grapes.

Dried fruit in the kitchen
Dried fruit is sweeter and richer than fresh fruit, which makes it invaluable in baking and desserts. It is most often used in fruit cakes and scones and occasionally in stuffings. It can be eaten on its own, candied as a confectionery item, mixed with cereals, or topped with cream, yoghurt or custard.

Packets of ready-mixed dried fruit can be bought in most supermarkets and health food stores, but the fruit can also be bought separately. Currants, raisins and sultanas are usually sold washed and ready to use; other dried fruits may need washing and soaking, preferably overnight. Keep the liquid in which they were soaked and use it to cook the fruit.

FIGS
California and the Mediterranean countries (particularly Turkey) are the world's main producers of figs, which are usually sun-dried. They can be eaten as they are, reconstituted with water in compotes, or chopped and used for baking and confections.

PEARS
Dried pears are now available in many health food and wholefood stores. They are used for making compotes and the famous Swiss *birnenbrot* (pear bread).

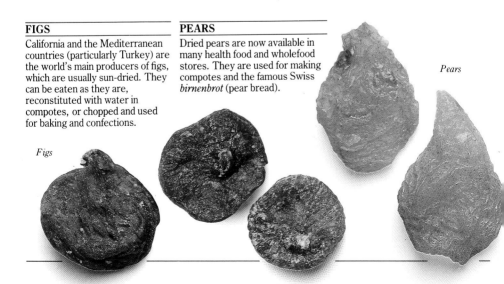

Pears

Figs

PEACHES

Although peaches are usually preserved by canning, a small part of the crop is halved and dried for use in fruit compotes, baking, jams and other preserves.

Peaches

PRUNES

Like dates, prunes (dried plums) vary widely in quality. Long enjoyed as a breakfast compote with great digestive qualities, they can be eaten on their own or used in cakes, puddings, sauces, the Arab stew *tadjub ahmar*, and also as a filling for dumplings and fritters. They can be canned or preserved in brandy or vinegar, and are sold stoned and unstoned. Prunes also make a fine brandy.

Prunes

APRICOTS

Dried apricots are almost preferable to the fresh fruit, unless the latter is very ripe and sweet. They vary in form from the withered yellow "rags", which must be soaked and cooked with sugar to make them palatable, to plump, sun-dried sweet fruit which can be eaten as it is.

Apricots

DATES

Dried dates vary in quality and form from the large, plump table dates, stoned or unstoned, to pressed slab dates, which are considerably cheaper. They are classified into dry, semi-dry and soft types, of which the soft is the most popular. Dried dates can be eaten as they are or used in baking and confections.

BANANAS

Drying concentrates the elusive taste of the banana to produce a deliciously chewy and highly nutritious sweetmeat. The fruits are usually split lengthwise and dried in the sun. Dried bananas are also used in baking, and the vacuum-dried purée of the ripe fruit produces a type of flour.

Bananas

Dates

CURRENTS

The dried fruit of the small, seedless grape of Corinth in Greece, from which they take their name, currants are used mainly for baking.

RAISINS

A type of dried grape and one of the most popular of all dried fruits, raisins are produced mainly in California and the Middle East. They make a good snack, especially if mixed with nuts, and also have a wide application in all kinds of baking.

SULTANAS

Another type of dried grape, these are larger and sweeter than raisins, and are used when the acidity of raisins and tartness of currants is not required.

Currants

Raisins

Sultanas

Apples

APPLES

Dried apples have been a winter standby of country housewives since ancient times, when cold storage and other modern methods of preservation were unknown. They attract moisture, however, and so have a shorter shelf life than other dried fruits. They can be eaten on their own or used in baking.

OTHER DRIED FRUIT

RED DATES

Although called "dates", these are in fact jujubes (native to China but also cultivated in the Mediterranean area). Usually sun-dried, they are used in oriental and Indian cooking as flavourings for both sweet and savoury dishes.

NUTS

BOTANICALLY, NUTS ARE single-seeded, dry, hard-shelled fruits that have to be cracked to open them, such as chestnuts and filberts. However, the term "nut" is also used for any seed or fruit with an edible kernel in a hard or brittle shell; for example peanuts – strictly speaking a legume – almonds, walnuts and coconuts. Since the earliest times, nuts have been used as source of food and oil. They were collected by food-gathering peoples before the birth of agriculture, were used extensively by the Greeks, and there is evidence that they were cultivated by the Romans.

Nuts are also an important feature of Middle Eastern cookery. In fact, medieval Europe learned the use of nuts in cooking from the Arabs, who not only used them in sauces with meat and poultry, but in marzipan, nougat and other sweetmeats. Spain, occupied for almost eight centuries by the Moors, also adopted the use of nuts in cooking, and took the technique to the Americas after the Conquest. They found the Aztecs already using pumpkin seeds and peanuts, and probably pecans, as thickeners for poultry and fish and shellfish sauces. Almonds are used extensively in Scandinavian cooking, and they are also important in Indonesian, Far Eastern and African cooking. In fact, the use of nuts is universal: they are present in every aspect of cooking from hors d'oeuvres through to desserts.

Using nuts
Some nuts, such as pecans and Brazil nuts, can be shelled more easily if they are allowed to stand in boiling water for 15 to 20 minutes. To blanch (remove the thin inner lining of) shelled nuts such as almonds, pistachios and walnuts, pour boiling water over them and then follow immediately with a cold rinse. Filberts need to be put under the grill for a few minutes before peeling. Nuts are more easily chopped if they are warm and moist. Roasting nuts brings out their flavour. Once shelled and skinned (if desired), they can be placed in a medium oven – 175°C (350°F) – for 10 to 20 minutes.

Storing nuts
The length of time nuts will keep varies according to the type: unshelled nuts are protected from heat, air, light and moisture, and therefore will keep almost indefinitely anywhere; but shelled nuts do not keep as well, and should be stored tightly covered in a cool, dark, dry place or freezer. Both salted and unsalted nuts should be refrigerated although, of the two, unsalted nuts last longer.

WALNUT (*Juglans regia*)
Also known as the English walnut and Persian walnut, this is available in the shell, shelled, ground or chopped. It can be used when immature or ripe, and dried or toasted. Young green nuts are pickled in vinegar (page 68); immature walnuts are an important ingredient in the Mexican national dish, *chiles en nogada* (peppers in walnut sauce); ripe walnuts are eaten as a dessert nut and are used in stuffings, confectionery, baking, salads, and vegetarian cooking. A liqueur, brou, is made from the shucks or casings of the nuts. Walnut oil (page 75), which has a pronounced flavour, is used for salad dressings. Black or American walnuts (*Juglans nigra*) have thick, hard shells and are usually larger than European walnuts. Stronger-tasting than the latter, they are used in confectionery and ice creams. Butternut (*Juglans cinera*), also known as white walnut, has a rich and pleasant flavour and is often used in confectionery.

Shelled walnut

Ground walnut

Chopped walnut

BRAZIL NUT
(Bertholletia excelsa)

The seeds of a tall forest tree of South America, Brazil nuts are sold whole and shelled. They can be eaten on their own, and are also used in confectionery and cakes.

Whole brazil nut

Shelled brazil nut

PECAN NUT (Carya illinoensis)

The pecan nut, indigenous to North America, is related to the walnut. It is eaten in large quantities as a dessert nut, plain or salted, and used to make nutbreads, confectionery, ice creams and in vegetarian dishes. Its best known use is in the popular American dessert, pecan pie.

Whole pecan nut

Chopped pecan nut

Shelled pecan nut

CASHEW NUT
(Anacardium occidentale)

The fruit of a tropical tree native to America, the cashew grows as a single, hard protuberance beneath a fleshy fruit. The nuts are used in baking, in cashew butter, or are eaten as a cocktail nut. They are usually sold shelled and salted.

Cashew nut

FILBERT (Corylus maxima)

Both this and the hazelnut (*Corylus avellana*) are fruits of the hazelnut or cobnut bush; filberts are the cultivated variety and the more robust of the two. Filberts are named after St Philbert, a French abbot whose feast day in August coincides with their ripening time. Both filberts and hazelnuts are rich in oil and may be eaten on their own or used in butters, confections and desserts.

Whole filbert   *Shelled filbert*

Chopped filbert   *Ground filbert*

ALMOND (Prunus dulcis)

The seeds of a Mediterranean tree of the peach family, almonds, when growing, are covered with a green outer skin which is later removed. One of the most popular nuts worldwide, there are two types, sweet and bitter. The latter contains prussic acid and is never eaten raw, but its essence can be distilled and used as a flavouring. Sweet almonds are used whole for baking and confectionery, ground into a paste for butters, pralines, fillings, and nougat, chopped, diced and shredded for coating and garnishing, roasted, salted or sugared. Sugared almonds may be covered in sugar, syrup or honey.

Chopped almond

Whole almond   *Ground almond*

PEANUT (Arachis hypogaea)

Native to South America, the peanut (or groundnut or monkey nut) is not, strictly speaking, a nut but a highly nutritious underground legume. Its outer "shell" is the dried fibrous pod of the plant, and contains the seeds or "nuts". It can be eaten raw or roasted and is used primarily for peanut butter (page 69) and peanut oil (page 75).

Whole peanut

Shelled peanut

TIGERNUT (Cyperus esculenta)

Always referred to, and thought of, as nuts, tigernuts or earth almonds are really the starchy rhizomes of a plant native to Africa. Usually sold dried, they have an almondy taste and can be eaten on their own, like peanuts, or cooked or made into a flour.

Tigernut

Shelled bitter almond   *Shelled almond*

Blanched almond   *Flaked almond*

CHESTNUT (*Castanea sativa*)

Native to southern Europe, the sweet chestnut has been grown for many centuries and used in soups, cereals, stews and stuffings. It is the only nut which is treated as a vegetable – because it contains more starch and less oil than other nuts it can be cooked differently. It can be eaten whole, either roasted, boiled, or steamed. Once shelled, they are preserved whole in sugar or syrup as marrons glacés (page 124), used chopped in stuffings or with vegetables, or ground into a flour.

There are two types of water chestnut. *Trapa natans* has an edible seed and a floury texture and is eaten raw, roasted or boiled in central Europe and Asia. A related aquatic plant, ling (*Trapa bicornis*), is grown in China, Korea and Japan. Its seeds are eaten boiled, or preserved in honey and sugar or used for making flour.

The Chinese water chestnut or *pi tsi* is a tuber which is cultivated in the East Indies, China and Japan. It is used sliced as a vegetable and, outside Asia, is usually bought canned.

Shelled chestnut

Whole chestnut

PISTACHIO NUT (*Pistacia vera*)

The fruit of a small tree native to the Middle East and central Asia, pistachios are prized for their pleasant, mild flavour and ornamental colour. They may be used in stuffings, sauces, confectionery, baking and ice creams, but are commonly eaten salted as a cocktail or dessert nut. To preserve their brilliant colour, shell them and boil in water for a few minutes, then remove their skins.

CHUFA NUT (*Cyperus esculenta*)

Related to the tigernut, this is fairly popular in Europe. When ground it is used in the Spanish drink *horchata de chufa*.

Chufa nut

COCONUT (*Cocos nucifera*)

All parts of the fruit are used, but only the milk and meat as food. Coconut milk is a refreshing and nutritious drink, and can be used in curry sauces. Coconut meat can be eaten fresh, or dried and used in baking and confectionery (page 124). Most coconut meat, however, is dried to form copra, from which coconut oil (page 75) is extracted. The sap of the coconut palm can be fermented to produce arrack.

MACADAMIA NUT (*Macadamia ternifolia*)

Native to Australia and now also grown in Hawaii, macadamia or Queensland nuts are usually sold shelled and roasted in countries where they are not grown.

Macadamia nut

PINE NUT (*Pinus pinea*)

The seed of the stone pine, native to the Mediterranean, pine nuts are eaten raw or roasted and salted like peanuts. In Italy they are used to make soups and sauces, such as the famous *pesto* sauce, in the Middle East they are popular in *dolmas*, and they can be eaten raw in salads.

Pine nut

Coconut

Pistachio nut

CEREALS

CEREALS ARE NAMED after Ceres, the Roman goddess of agriculture, and comprise edible grains such as wheat, oats, and corn, and foods prepared from such grains. When agriculture first began in the Middle East, Central and South America in about 7000 BC, cereals figured prominently – wheat and barley are Middle Eastern crops, and corn is Mexican.

The starchy carbohydrates which are provided by cereals are essential in human nutrition. Rice is a staple food for half the world's population, the remaining half cultivating wheat, oats, corn, barley, millet and so on, depending on soil and climate. There are starchy dishes in every cuisine in the world, including Mexico's corn tortillas, Italy's many pastas, and Brazil's farofas, made from cassava (manioc) meal.

Cereals come from the cultivated grasses (*Graminaceae*) wheat, corn, rice, oats, barley and rye. In addition, there are other meals that are good starch-providers, including tapioca and cassava meal from the root of the cassava plant and sago from the sago palm. Fecula or "flour" products also come from the roots of such plants as the lotus, arum lily, bracken, potato, and other tubers. From the cereal grasses we harvest the valuable grains – how we use these grains depends on their individual structure and their behaviour as foodstuffs.

RICE

There are about 7000 varieties of rice (*Oryza sativa*). Probably native to India and Indo-China, it comes in many forms. Brown rice is simply the rice plus bran, which is removed during the secondary stage of milling (or "pearling") to give us the familiar white polished grain. The bran in brown rice offers additional protein, plus traces of iron, calcium and vitamin B, but takes longer to cook. Not all rice varieties are white when polished: Carolina and some Italian rices are amber.

Rice is divided into three groups: long-, short- and medium-grain. Long-grain rice is four to five times as long as it is wide and, when cooked, the grains are separate and

fluffy. It is used in salads, curries, stews, chicken or meat dishes. Short- and medium-grain rice have short, plump grains which become tender and moist when cooked with the grains clinging together. Each type of rice is suited to traditional cooking styles: Indian cooks prefer a dry rice, especially for pilaus; Japanese and Chinese cooks use short-grain rice which can be shaped by the fingers, and is easily handled with chopsticks.

Under the general classification of long-grain rice are the American Carolina and the delicate Basmati from Pakistan. The short-grain rices include Japan's kome, and the stubby round Italian rice. There is also wild rice, which, despite its name, is a water grass, not a grain. Native to North America and known to botanists as *Zizania aquatica*, it is long-grained and grey-brown in colour, with a "nutty" flavour. Wild rice is used mainly for stuffing game and poultry. Converted, precooked or prefluffed brand-name rice is a commercial product that has been parboiled then dried, and though its cooking results are more easily determined, there is some loss of flavour.

Rice in the kitchen
Rice will keep almost indefinitely, a fact only important to western households that do not use rice as a staple food. In cooking, long-grain rice will absorb one and a half times its bulk in liquid, depending on the type of grain. Basmati, for example, will absorb less water than Patna or Carolina. Short-grain rice will absorb over four times its bulk in liquid.

Rice can be cooked separately or processed to make rice flour, flaked rice and ground rice, for use in puddings, cakes and as a thickening agent for sauces, soups and stews. Fermented rice makes some potent Chinese spirits, and the famous Japanese *sake*.

WHEAT AND FLOUR

Wheat is a cereal grass, and was probably first cultivated in Mesopotamia. There are two main varieties, bread wheat (*Triticum aestivum*) and hard wheat (*T. durum*), used for making pasta (page 108), and semolina.

Bread wheat is the world's most important cereal crop; its unique quality is due to the high gluten content of the wheat berry. Gluten is a muscular substance of great elasticity that strengthens the cellular structure of bread. When yeast liberates carbon dioxide gas during "proving", and water releases steam during baking, the gluten helps the bread to expand – without gluten, bread would be flat and heavy.

The wheat berry, and the way it is milled, gives us our flours in different varieties and grades. The berry consists of the outer husk or bran, the endosperm, containing most of the starch to make flour, and the inner core or wheat germ embryo. When the entire grain is milled we obtain a brown flour rich in nutrients and protein. In America this flour is known as Graham or whole-wheat flour; in Britain it is wholemeal flour. The "brownness" of the flour depends on the amount of bran included, white flour being the product of the endosperm only.

Strong, hard or bread flour is milled from certain varieties of bread wheats, while all-purpose, soft, plain or cake flour has less gluten, and comes from soft types of flour. Self-raising flour contains an aerating agent.

Flour in the kitchen

Flour provides the basic structure of bread, cakes, batters and pastry, but the structure is further dependent upon the type of flour and the raising agent. Bread flour must be aerated by yeast, although brown flour can be leavened either with yeast or with baking soda. Bread also requires kneading to strengthen the gluten. The soft flour in cakes is raised by the dispersal of air or gas by baking powder or whisked eggs. Steam is liberated in oven-cooked batters by whisked eggs, while pastry owes its texture to the plasticity of fat, and steam released by water in the dough, depending on the type of pastry. Soft flours produce a softer, spongier texture – you cannot beat air into bread flour, but soft flours are more easily leavened by thorough beating which introduces aerating.

Grains

RYE (Secale cereale)

Probably of south-west Asian origin, rye is similar in composition to wheat. In Europe it is used mainly for making rye bread and crispbread (particularly in Scandinavia). It is also used in the manufacture of drinks such as whiskey in America, gin in Holland and beer in Russia.

MILLET (Panicum miliaceum)

Native to Asia, millet was once the principal cereal of Europe, rivalling barley. It is the seed of an annual gluten-free grass which is widely eaten as a cereal in Africa and Asia, and is also used as a source of starch in Russia. Millet has as high a protein content as wheat, but its lack of gluten makes it inferior for baking. Millet flour is used for flat breads and griddle cakes. The grains can be mixed with pulses and vegetables, and used in soups and stews.

SWEETCORN (Zea mays)

Indigenous to Mexico, sweetcorn (also known as corn or maize) has been cultivated for thousands of years, both as a vegetable (page 36) and a source of meal. It is one of the most important cereals in the form of grain, meal and flour. It is used in many American recipes such as corn bread and hominy, and is also an important source of starch, corn syrup and cooking oil. The fermented grains are used to make Bourbon.

Rye

Millet

Sweetcorn

Grains and Cereal Products

BUCKWHEAT
(*Fagopyrum esculentum*)
An annual grain plant thought to be native to China, its seeds are roasted and made into flour used for pancakes, crisp thin cakes, and noodles called "soba" in the Far East. Buckwheat groats, or "kasha", are used in soups.

Buckwheat

BARLEY (*Hordeum vulgare*)
Barley is native to Mesopotamia, where it was milled to make bread and fermented to make beer. Malting barley is used in the production of whisky, gin and beer. In countries where barley and rye crops flourish, you will find barley porridge and barley bread. It is not, however, usually used to make bread flour.

Barley

GLUTINOUS RICE
(*Oryza sativa*, spp.)
Despite its name, this rice, widely used in Chinese cooking, is completely gluten-free. When boiled it becomes sweet and sticky and is thus used mainly in baking and confectionery, and also for making beer. Two varieties are shown: black and white. The white variety is dehulled in processing.

Black glutinous rice

OATS (*Avena sativa*)
Native to central Europe, oats are a Scottish staple, and are milled to varying degrees of fineness. Cooked with water, oats become porridge; oatmeal is an ingredient in haggis, oatcakes, and the whisky drink Athol Brose.

Oats

WHEAT
(*Triticum aestivum, durum*)
Thought to have first been cultivated in the Nile region, it is the source of the highest quality bread and baking flours. There are many different varieties: the durum wheat type is best known for making pasta and semolina.

Wheat

White glutinous rice

CONVERTED RICE
(*Oryza sativa*, spp.)
This rice is parboiled to remove its surface starch, thus leaving most of the nutrients and vitamins in the grains, unlike other white rice varieties. It provides the best of all possible options, since it has the nutritional value of brown rice, without its chewy texture and longer cooking methods.

BASMATI RICE
(*Oryza sativa*, spp.)
Grown in the foothills of the Himalayas, this narrow long-grain rice is one of the finest. It should be washed and soaked before cooking and is the best rice to eat with Indian food.

Basmati rice

Converted rice

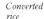

ITALIAN RICE
(*Oryza sativa*, spp.)
A large, round-grained type of rice, the texture makes it ideal for the classic Italian rice dish, *risotto*. Brown and white varieties, shown here, are available.

Brown Italian rice

White Italian rice

BROWN RICE
(*Oryza sativa*, spp.)
This is the whole natural grain of the rice before it is processed. It needs more water and longer cooking than white rice.

Brown rice

COUSCOUS
A cereal processed from semolina into tiny pellets, this is best known for its use in the traditional North African dish of the same name.

Couscous

CAROLINA RICE
(*Oryza sativa*, spp.)
Grown all over the world, Carolina or Patna rice is the most versatile and popular of all. The grains, which are hulled and polished, remain firm, fluffy and separate when cooked.

Carolina rice

PUDDING RICE
(*Oryza sativa*, spp.)
A short-grain strain of polished rice which becomes soft and mushy when cooked, this is usually reserved for cream and milk puddings.

Pudding rice

PEARL BARLEY
Dehulled and polished barley grains which may be added to soups, used to make invalid beverages or served as a pilaf in place of potatoes.

Pearl barley

SEMOLINA
The hard part of durum wheat sifted out of flour and used for pasta, which would be difficult to make with "soft" or cake flour. It is also used in puddings.

Semolina

OTHER GRAINS

SORGHUM
(*Sorghum vulgare*, spp.)
A type of millet cultivated in in Africa and Asia, the seeds when ground are made into bread, porridge and flat cakes and are used in soups. Another variety of sorghum, *Holcus sorghum* var. *saccara*, produces a smooth sweet syrup.

WILD RICE
(*Zizania aquatica*)
Native to North America, wild rice looks like rice and is used in the same way, although it is in fact not a variety of rice. The dark brown grains are longer and thinner, and turn slightly purple when they are cooked.

Cereal Products

MATZOH MEAL

Ground *matzohs* (unleavened crispbreads), made of wheat flour and water, are used in place of leavened breadcrumbs during the Jewish Passover.

Matzoh meal

POLENTA

A type of meal ground from sweetcorn or maize, polenta, or cornmeal, can be eaten on its own as a type of porridge or used to garnish meat and fish dishes.

Polenta

TAPIOCA

These are pellets made of manioc flour, a starch extracted from the root of the manicc or cassava plant (*Manihot esculenta*). They form the basis of nursery milk puddings, and are used also to thicken soups and stews.

Tapioca

SAGO

The dried, starchy granules obtained from the sago palm (*Metroxylou sagu*) grown in the Far East, sago is used as an invalid food, in milk puddings, and as an ingredient, particularly in Scandinavian recipes, such as the Danish dish *sagosuppe*.

Sago

CRACKED WHEAT

Also known as burghul or bulgur, this processed wheat is popular throughout the eastern Mediterranean and the Middle East. It may be baked, cooked as a pilaf, soaked and served as a raw salad (Lebanese *tabbouleh*) or pounded into a paste with lamb to make the Lebanese *kibbi*.

Cracked wheat

OATMEAL

Dehulled oats maybe ground to make oatmeal of varying degrees of fineness (as shown), or softened and rolled to make rolled oats.

Medium oatmeal

WHEATGERM

The germ or "embryo" of the wheat grain, from which new wheat plants can be grown, wheatgerm is usually extracted from the grain during flour-making. Although it only forms a small part of the grain it is considered to be high in nutritional value, and can be eaten on its own or used to make the basis of a flour. It is used in soups and stews and as a thickening agent.

Wheatgerm

BARLEY FLOUR

Once the main ingredient of bread, this is now usually combined with wheat flour to increase its gluten content (bread made exclusively from barley flour tends to go dry very quickly).

Barley flour

Coarse oatmeal

MAIZE FLOUR

A gluten-free flour that must be reinforced with wheat flour for bread-making. It is also used to make cakes.

Maize flour

LOTUS ROOT FLOUR

A gluten-free flour milled from dried and powdered lotus root, it is used in Chinese and Japanese cooking as a thickener for sauces.

Lotus root flour

RICE FLOUR

A gluten-free flour milled from both ordinary polished white and brown rice grains, this is widely used as a thickening agent, both alone or in conjunction with other flours for cakes and biscuits, and in the Chinese kitchen for making a variety of noodles called "fun".

Rice flour

RYE FLOUR

Frequently used in combination with wheat flour because of its unsuitable gluten content, rye flour makes the characteristic "black" breads of northern and eastern Europe.

Rye flour

BRAN

The brown outer layer of any cereal, usually separated from the grain during flour-making, this is a valuable source of fibre in the diet, and can be used to make a flour in its own right.

Bran

WHOLEMEAL FLOUR

Wholemeal flour is milled from the whole grain of the wheat, including the bran and wheatgerm, which are removed in ordinary flours.

Wholemeal flour

SOY FLOUR

This is not a flour in the conventional sense, but a highly nutritious food supplement which can be added to soups and cakes.

Soy flour

WHEAT FLOUR

There are many varieties of wheat flour, ranging from the all-purpose plain (as shown) to fine cake flour.

Wheat flour

POTATO FLOUR

Made from cooked potatoes that have been dried and ground, this flour is often used as a subtle thickening agent.

Potato flour

BUCKWHEAT FLOUR

A type of pancake flour particularly popular in America, France and eastern Europe.

Buckwheat flour

PASTA, NOODLES AND DUMPLINGS

ASTA – THE WORD SIMPLY means "dough" – is the staple diet of Italy, essential to the Italian kitchen and far more popular than its rivals, bread, polenta (corn meal) and rice. Pasta, or to give it its official title, *pasta alimentari*, falls into two main types: the factory-made flour and water paste, called *pasta secca*, "dry" pasta, as sold in packages, and the fresh paste made with flour and eggs called *pasta all'uovo*, or *pasta fatta in casa*, "home-made" pasta.

Pasta secca begins as a springy dough of flour, salt and water which is then cut, pressed or moulded into a variety of shapes, sizes and designs which include tubes, ribbons, spirals, shells, bows and wheels, to provide a versatile foundation for an equally bewildering number of sauces. Even the Italians find the study of pasta confusing, since names and shapes vary from province to province.

Pasta uses the flour milled from the hard, translucent *Triticum durum* wheat, although there is also a type which is made with buckwheat. Durum produces fine, gritty particles of amber-coloured semolina flour (page 105), which is more durable than bread flour. When mixed to a dough with water this makes a nutritious paste that can be dried and kept indefinitely; you can test for good-quality pasta by running your finger along the surface – it should be silky smooth and quite pliant.

Strictly speaking, home-made *pasta all'uovo* should also be made with semolina flour, but all-purpose flour is a good substitute, and with the addition of eggs, salt, and perhaps a little water or oil to soften the dough, makes a good-quality *sfoglia*, as the rolled-out sheet of finished pasta is called.

Some pasta-makers, especially from the region of Emilia-Romagna, colour their paste with spinach purée which, not unnaturally, turns the pasta green – *lasagne verdi* or *tagliatelle verdi* are examples. There are also wholemeal versions.

Pasta's origins and development
Historians will always argue over the provenance of pasta. It is probably indigenous to Italy, having been developed by the Etruscans from a Greek recipe, a dough cake cut into strips and called *laganon*, from which the word *lasagne* is ultimately derived. Yet one of the earliest words for pasta was *tri*, from the Arabic *itriyah*, "string", which, as a description of spaghetti (literally "little threads"), hints at an Arabic origin.

By the fifteenth century, pasta was known as *vermicelli*, or "little worms", and in Sicily as *maccheroni*, a word of disputed origin. Today, macaroni is a generic term for all types of *pasta secca*, and recipes and sauces have swollen the ranks of pasta into a confused legion of nearly 600 different shapes.

The Italians, artists in the kitchen, found that some shapes were particularly suited to certain sauces; that *spaghetti* from Naples complemented the meat *ragù* of Bologna; that delicate *fettucine* noodles went best with a cream and mushroom sauce; and that the ribbons of pasta called *trenette* were the life partner to the Ligurian *pesto* made with basil and pine nuts. The majority of pasta shapes are, however, successfully interchangeable with the infinite variety of sauces – the spirals of pasta called *fusilli* or *archimede* are just as companionable to *vongole* (clams) as is the traditional *spaghettini*.

Some shapes are particularly well suited to oven cooking and to stuffing. The tubes of *cannelloni* and *rigatoni* are filled with meat, or minced vegetables, covered with a cheese-flavoured béchamel sauce and finally baked *al forno*. *Lasagne*, the large sheets of pasta, are alternately layered with minced meat and béchamel, and then baked as before. Smaller shapes, such as *ravioli*, hats (*cappelletti*) or half-moons (*tortellini*) are stuffed and may be cooked *in brodo* (broth) or water.

Pasta in the kitchen
The basic types of pasta, dry or fresh, can be further divided into categories according to their use: *pasta asciutta* and *pasta in brodo* or *pastina*. Briefly, the term *pasta asciutta* describes all those substantial daily dishes such as the familiar spaghetti or macaroni served with a sauce; pasta stuffed with meat, cheese or puréed vegetables, such as *ravioli* or

cannelloni (*pasta ripieni*, meaning "stuffed"); pasta dishes baked in the oven – *al forno* – such as *lasagne*.

Pasta in brodo, the second category, is pasta in miniature; tiny shapes of pasta (*pastina*) that find their natural element in soup – *in brodo* – such as wheels (*ruote*), shells (*conchiglie*), butterflies (*farfalle*), and a host of other motifs. Thrifty cooks sometimes employ broken scraps of *pasta secca*, that have dropped to the bottom of the grocer's bin or sack, to make a rustic dish of pasta, cheese and tomatoes called *tuoni e lampo* or "thunder and lightning".

Whereas opinions might vary about which pasta goes best with which sauce, everyone is united on the topic of how pasta should be cooked. *Pasta asciutta* needs plenty of salted boiling water, roughly 4.5 l (4qts) of water and 30g (1oz) of salt to each 0.5kg (1lb) of pasta, otherwise the pasta goes gluey since the water cannot cope with the excess starch. Some experts demand that salt be added after the pasta, otherwise a slight aroma of phenol is liberated, but the majority of cooks ignore such finesse, merely insisting that pasta should be cooked to a precise minute – give or take a second or two.

Cooking times vary according to the pasta, but the end result should be *al dente* – in other words, not soft but with firmness to the bite. Some people like their pasta firmer, even hard; the term for this is *fil de ferro* ("wire"). Pasta should not be drained too thoroughly, otherwise you will find that it sticks together, especially lasagne. As a further precaution, cooks may add a teaspoon of oil to the pasta while it is still boiling to prevent sticking.

NOODLES AND DUMPLINGS

The Chinese, pioneer inventors that they were, must have discovered the value of starch pastes early in history, and celebrated noodle reports followed Marco Polo's visit to China in 1270. We may assume that pasta was an independent invention: *vermicelli* was a staple in the Italian diet long before the thirteenth century.

Since there has been domestication of cereals for over 8000 years it can be assumed that the production of noodles is quite ancient. Familiarity with cereals would have proved

that grains make flour, and flour plus water produces a pliable paste that can be cut and dried and kept.

The word "noodle" derives from the German, Bavarian and Austrian words for dumplings – *nudeln, knödl* and *knödel* – and dumplings seem to have originated from the practice of nipping off pieces of uncooked dough or bread (*croûtons*), and dropping them into soups or stews; variations on this theme exist from Hungary across Europe to Britain.

Types of noodles
While noodles and pasta have much in common they fall into different categories. Noodles are defined as a food paste made of flour, water and eggs which may be sold and used either dried or fresh. Most Italian pasta, when made commercially, contains no eggs. In many western countries, particularly in Germany and America, noodles must include eggs, unless sold as "plain noodles". Noodles are also referred to as "vermicelli", regardless of whether they come from Italy or Hong Kong, and the main areas of production are central Europe, America and the Far East.

The Germans are credited with being the first to make a noodle dough with eggs, and in the familiar ribbon-shape of commercial noodles. This type of egg noodle paste is also popular with the Italians and the Chinese. Asian noodles, however, may be based on a number of different flour pastes, with or without eggs, including the flour of mung beans, soy-beans, buckwheat, seaweed, corn, chick-peas, rice and durum wheat, and sold in skeins of fine threads that are typically Eastern. The Japanese have an impressive range of *menrui* (noodles) made of white wheat or golden buckwheat such as *soba, somen*, and *udon*. Japan shares with China a fondness for bean-gelatine or cellophane noodles, called, in Japan, *harusame*. Another popular Japanese noodle is *shirataki*, made from *konnyaku* (devil's tongue or snake palm plant), a member of the arum family.

Noodles in the kitchen
Commercially made noodles will last almost indefinitely, kept in a cool, airy place. Noodles should be cooked according to the recipe or instructions on the package. Presoaked

noodles need less cooking than dried ones, and they are usually soaked to facilitate cooking in stir-fried dishes – 5 minutes is usually sufficient. *Harusame* noodles and Chinese cellophane noodles may need presoaking for 30 minutes. Straight from the package, *soba* noodles need about 7 minutes, *somen* 7 minutes, and *udon* 20 minutes. Unlike *vermicelli*, they are preferred soft, and not *al dente* in the Italian style.

Pasta

Capellini

FEDELI (*pasta asciutta; secca*)

This is a very fine, cylindrical pasta, similar to *vermicelli*. It is available fresh or dried. *Fedelini* is even finer.

CAPELLINI
(*pasta asciutta; secca*)

The finest ribbon pasta, *capellini* (or *vermicelli* or *capolnevere*) can be home-made or bought ready-made in a shop. *Capelli d'angelo*, meaning "angel's hair", is the thinnest variety.

Fedeli

Lasagnette

LASAGNETTE
(*pasta asciutta; secca*)

A smaller version of *lasagne*, this is a flat, ribbon pasta about 18mm (¾in) wide, with a ruffled edge.

Buckwheat spaghetti

SPAGHETTI
(*pasta asciutta; secca*)

Known as *vermicelli* in southern Italy, the word *spaghetti* means "little strings". It remains the most popular type of pasta and is available fresh or dried.

Wholewheat spaghetti

Extra-long spaghetti

Tagliatelle verdi

Tagliarini verdi

Tagliatelle

Tagliarini

Spaghetti

TAGLIATELLE
(*pasta asciutta; all'uovo*)

Tagliatelle or *fettucini* is the pasta speciality of Bologna. These flat, 6mm (¼in) wide ribbon noodles are, like all pasta, made from durum wheat and can easily be made at home or bought fresh or dried. They are served with a variety of sauces, ranging from a simple milk and butter mixture to one with a rich meat, fish or poultry base. *Tagliatelle verdi* (top) has puréed spinach added to the basic dough.

TAGLIARINI
(*pasta asciutta; all'uovo*)

A flat, ribbon-like pasta, similar to *tagliatelle*, but slightly smaller in width. It can be home-made, obtained fresh in a speciality shop or bought ready-made and is also available as *tagliarini verdi* (top). It is usually served with a sauce as for *tagliatelle*.

CASARECCIA
(pasta asciutta; secca)

Pasta lengths that are curled into shape, with a twist at one end.

Casareccia

BOZZOLI *(pasta asciutta; secca)*

This pasta is named for its cocoon-like shape.

Bozzoli

CRESTI DI GALLO
(pasta asciutta; secca)

This is named for its ridged mane that looks like a cock's comb.

Cresti di gallo

LUNGO-VERMICELLI COUPE *(pasta asciutta; secca)*

This name describes the pasta accurately as long *vermicelli*, cut into pieces.

Lungo-vermicelli coupe

RICCINI *(pasta asciutta; secca)*

This ridged, shell-like pasta takes its name from the Italian word *riccio*, meaning "curl".

Riccini

GRAMIGNA
(pasta asciutta; secca)

This has small, grass-like shapes. The name actually means "grass" or weed.

Gramigna

FESTONATI
(pasta asciutta; secca)

The word *festonati* means "festoon" or "garland".

Festonati

CAVATAPPI
(pasta asciutta; secca)

Ridged pasta in a twisted shape.

Cavatappi

FUSILLI BUCATI
(pasta asciutta; secca)

This pasta is made in the shape of tiny springs.

Fusilli bucati

GNOCCHI *(pasta asciutta; secca)*

These small dumplings, shown made from durum wheat, are also available made from potato or semolina flour.

Gnocchi

ORECCHIETTE
(pasta asciutta; secca)

Pasta shaped like an ear. The name derives from the Italian word *orecchio,* meaning "ear".

Orecchiette

GNOCCHETTI SARDI
(pasta in brodo; secca)

A smaller version of gnocchi, this is named for its sardine-like shape.

Gnocchetti sardi

PIPE RIGATE
(pasta asciutta; secca)

A ridged pasta made in the shape of a pipe.

Pipe rigate

SPIRALE *(pasta asciutta; secca)*

Pasta lengths twisted together to form a spiral.

Spirale

ANELLI *(pasta asciutta; secca)*

Anelli, meaning "ring", is an appropriate title for these pasta shapes, shown made from wholemeal flour (brown) or durum wheat (pale).

Anelli (wholemeal)

Anelli (durum wheat)

LUMACHE MEDIE
(pasta in brodo; secca)

These shapes resemble snails' shells, thus the name *lumache,* which means "snail".

Lumache medie

VEGETABLE-DYED MACARONI
(pasta in brodo; secca)

Made from durum wheat, this may be dyed green with spinach or red with tomatoes.

Vegetable-dyed macaroni

FARFALLE
(pasta asciutta; secca)

The name means "butterfly". *Farfallini (pasta in brodo)* are the same, but smaller.

CAPPELLETTI
(pasta asciutta; secca)

Little pastry hats made, like most pasta, from durum wheat.

Farfalle

Farfallini

Fusilli

Conchiglie piccole rigate

Cappelletti

FUSILLI *(pasta asciutta; secca)*

Pasta made in the spiral shape of a corkscrew.

CONCHIGLIE RIGATE
(pasta asciutta; secca)

This ridged pasta is made in the shape of sea shells. *Conchiglie piccole rigate* are smaller versions.

RUOTI *(pasta asciutta; secca)*

These resemble wheels, and are available in wholemeal and durum wheat versions.

Ruoti (wholemeal)

Conchiglie rigate

Ruoti (durum wheat)

TUBETTI LUNGHI
(pasta asciutta; secca)

This pasta is made in short lengths with a slight bend resembling an elbow joint. Wholemeal (top) and durum wheat (below) variations are illustrated.

Ditali

Ditalini

Tubetti lunghi (wholemeal)

Tubetti lunghi (durum wheat)

MACARONI
(pasta asciutta; secca)

This is a generic term for all types of *pasta secca*, but is commonly used to describe this wider hollow version of spaghetti.

SMALL MACARONI
(pasta asciutta; secca)

This is also known as *bucatini*.

PENNE *(pasta asciutta; secca)*

Small or large sizes and ribbed versions of this pasta shape are easily obtained.

DITALI *(pasta asciutta; secca)*

The Italian word *ditali* means finger of a glove, or thimble. *Ditalini (pasta in brodo)* are merely smaller versions of *ditali*.

Macaroni

Penne

Small macaroni

Rigatoni

RIGATONI *(pasta asciutta; secca)*

This name is derived from the Italian word *riga*, meaning "line".

Elicoidali

ELICOIDALI
(pasta asciutta; secca)

This is similar to *rigatoni*, but is smaller in size with a spiral (helical) line pattern.

Ziti

ZITI *(pasta asciutta; secca)*

Another version of macaroni, but cut into short lengths.

LASAGNE (*pasta asciutta*)

Often home-made, but widely available dried, this is the broadest of the ribbon pasta. *Lasagne* can be bought smooth, ridged or with a ruffled edge and can be made with wholemeal dough or with the addition of puréed spinach.

Pasta all'uovo

Pasta secca

Pasta secca

Pasta secca

Wholemeal lasagne
(pasta secca)

TORTELLINI
(pasta asciutta; all'uovo)

A small, stuffed pasta dumpling which, according to legend, was modelled on Venus's navel. It is usually stuffed with a variety of the following: chopped chicken breast, pork, Mortadella or Bologna sausage, cheese and nutmeg. Tortellini is widely available ready-made, either dried or fresh.

RAVIOLI
(pasta asciutta; all'uovo)

This is the most well-known pasta dumpling. Square in shape, it is traditionally stuffed with spinach and ricotta cheese or herbs, but can be filled with a savoury meat mixture. Cooked in boiling water, it is often served with a gravy or sauce, or small *ravioli* may be cooked *in brodo* (in soups). *Ravioli* is usually served fresh, but can be bought ready-cooked in a can.

CANNELLONI
(pasta asciutta; secca)

The word *cannelloni*, meaning "big pipes", describes this hollow, cylindrical pasta shape, which is stuffed and baked *al forno*.

Tortellini

Ravioli

PASTINA *(pasta in brodo; secca)*

Pastina is the general term for the wide variety of tiny pasta shapes that are usually cooked *in brodo*.

Pastina

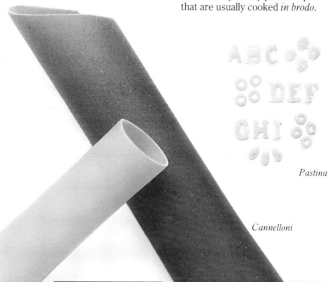

Cannelloni

Egg Noodles and Dumplings

Egg noodles

All of these noodles are made with eggs, the darker yellow ones containing more egg than the others. These noodles are normally sold in compressed bundles of varying size and have usually been pre-cooked by steaming so they require only a minimal amount of preparation at home. The main difference between noodles and Italian pasta lies in the way they are prepared rather than their substance or shape. Most of the noodles shown are dried.

Commercial noodles are made from about 5.5kg (12lb) fresh eggs to every 44kg (96lb) semolina flour. The dough is mixed, kneaded, rolled, laminated, cut and dried, all by machine.

European noodles may have ultimately derived from the *spätzle* (little sparrows) of Württemberg, where egg dough is forced through the holes of a colander into boiling water. They accompany veal, cabbage, or are mixed with chopped meat or herbs and served as a salad.

Fresh egg noodles

Dried egg noodles

Dried egg noodles

Chinese noodles

CHINESE NOODLES

These vary considerably, but typically they are 3mm (⅛in) wide, dried and sold like loosely tangled balls of wool. Noodles are *mein* and *mee* in Chinese cooking, and feature in chow mein dishes, incorporated with meat and vegetables.

Dried egg noodles

Dried egg noodles

Dried egg noodles

EGG DUMPLINGS

CSIPETKE
These Hungarian egg-flour dumplings are scraps of dough dropped into boiling water and served with soups and goulash.

KASNUDLN
From Austria, these are a variety of Uszka, made either with a savoury filling such as cheese or meat, or with a sweet filling such as fruit and spices.

USZKA
This is a type of *ravioli* from Poland. It is an egg-flour dough which is stuffed with mushrooms, then dropped into soup. *Uszka* means "little ears" and describes the shape of the dumplings.

Rice, Bean and Wheat Noodles

RICE NOODLES

Noodles are a symbol of longevity in China and are often served at birthday parties as a wish for long life. These rice noodles are made in long strands before being folded over and packaged.

Rice noodles

RICE NOODLES

These flat, ribbon-like rice noodles are made in long strands and are often called rice sticks.

Rice noodles

Rice noodles

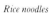

Rice noodles

Rice noodles

RICE NOODLES

Noodles made from rice are more commonly eaten in southern China, where more rice is grown. The curled pad of noodles illustrated here is commonly known as "rice vermicelli".

WHEAT NOODLES

These flat, stick-like wheat noodles are available in different widths, and are interchangeable with rice noodles according to taste.

TRANSPARENT NOODLES

Chinese and Japanese transparent noodles are made with mung bean paste (shown here), pea starch or wheat flour. In Japan they are known as *harusame* ("spring rain"), and feature in *yosenabe*, a kind of chop suey of fish and vegetables in broth. In India, transparent noodles are called *sevian* or "China grass" and are used to make sweet dishes.

Wheat noodles

Transparent noodles

OTHER NOODLES AND DUMPLINGS

BIJON

These noodles are produced commercially in south-east Asia from corn kernels. The kernels are steeped in water for 4–7 days to encourage the fermentation of butyric acid, then mashed and formed into "dumplings" with cornflour. The dough is extruded into long strands, parboiled for 2 minutes, then sun-dried for about 4 hours.

Other noodle types from the same area include Canton noodles made from wheat flour, duck eggs, salt and vegetable oil, *miki*, made with wheat flour, eggs and soda, ash and *misua*, which are fine wheat noodles like the Japanese *udon sotanghon*, a version of transparent noodles. These noodles would

be served with such typical dishes as *laksa*, a fish and coconut milk soup.

BREAD DUMPLINGS

Bavarian *knödl*, Austrian *knödl*, and Czech *knedliky* are all made with stale bread or yeast dough, and may be sweet or savoury. The English Norfolk dumpling falls into this category, being a boiled yeast dough that accompanies meat broths and stews, or is served with sugar, honey or treacle as a dessert.

SHIRATAKI

These are noodles made from the starch of the devil's tongue plant (*Amorphopallus rivieri*), cultivated in China and Japan. The tubers are dried to make *konnyaku* flour, used to make

shirataki ("white waterfall"). They feature in the well-known *sukiyaki* dish.

SOBA

These are the most popular type of noodle in Japan, made with golden buckwheat, and served in the many *sobo-ya* restaurants. The noodles may be presented in *zaru* bowls, accompanied by *nori* (seaweed) and horseradish.

SOMEN

These are thin, very fine, white wheat noodles which are often served cold.

UDON

Very narrow, ribbon-like white wheat noodles, these are served in hot soups and mixed meat and vegetable dishes.

Baking Goods

Some ingredients, though unobtrusive, play a vital role in baking; others are more decorative. In the first category are the raising and thickening agents – the ingredients responsible for the "inside" chemical changes in baking. In the second are those that provide the additional touches, the colourings and the confections.

Uses in the kitchen

Yeast is used to raise the strong gluten flour of bread doughs, and baking powder is used for most cakes and some breads. Fresh yeast should be greyish-brown and crumble easily. When old, the brownish shade darkens. It should be dissolved in warm water before being combined with other ingredients. Dry yeast should be sprinkled on the water and greater heat and more moisture are needed than with fresh.

Many thickeners, such as arrowroot and cornflour – so important in gravies and sauces – are used in baking as well, while gelatine, sold in powder and in sheets, is used to set both aspics and gelatine-based desserts. Generally, dried baking goods, such as yeast, baking powder and cornflour, will keep indefinitely, stored in tins in a cool dry place.

There is a wide range of confections and colourings for the pastry cook to call upon. Many of the traditional colouring dyes, such as chlorophyll and cochineal, are being replaced and augmented by synthetic colours which give a huge range. There are also many commercial products available in hard and soft sugar as well as candied fruits.

FRESH YEAST

Yeast is a plant with active living cells which feed on sugars and produce alcohol and carbon dioxide. One of the main raising agents used in bread, fresh yeast should be bought in small quantities, as it loses its potency quickly once broken. It is also available frozen.

Fresh yeast

YEAST CAKES

This is another form of fresh yeast, compressed into a rounded shape rather than being sold in a block. It can be bought in most specialist oriental food shops.

Yeast cakes

BREWERS' YEAST

In spite of its name, this is not a raising agent, but is used mainly for brewing wines and beers, as its name implies. It is available dried, powdered or in tablets.

Dried brewers' yeast

Powdered brewers' yeast

RED YEAST

A type of wild yeast, red yeast is sold dried and used mainly for fermenting purposes, in particular to make oriental vinegars.

Red yeast

DRIED YEAST

Today, dried yeast is manufactured only in factories and is almost always based on a solution of molasses and water. It is used for the same purposes as fresh yeast, but it will keep for much longer. It is also available in an instant form.

Dried yeast

PECTIN

A carbohydrate that occurs naturally in certain fruits, pectin is used mainly in jams and jellies to help them set. Pectin extracts can be bought commercially or can be made at home.

Pectin

SODIUM BICARBONATE

Sodium bicarbonate (also known as bicarbonate of soda and baking soda) has no leavening properties, but can be used as a raising agent when combined with an acid such as sour milk.

Sodium bicarbonate

CREAM OF TARTAR

This substance is found in the juice of grapes, after they have been fermented in wine-making. It reacts with baking soda to produce carbon dioxide to leaven batters.

Cream of tartar

BAKING POWDER

There are several kinds of this leavening agent, but basically they are composed of sodium bicarbonate plus various acids or acid salts. It can be bought commercially or made at home from cream of tartar, sodium bicarbonate and salt. When water is added to baking powder, carbon dioxide is given off and the mixture to which the baking powder has been added is aerated. Too much baking powder can spoil the texture and flavour of a cake, so it is important to use only the amount stated in a recipe.

Baking powder

CORNFLOUR

A fine, white flour obtained from corn, used for thickening puddings and sauces and for baking cakes.

Cornflour

ARROWROOT

This delicate nutritive starch is obtained mainly from the West Indian plant of the same name (*Maranta arundinacea*). It is most often used as a thickening agent.

Arrowroot

KUZU

The tuberous roots of the Kuzu vine are rather bitter-tasting, but when boiled and mashed are often used as a thickener in Chinese and Japanese cooking.

Kuzu

AGAR-AGAR

A neutral-tasting gelatinous product obtained from various Far Eastern seaweeds, agar-agar has a variety of names: Bengal isinglass, Ceylon moss, Japanese moss and Macassar gum. It is used mainly in the making of jellies, and gelatine-like desserts. Sold in threads, flakes or powder form, it is only partially soluble in water, unless boiled.

Agar-agar

GELATINE

Extracted from boiled beef bones and tendons, gelatine is available as powder or in transparent sheets. It is a setting agent, most often used in the making of desserts and prepared meats.

Powdered gelatine

Sheet gelatine

OTHER BAKING GOODS

AMMONIUM BICARBONATE

The predecessor of modern leaveners, this renders non-fermented dough spongy.

GUM ARABIC

A product obtained from the *Acacia senegal* tree, gum arabic prevents the crystallization of sugar and is used to glaze marzipan fruits.

GUM TRAGACANTH

A gum used in making pastillage gum paste for sugar flowers and cake decorations. It comes from a plant found in the Middle East.

Colouring Agents and Confections

MARZIPAN FRUITS
Almond paste is shaped and then tinted with food dyes to resemble fruits. These are used as cake decorations or often are boxed as gift confectionery.

COCONUT
Dried (desiccated) coconut in flaked or finely shredded form is often used plain or toasted as a garnish, or it may be included in baking recipes such as macaroons.

GUMDROP DIAMONDS
Soft and chewy in texture, these sugar decorations, also known as diamond jellies, are particularly useful for making patterns on cakes and desserts.

NON PAREILS and HUNDREDS AND THOUSANDS
Available in tiny tube (non pareils) and ball (hundreds and thousands) shapes, these hard sugar sprinkles are quick and easy to apply as dessert and cake decorations.

FOOD DYES
These are sold in a powdered form or, more commonly, as a liquid. They may be of artificial or natural origin and should be used sparingly as too much can give food a vivid tint. Natural food dyes include alkannet (a red or blue colouring from the root of *Anchusa tinctoria*), annatto (an orange dye from the seeds of the West Indian *Bixa orellana*), carotene (a yellow pigment linked to vitamin A, found in carrots), chlorophyll (green pigment from leaves, such as spinach and nettles), and cochineal (a pink pigment obtained from the female of an insect species, *Dactylopius coccus*, found in Mexico and Iran).

Marshmallow

Marzipan fruits

(flaked)

Coconut

Chestnut purée

(finely shredded)

Gumdrop diamonds

Non pareils

Dragees

Sugar drops

Hundreds and thousands

Sugar violets and rose petals

Powdered food dyes

Crystallized violets, rose petals and mint leaves

Liquid food dyes

MARSHMALLOW
A soft white confection that is eaten plain or toasted. It is made of sugar, egg white and gelatine and coated in powdered sugar. Originally made from the roots of the marsh mallow plant.

CHESTNUT PUREE
Cooked shelled chestnuts are puréed (sometimes with cream) and added to smooth-textured desserts or may be used as a poultry stuffing.

DRAGEES
Shiny and smooth-coated hard sugar balls are often used on cakes for special occasions.

SUGAR DROPS
Sugary sprinkles, available in different shades, are useful for small and large cakes.

SUGAR VIOLETS and ROSE PETALS
These hard sugar flowers, popular cake decorations, are available in different sizes and shades.

CRYSTALLIZED VIOLETS, ROSE PETALS and MINT LEAVES
Dipped in egg white and granulated sugar, these flowers and leaves are used to decorate small cakes and ice creams.

MARRONS GLACES
Often boxed as a gift confection these chestnuts are first preserved – a lengthy process – and then glazed with syrup.

Marrons glacés

GLACE CHERRY

Cherries, coated in a sugar and glucose syrup mixture, are used as ingredients in fruit cakes and chocolates and as decorations.

MIXED PEEL

A mixture of citrus fruit peel, sugar and glucose syrup, mixed peel is included in rich fruit cakes and Christmas puddings.

CRYSTALLIZED PINEAPPLE

Pineapple with a sugary coating can be eaten as a confection or used chopped as a decoration.

CANDIED FRUIT

Simulated fruit slices made of sugar and gelatine make decorative finishes for desserts and cakes.

COOKING CHOCOLATE

This slab chocolate is produced when crushed cacao bean liquid is cooled and shaped into blocks. It is also known as baking or unsweetened chocolate. Sweet and semi-sweet chocolates, which contain more sweetening and cocoa butter, are also available and used for baking and making sauces.

ALMOND PASTE

Crushed, blanched almonds mixed with vanilla and sugar. Also known as almond icing or marzipan, the mixture is rolled out and used to cover fruit cakes before they are iced. It is believed to have originated in the Middle East.

CHOCOLATE FLAKE

Served whole or crumbled, it is used as an accompaniment to vanilla ice cream.

ANGELICA

The stalk of the herb angelica (page 55) is coated in sugar and used chopped or cut into slivers as a cake decoration.

Glacé cherry

Sugar-coated cumin seeds and mimosa balls

Mixed peel

Strawberry and chocolate crunch

Chocolate chips

Crystallized pineapple

Crystallized ginger

Candied fruit

Cooking chocolate

Almond paste

Rice paper

Chocolate flake

Angelica

SUGAR-COATED CUMIN SEEDS and MIMOSA BALLS

These are seeds with a coating of tinted sugar. Hard and crunchy, they provide a contrasting texture to a creamy dessert.

STRAWBERRY and CHOCOLATE CRUNCH

Sugar crunch for cakes and ices.

CHOCOLATE CHIPS

Tiny chocolate chips used in cakes and biscuits and for decoration.

CRYSTALLIZED GINGER

Stem ginger with a sugary coating that can be eaten as a confection or used chopped as a decoration.

RICE PAPER

A very fine paper used to coat the undersides of certain confections.

OTHER USEFUL CONFECTIONS

NOUGAT

Originally from Europe, nougat is made of sugar, syrup, egg whites, and often nuts and glacé cherries.

PASTILLAGE

A gum paste used on cakes, this is prepared with icing sugar, gum tragacanth or gelatine and cornflour. It may be coloured.

COFFEE

COFFEE ORIGINATED IN Ethiopia, where *Coffea arabica*, one of the three main species, grows wild. The others, *C. robusta* and *C. liberica*, come from the Congo and Liberia respectively. The coffee tree requires a hot, moist climate and a rich soil.

The word "coffee" comes from the Arabic *quwah*. *C. arabica* was first cultivated about 575 AD but it was not until the fifteenth century that the plant was extensively grown in southern Arabia. From there it spread to countries bordering the Indian Ocean and the Mediterranean. By the mid-seventeenth century it had reached all of Europe, where innumerable coffee-houses, forerunners of the modern club, sprang up. It reached North America by 1668. Early in the eighteenth century it was taken to the French West Indies and from there was introduced to Brazil and the rest of South and Central America. Today, coffee is grown in the West Indies, Mexico, Central America, tropical South America, Africa, India and Indonesia. *C. arabica*, *C. robusta* and *C. liberica* are all grown commercially and each has its own varieties.

The green coffee beans are extracted from the ripe red berries of the tree, each berry containing two beans or seeds. Approximately 4000 berries produce 1kg (2.2lb) of coffee.

Extracting the brew

Coffee beans are classified into three main types. The finest coffee comes from *C. arabica* and has a low caffeine content. *C. robusta* is a strong, high-caffeine type, but of inferior quality. Finally, there is *C. liberica*, which is very productive but mediocre in taste.

Taste and aroma are induced by roasting the raw green beans. The beans turn a pale yellow at around 100°C (212°F) and on reaching 230°C (450°F) swell to almost double their size, turn dark brown, and sweat oil on the surface, giving them an attractive glossy appearance.

There are four main types of roast. The high or double roast has a strong, bitter taste and should always be drunk black. The full roast has a slightly bitter taste but lacks the "burnt" taste of a high roasted bean. Medium roast produces a strong-tasting coffee without the bitter taste, while the light or pale roast allows the milder beans to develop a full, delicate taste and aroma which is good with milk.

Strong, black coffees, especially those from *C. robusta*, tend to be more stimulating on account of the caffeine present. Decaffeinated coffees are made in one of two ways: naturally by washing out the caffeine alkaloid, and chemically by the use of a solvent. Other plants used to flavour coffee or as coffee substitutes include the dried roots of the dandelion (*Taraxacum officinale*), a relative of chicory.

Instant coffees are available in powder form or granules, and have been in use since the 1930s, heralding the era of convenience foods. They are produced by brewing freshly roasted and ground coffee to obtain a strong concentrate. This is then passed through an atomizing spray into a stream of hot air which evaporates the water and leaves behind a fine residue powder.

Freeze-dried coffee is the most successful method of making an aromatic instant coffee. The coffee is brewed, frozen into slabs and ground into particles which are then put into a vacuum with a small amount of heat. This turns the ice directly into steam, leaving the ground particles dry, chunky and ready to use.

Coffee in the kitchen

Raw coffee beans will keep indefinitely in a cool, dry place. Once roasted and ground, the coffee should be used as soon as possible; the finer the grind, the more rapid the loss of taste.

Brewing coffee is merely a matter of infusion or boiling. Boiling coffee gives it a strong, bitter taste, as much of the aroma is steam-distilled from the brew and the bitter components are dissolved into it.

Coffee used in recipes should be made very strong and concentrated, or you can use instant coffee powder, with excellent results. Any recipe that includes the term "mocha" will have a predominantly coffee taste. Coffee also features in several alcoholic drinks, for example Irish coffee and such liqueurs as Tia Maria, kahlua, crème de café, crème de mokka, and Bahia, mostly made from the pulp of the coffee berry.

HIGH ROAST BEANS

High roast beans

Shown here is an Algerian *C. arabica* bean. Like all high or dark roasts it has a rather bitter taste as the oil, which sustains a coffee's sweetness, has come out.

COARSE GRINDS

High roast coarse grind

Coarse grinds are better for percolating. Use high roasts, which are stronger, at dinner; light ones at breakfast.

MEDIUM GRINDS

The best texture to preserve the delicate taste and aroma. Medium grinds are suitable for percolator, Cona and jug methods.

High roast medium grind

FINE GRINDS

Ideal for infusion, espresso machines and filter methods which use papers to strain.

High roast fine grind

DANDELION COFFEE

Extracted from the root, it can be brewed as a caffeine-free substitute for coffee.

Dandelion coffee

DECAFFEINATED

When ground, treated with solvent and dried, coffee loses most of its caffeine.

Decaffeinated

INSTANT FREEZE-DRIED

Made by freezing a brew of good coffee, grinding it to particles and removing the water in a vacuum.

Instant freeze-dried

LIGHT ROAST BEANS

Shown here is a Kenyan *C. arabica* bean. The light roasts have a delicate taste and can be drunk with milk.

Light roast beans

FULL ROAST BEANS

Shown here is the Mocha bean. Highly regarded, it has a strong distinctive taste on its own but blends well with milder beans.

Full roast beans

MEDIUM-LIGHT ROAST BEANS

Shown here is a bean from Turkey, where the unique style of brewing strong coffee from powdered beans originated.

Medium-light roast beans

COSTA RICAN UNROASTED BEANS

Beans can be stored for two to three years before roasting which gives them aroma and caramelizes them. All coffee is best when freshly roasted.

Costa Rican unroasted beans

COSTA RICAN ROASTED BEANS

A fine, mild and rich-bodied *C. arabica* bean, it has a slightly acid taste. Always medium or lightly roasted, it is good unblended.

Costa Rican roasted beans

INSTANT

Usually made with cheaper grades of coffee, it's harsher tasting but more convenient.

Instant

OTHER COFFEES

COLOMBIAN
A full-bodied coffee bean that has little acidity.

JAMAICAN
A large yellow bean *C. arabica* coffee with a delicate flavour.

KENYAN
The pale green African *C. arabica* beans give a rich liquor with a sharp taste when roasted.

MOCHA
A *C. arabica* type, originally from the old port of Mocha in Yemen, this is one of the world's finest coffees.

MYSORE
East Indian bluish-grey *C. arabica* beans, giving a liquor with a fine, strong taste.

SANTOS
Santos and Rio, both from Brazil, have green-yellow beans which give a smooth, mellow liquor.

TEA

TEA IS THE WORLD'S most popular drink. It is the name given to the leaves of the tea plant *Thea sinensis*, an evergreen tree or shrub which grows in damp tropical or subtropical regions at altitudes of up to 2000m (7000ft). Though the plant may have originated in India it had reached China (where as *cha* it is the national drink), by 200 AD and Japan (where it was not only a popular drink but had reached great ritual significance in the *cha-no-yu* – tea ceremony) by the eighth century. It was brought to Europe by the Dutch in 1610, reached England in 1644, and America at the beginning of the eighteenth century. It has subsequently spread throughout the world. It is grown principally in China, Taiwan, Japan, India, Sri Lanka and south-east Asia, and, to a lesser extent, in Africa.

There are two main types of tea, black and green, produced from different treatments of the leaves after they are picked. For black tea, which is amber-coloured and strongly flavoured, the leaves are fermented. For green tea, greenish-yellow in colour and rather bitter in taste, this step is omitted. There is another category of tea: Oolong, grown in China, Taiwan and Japan, which is partly fermented with a subtle flavour combining the characteristics of both black and green tea. Oolong is often perfumed and flavoured with jasmine flowers.

The prime part of the tea shrub is the bud, enclosed by two downy leaves (*pekoe* in Chinese means "downy"). Tea planters refer to the "two leaves and a bud", while the word "pekoe" is employed to describe leaf sizes and grades. The leaves are plucked from the shrub by hand, and it takes about 2kg (4lb) of leaves to produce 450g (1lb) of black tea.

Processing the leaves

The plucked leaves are swiftly transported to the factory, where they are spread on racks to dry, losing about 50 per cent of their moisture content. After this "withering" process, the leaves are machine-rolled to break up the cellular structure, which releases the fermenting enzymes and encourages absorption of oxygen; the rolling technique was also designed to give a decorative twist to the leaf, imitating the original hand-twisted leaves of China. After rolling, the pulped leaves are left to ferment at about 27°C (82°F), and they gradually assume a coppery hue; fermentation is necessary to produce the characteristic taste and strength of tea. The fermentation is checked by "firing" in chambers, that is, passing a current of hot air over the leaves for about 30 minutes, at a carefully regulated temperature.

Once fired, the black and broken leaves are sifted by machine to be sorted into two main grades – "broken and small leaf" teas, and "leaf" teas. Usually, the larger the leaf size, the better the taste of the brew, while smaller leaves give stronger and darker brews.

Broken leaf teas are separated from the leaf teas by sifting, then further graded into broken orange pekoe, flowery broken orange pekoe, broken pekoe, and so on down to "fannings" and "dust", while leaf grades are flowery orange pekoe, orange pekoe, and pekoe.

These orthodox grades apply to both China and India teas, but in recent years, Indian manufacturers have gone over to machine-cutting, called "legge-cut" leaves. Such teas are quick to infuse and thus are particularly suitable for use in the tea-bag industry.

Tea in the kitchen

Tea is used as a hot beverage, as iced tea or tea punch. Ceylon tea is best for making iced tea or tea punch, since it is the only type that does not cloud. Black tea may be served with lemon and sugar or with milk, green tea with lemon and sugar or plain. In North Africa, tea is infused with mint leaves and a great deal of sugar added; in the Himalayas a kind of tea soup is concocted with yak butter and salt.

Tea is rarely used as an ingredient in recipes, but tea ice cream and tea soufflé are examples. The habit of taking soothing or stimulating beverages by infusion is universal; tea, coffee, Paraguayan maté (*Ilex pape*), Yapon tea (*L. cassine*) and guarana bread (*Paullinia sorbilis*) all contain tannin, theine or caffeine, but the majority of infusions, the tisanes or herbal teas, are free from stimulants. Tea should be kept in airtight containers.

KEEMUN

A black tea from China with a large black leaf that makes a light infusion with a smoky taste and a special bouquet – "the fragrance of an orchid". Good to serve with food, it is best without milk.

Keemun tea

ORANGE PEKOE

The finest grade of black Indian tea, it is picked from the buds and top leaves of the plant. Sometimes scented, it has a jasmine taste and is rarely used in blends.

Orange pekoe tea

LAPSANG SOUCHONG

A black China tea with large leaves and a rich smoky taste. Lapsang souchong needs slow brewing, is best without milk or lemon, and is often used in blends.

Lapsang souchong tea

ASSAM

A high-quality, full-bodied, all-purpose black tea from Assam in north-east India. Usually drunk unblended, it makes a reddish brew with a full, malty taste. It is good with milk or on its own. Shown here is new season Assam.

Assam tea

GREEN

A greenish-grey China tea made in China, Taiwan and Japan, the leaves of green or gunpowder tea are characteristically rolled in pellets. Unfermented, it has a delicate taste and fine aroma, and is best drunk on its own.

Green tea

FAN YONG

This is an unscented tea from China. Its black leaves make a mild, light infusion low, in tannin. It is best without milk and good with food.

Fan yong tea

JASMINE

A green tea from China with a distinctive fragrance, it is delicately scented with dried jasmine blossoms. A tea to enjoy on its own, never with milk.

Jasmine tea

KANOY

This is a black, unscented tea with tiny black leaves from the island of Sri Lanka, once called Ceylon. It makes a bright golden infusion.

Kanoy tea

FORMOSA OOLONG

A black semi-fermented tea from Taiwan, it has the biggest leaf, but makes quite a light infusion tasting of ripe peaches.

Formosa Oolong tea

DARJEELING

A black, slow-brewing Indian tea with a rich, rather fruity taste. Considered the best and most delicate of all the Indian teas, it is grown around Darjeeling.

Darjeeling tea

HIBISCUS

Made from hibiscus flowers, the brew is red, tart and fruity.

Hibiscus tea

ROSEHIP

Made from the fruit of the wild rose plant crushed with the seeds, it makes a tart brew.

Rosehip tea

BAMBOO

A strong-tasting, bitter black tea from China, so-called because it is encased in dried bamboo leaves.

Bamboo tea

OTHER TEAS

CAMOMILE

This herbal tea, made from the flowers only, has a delicate flavour. Other herbal teas commonly available include peppermint, made from the leaves, which has an excellent flavour.

CEYLON

Delicate and fragrant high quality teas grown in altitudes of over 1200m (4000 feet).

EARL GREY

A well-known blended tea scented with bergamot to give it a distinctive taste.

SUGARS, SYRUPS AND HONEYS

UNTIL THE SIXTEENTH century, when cane sugar from the West Indies became readily available and inexpensive, the world depended mainly on honey as its sweetener. Like honey, sugar cane is of ancient origin. It was first cultivated in India 2500 years ago and called, in Sanskrit, *karkara*. Sugar derives from the Arabic form of the word *sakkara* (*sukkur*), and appeared in the thirteenth century in England. The recorded history of cane sugar begins when a member of Alexander's army mentions it in 325 BC. It reached China by 100 BC but the Japanese did not get it until 700 AD, though by 400 AD it was being widely cultivated in the Middle East. Pliny the Elder called it a kind of honey made from reeds. So did the Crusaders, who encountered it in the eleventh century and introduced it to Europe. It remained expensive until Columbus introduced the canes into Hispaniola, now Haiti-Dominican Republic, in the West Indies in 1493. Its cultivation spread throughout the islands and cane sugar became, and still is, a main source of sweetness.

There are several types of sugar. The white crystalline product used in the kitchen or found on the table as "sugar" is a purified chemical, a carbohydrate consisting of almost pure sucrose or cane sugar, which in its turn contains glucose (dextrose or grape sugar) and fructose (fruit sugar).

Sugar is created in green plants by photosynthesis. The plants convert carbon dioxide and water into carbohydrates, using the energy provided by the sun. The carbohydrates are synthesized in the leaves and converted to sugar – sugar is the main source of the plant's energy and is important to its metabolism. Some plants have an additional reserve of sucrose, and these sugar-rich varieties are used by the sugar industry. They are the sugar cane, sugar beet, the maple, and several varieties of palm tree.

Sugar from canes
Sugar cane (*Saccharum officinarum*) is the world's principal source of sugar. The cane is harvested mechanically; only in a few places is it still gathered by the traditional method of hand-cutting. The cut cane is fed into a crushing machine to extract the juice, which is then chemically treated to precipitate the impurities, and boiled to give a saturated solution. This syrup must then be processed to allow the "cropping out" of sugar crystals. The technique is progressive, so that the residue mother liquor, or molasses, may yield a further crop of crystals.

Brown sugar is produced when cane juice is boiled to provide the first crop of sugar crystals and molasses. The crystals are brown simply because they are coated with liquid molasses. Washed, the crystals would be almost white, with a faint golden tint.

During the cropping out process in the refinery, sugar crystals are produced that leave a residue of syrup. These syrups are variable in quality – a secondary syrup is bound to be more concentrated than a primary one. Such syrups also vary in colour from very light to dark brown, almost black. The final, non-yielding syrup is blackstrap molasses, a concentrate of about 50 per cent sugars with minerals and organic materials. Molasses may be a blend of syrups from different varieties of cane, and marketed in grades according to quality, or a blend of refinery syrups obtained during the refining of white sugar.

Sugar from roots and trees
The sucrose obtained from the sugar beet (*Beta vulgaris*) is identical to the sugar processed from the cane, both in strength and quality. It is extracted by pulping or slicing the washed roots, which are soaked in hot water to provide a sugar solution, processed in the same fashion as cane sugar. Sugar beets will not, however, produce brown sugars, though a bitter-tasting molasses is obtained from them.

American settlers learned from the Indians to exploit the maple tree as a source of sugar. Straight from the tree, the sap is sweet but without colour or flavour, and it must be boiled to produce the dark syrup with its characteristic maple taste.

Palm sugar comes from the date, coconut, toddy and palmyra palms. The sap is collected by tapping the trunk or top of the tree, and reducing it to syrup, a clear and transparent product which is then allowed to crystallize.

Sugar in the kitchen

Brown sugars are used for their characteristic taste and for the fact that they add moistness to the finished product; brown sugars are often specified in recipes for bread and cakes. Icing sugar is used to make confectionery and replaces castor sugar in some cake recipes. Typically it is used for icing. Treacle, molasses, corn syrup and maple syrup all have important applications: they are used in baking and confectionery and as toppings.

Icings and syrups may need boiling, as will many types of confectionery, jams and jellies, reaching temperatures that are critical to the success of the recipe. Temperatures can be checked with a sugar thermometer, and the density of the syrup with a saccherometer. Boiling sugar syrups are inclined to crystallize or grain if the crystals are not entirely dissolved before bringing to the boil. Any stray crystals clinging to the side of the pan may precipitate graining and should be brushed down into the syrup with a brush dipped in water. The addition of a little cream of tartar and glucose will help to prevent graining, and scum forming on the syrup.

HONEY

Honey is the oldest sweetening substance; it was used long before sugar. Ancient brewers used it to make the fermented drink, mead (from the Sanskrit *madhu*, a honey drink), which sustained Beowulf and lesser mortals during the Age of Heroes. Its traditional use, however, has been in baking. The ancient Greeks used honey in a bread called *melitutes*, which the Romans subsequently borrowed, and called *panis melitus*, and also baked a sacrificial honey cake known as *libum*.

The practice of sweetening bread with honey led in turn to a wealth of spice-honey cakes, such as the French *pain d'épices*, the German *lebkuchen* and the English gingerbread. Eastern confectioners discovered the happy marriage of almonds with honey, and the recipes spread far and wide – to Italy, where the sweetmeat *torrone* was fashioned, to France, where nougat was produced at

Montélimar, and to Spain in the form of *turrón*. The Maya made a liqueur, *Ixtalseutun*, out of it; the Aztecs sweetened their chocolate with it.

Although honey can be made artificially, it is the natural product made by the bees which is normally used. The honey-combs are uncapped by machine and the honey extracted from the combs by a centrifugal force which spins it out, or by heat extraction. The honey is then strained, filtered and packed.

Types of honey

Honey is produced by the bee from nectar taken from a variety of flowers and trees. It is the true essence of flowers, and each species of flower in different parts of the world will produce a honey of characteristic flavour. For example, the famous Hymetus honey of Greece is produced as a result of bees visiting sage, marjoram, thyme and savory, and, as you might expect, combinations of orange blossom, lemon and lime produce citric lemony-tasting honeys.

There are many types of honey, and they can vary a great deal in flavour and appearance. Apart from the fact that they are available in wax combs or as liquid in jars, the actual liquids can differ greatly, ranging from very thin to almost hard, and may be white, golden, amber, varnish-brown, and even black.

The difference in the consistency of honeys is due to a variety of factors: plant sources, water content and temperature while processing. Flavours too, are easy to analyse, but it is not known why honeys each develop a particular colour.

Honey in the kitchen

Honey can be eaten on its own or used as an ingredient. Its main use is still in baking: it is the sweetener for many oriental and Arab cakes, also for the Turkish *baklava*, the Greek *pasteli* and the popular *halva*, as well as for those sweetmeats already mentioned. It is used for curing ham, making honey butter, coating breakfast cereals, and is delicious cooked with chicken and almonds.

When cooking with honey, bear in mind that its sugars tend to caramelize when heated, and that some of its delicate aroma may also be driven off. Also, all honeys tend to crystallize and harden with age.

Sugars and Syrups

CASTOR SUGAR

Much finer than granulated sugar, castor is used generally for baking in cakes and pastries. Because of its texture, it dissolves quickly and so is also popular for use with fruits and cereals.

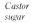

Castor sugar

GRANULATED SUGAR

Several textures of white refined sugar are available. The most common is granulated, a general-purpose sugar used both for the table and in cooking.

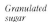

Granulated sugar

PRESERVING SUGAR

A sugar boiled in the refinery to obtain a large grain or crystal, which helps to eliminate scum forming when making preserves and jellies.

Preserving sugar

ICING SUGAR

This is powdered sugar with the addition of tricalcium phosphate or cornflour as a conditioner against damp, which may cause the sugar to go lumpy or to solidify. It is used to make meringues, cakes, cake icing and confectionery.

Icing sugar

GLUCOSE

Natural glucose occurs in large quantities in grapes and honey. Commercial glucose is available as a powder, a syrup and in chips. Used in jam and confectionery, it is also useful to athletes as a quick source of energy because it is easily absorbed.

Glucose

RAINBOW SUGAR CRYSTALS

Vegetable dyes are added to white sugar to produce pastel-shaded crystals. They may be served with coffee for an attractive table presentation and are often used for decorating cakes and other baked goods and confections.

Rainbow sugar crystals

SUGAR CRYSTALS

These fairly large brownish crystals are particularly popular with coffee drinkers because they dissolve slowly. The coffee retains some of its bitter taste and is sweetened gradually as it is drunk.

Sugar crystals

DEMERARA SUGAR

One of several raw brown sugars – Barbados is another – which go through a preliminary cleaning process in their country of origin and are exported already packaged. They vary in taste and appearance and are used mainly in rich, dark fruit cakes.

Demerara sugar

SOFT BROWN SUGAR

Several manufacturers produce a variety of brown sugars which differ in shade and texture. These are refined sugars with cane molasses added. The refining process leaves a coating around the crystals (which is soluble in water) whereas with raw brown sugars the molasses is in the crystals. Both the light and dark types shown here are used with cereals and coffee and also in fruit and spice cakes. There are other brown sugars on the market which do not contain cane molasses. These consist of white sugar with a vegetable dye added, and this will be stated on the packet.

Dark soft brown sugar

Light soft brown sugar

CUBE SUGAR

This is refined and crystallized sugar that has been moistened and compressed into square or rectangular blocks. Brown varieties are also made in Europe. Cube sugar is used for the table to sweeten hot drinks.

Cube sugar

MOLASSES SUGAR

The darker the sugar, the more molasses it contains. This lightly processed brown sugar is moist and soft in texture. It is generally used in rich, dark fruit cakes.

Molasses sugar

MUSCOVADO SUGAR

A lighter brown than molasses sugar, muscovado is also soft and moist. It is used in fruit cakes and a variety of it is an important ingredient in many Indian dishes.

Muscovado sugar

LUMP SUGAR

The large golden crystals of yellow lump sugar, popular with Chinese cooks, are also used in desserts and drinks. Dark brown concentrated lump sugar is used in many Chinese and Indian dishes.

GOLDEN SYRUP

This is molasses residue that has been clarified. It is specially processed to obtain the golden colour, hydrolized to reduce the water content, and stabilized microbiologically to prevent fermentation in the tin. It is used to make treacle tart in the UK.

Golden syrup

MAPLE SYRUP

The processed sap of the maple tree, this syrup has a distinctive taste. Its best known use is for pouring over pancakes and waffles but it is also used in maple butter, maple sugar cake, biscuits, icing, in baked beans, ice cream, baked ham, candied sweet potatoes, baked apples. Enthusiasts claim there is no substitute.

Maple syrup

CANE SUGAR

The concentrated sap of sugar cane, it is sometimes substituted for molasses.

Cane sugar

Yellow lump sugar

Dark brown lump sugar

FRUIT SYRUPS

These simple preparations of white sugar, fruit and water, are especially popular in the Middle East. They are prepared from fruit pulp, such as rosehips (rosehip syrup) or blackcurrants (cassis syrup), or from the petals of flowers treated with a pectin enzyme that destroys natural yeasts, boiled, bottled and sterilized. Fruit syrups are used as a base for drinks, and to top ice creams and desserts.

Cassis syrup

Rose hip syrup

BLACK TREACLE

A darker and heavier version of golden syrup, this is used in rich fruit cakes and spicy sauces.

Molasses

Black treacle

MOLASSES

A by-product of sugar-making, dark or blackstrap molasses (shown here) improves the keeping qualities of breads and cakes and is rich in iron. Light molasses has a milder flavour and is used as a table syrup.

OTHER SYRUPS

CORN SYRUP

A by-product of sweetcorn (*Zea mays*) cultivation, corn syrup is converted from cornflour. It is used for a great variety of products, including beverages, canned fruits, ice cream, baby foods and preserves.

SUGAR SYRUP

This is granulated sugar which is dissolved in either hot or cold water.

Honeys

COMB

The natural form in which all honey is found, comb honey is eaten, wax and all. Normally the wax combs are cut by hand to remove the honey; when commercially processed they are uncapped by machine.

HONEY CONTAINING COMB

This luxury item – also known as chunk comb honey – contains a section of the comb in a jar topped up with clear honey.

ENGLISH

This is a blend of honeys gathered from a variety of English blossoms. Also available creamed, it is often thought essential for a "proper" afternoon tea.

ORANGE BLOSSOM

This comes from *Citrus anrantium*, and is produced mostly in Spain, but also California, Mexico, South Africa and Israel. It is a light, delicately citrus-tasting honey, especially good in custards.

MANUKA

This thick dark honey comes from the prolific "ti" or tea tree of New Zealand (*Leptospermum scorparium*). Its rich taste is good in cooking.

JAMAICAN

Clear and dark with an exotic tropical flower taste, this thick honey is good to use in cooking.

HUNGARIAN ACACIA

A thin, very pale honey from *Robinia pseudocacia*, Romania, France and Italy also produce this mild variety which tends always to remain liquid.

Honey containing comb

English

Comb honey

Pure orange blossom

Manuka

Hungarian acacia

Jamaican

OTHER HONEYS

ALCAHUAL

This amber-coloured honey with a fine flavour is exported from Mexico. Also from Mexico are Campanilla, Morning Glory and Aguinaldo.

BARBERRY

Another amber-coloured honey, this is derived from the flowers of *Berberidacae*.

BUCKWHEAT

Wild buckwheat honey is mainly produced in California as "Californian sage honey". Cultivated buckwheat makes a very dark brown honey with a strong flavour. It is the main type used for making honey cakes and Jewish honey wine.

ILEX

This honey comes from the holly tree and is mild and light-coloured. It is popular in Europe.

LAVENDER

A popular European honey, especially in the south of France, it is amber-coloured, often with a greenish caste and a butter-smooth texture.

HEATHER

Heather-covered heaths produce a creamy honey which liquefies when stirred. It is extremely popular in Britain and Europe, coming either from ling (*Calluna vulgaris*) or from bell heather (*Erica cinera*).

Eucalyptus

Heather

Hymetus

Sunflower

Clover

Tasmanian leatherwood

Rosemary

EUCALYPTUS

There are about 500 varieties of this creamy honey, all native to Australia. Some honeys are light to medium amber, others quite dark. Flavours range from the delicate *Eucalyptus albaros* to the extra light but sweet and cloying *E. melliodora* and the dark strong *E. tereticorius*.

HYMETUS

From thyme, marjoram and other herbal blossoms growing on Mt Hymetus in Greece, this dark, clear and slightly thick aromatic honey is considered to be one of the best in the world. It is a perfect complement to tart natural yoghurt and is excellent used in the confection *baklava*.

CLOVER

This is perhaps the commonest and most popular honey in Europe and America. It comes from the red or white *Trifolium repens*, is thick and pale amber. Also available clear, its mild taste is best for general cooking.

SUNFLOWER

Produced mainly in Greece, Turkey, southern Russia and Argentina, sunflower honey loses its excellent fragrance in cooking.

LOGWOOD

This honey, produced mainly in Jamaica, is made for export and is usually light in colour.

MANGO

This amber-coloured honey is dense in body.

POHUTAKAWA

A rare honey from New Zealand, this has a unique and salty flavour and comes from the tree *Metrosideros excelsa*.

SWEET BASIL

A honey of very light colour, with a characteristic herbal flavour, popular in Europe.

TULIP TREE

This honey is dark brown with a heavy body and delicate, quince-like flavour.

TASMANIAN LEATHERWOOD

From Australia, this rich, creamy honey has a distinctive taste and is high in glucose. If necessary, it can be put in warm water for 30 minutes to make it clear. It can be used for general cooking.

ROSEMARY

This strong, aromatic herb honey is produced mainly in the countries around the Mediterranean from the small blue flowers (once associated with the Virgin Mary) of *Rosmarinus officinalis*.

EGGS

EGGS, ONE OF THE most essential and versatile foods used in cooking, have been eaten and enjoyed since the beginnings of civilization. Often venerated as a symbol of life and fertility, many ancient philosophers saw eggs as a symbol of the world and the four elements, since they held that the shell represented earth, the white, water, the yolk, fire, and air was found under the shell at the round end of the egg. To early Christians, eggs were a symbol of rebirth and were hard-boiled, decorated and given as presents at Easter.

The eggs most often used today come from the domestic hen – either the farmyard or "free-range" variety, or the modern "battery" variety. There is no nutritional difference between free-range and battery eggs and none between brown and white eggs, since the shell colour is related purely to the breed of hen. As far as culinary purposes are concerned, free-range eggs deteriorate more quickly.

Composition of the egg
The egg is made up of the outer shell (about 12 per cent of its total weight); the albumen, or white (about 58 per cent) and the yolk (about 30 per cent), which is held in place by a twisted strand of material called "chalaza", which is usable. There is also an air chamber at the rounded end of the egg. This gradually expands as the egg loses its freshness.

Egg white proteins, when whipped, break and expand, forming elastic-walled cells that trap air, which in turn expands when subjected to heat (as in the oven). This is what makes egg whites such a valuable leavening agent. Yolk proteins, on the other hand, bind and thicken. They are less stable than those of egg whites, and, when exposed to excessive heat, harden and separate from the yolk's fat and water molecules, and the yolk curdles.

Choosing eggs
All eggs are classified according to size. Under Common Market regulations there are seven sizes. Size 1 is the largest – 70g (2½oz) – and size 7, below 45g (1¾oz), is the smallest. Eggs are also graded A, B and C for quality and, if packed in cartons, these are stamped with the packaging date. Grade A are fresh, B less fresh and C means that they are suitable only for processing by the food industry.

Fresh egg white should be firm, thick and support the yolk. A less than fresh egg has a thin white that spreads away from the yolk and a yolk which breaks easily.

Eggs in the kitchen
Eggs are extremely versatile. Apart from their endless uses in main dishes, soufflés and baking, they can be used for a number of general culinary purposes: to thicken, emulsify, coat, bind or glaze other foods and to provide a foamy base. They can be boiled, poached, baked, fried or pickled, though some, because of their size, may be less suited to general cooking. Unless a recipe specifies otherwise use a large egg; two small ones can always be substituted.

Egg whites are more easily whipped when the eggs are at room temperature and at least three days old. Fat, even the merest trace from the yolk or any grease on the beater or bowl, will prevent whipping; salt acts similarly. A tiny amount of acid (such as cream of tartar) will make the whites stiffer and give greater bulk, while sugar keeps the proteins supple. Sugar or acid should be added when the egg white is just beginning to foam, otherwise it will remain as gritty particles. Do not over-beat or the whites will become dry and lose air.

Storing eggs
Eggs should be stored in a larder or at room temperature. They should not be kept in the refrigerator as the shells can become moist, which allows bacteria to penetrate. Also it is difficult to judge cooking time accurately if the eggs are colder than room temperature. Store eggs with the pointed end downwards so that the yolk rests on the white rather than on the air chamber. Do not freeze eggs unless separated as their shells crack at low temperatures. Eggs can be frozen for up to nine months, but allow them to thaw completely in unopened containers before use.

HEN

Both brown and white eggs have the same nutritional value and it is a matter of personal taste which you choose to buy. Hen or chicken eggs are the only eggs to be produced on a large commercial scale and are the familiar standard by which other eggs are compared, the average weight being about 50g (2oz). They are used in all aspects of cooking.

Hen eggs

GOOSE

The goose egg has a slightly oily taste and should always be used very fresh and cooked lightly. These eggs weigh 225–280g (8–10oz) – four to five times the size of a hen's egg.

Goose egg

QUAIL

Considered a delicacy, these small eggs are usually eaten medium- or hard-boiled, shelled and used in salads, pickled, or poached and set in aspic.

Quail egg

PHEASANT and PARTRIDGE

These eggs are usually solid white, buff or olive, although some species nest in open areas and their eggs are blotched with brown or black for protection against predators. They are most often served hard-boiled, shelled and used in salads, may be pickled or set in aspic and served as an hors d'oeuvre.

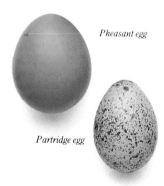

Pheasant egg

Partridge egg

1,000-YEAR-OLD

Raw duck eggs preserved in lime, pine ash and salt for between 50 and 100 days, these emerge translucent blue and green, looking much older than they are – hence the name. Firm in texture, they are rich with a slightly fishy taste. They are a Chinese delicacy, usually shelled, sliced, steamed and served cold.

DUCK

These eggs are oilier-tasting than hen eggs and can acquire a harmful bacteria as they are usually laid in a dirty spot. However, they are still suitable for eating if they are boiled for 15 minutes or used in baking. The white turns bluish and the yolk a reddish-orange after boiling. They should be eaten very fresh and are not suitable for meringues.

1,000-year-old egg

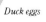

Duck eggs

GUINEA FOWL

Flecked with brown, this egg has a more delicate taste than the hen egg. It is best medium- or hard-boiled for 3 to 5 minutes, cooled, shelled and then tossed into green salads.

Guinea fowl egg

Gull egg

GULL

These eggs vary in size, depending on the species of gull, but are almost always camouflaged with dark blotches. They lack the strong fishy taste which is common to the eggs of most sea birds. They are usually hard-boiled for 5 minutes, cooled and eaten cold with a little celery salt.

OSTRICH

This egg is rarely available, but it is edible provided it hasn't been left to bake in the sun or been partially hatched. Up to twenty times the size of a hen egg and with a thicker shell, one egg can feed a family of four.

BANTAM

The bantam is a breed of chicken, and its eggs, similar in taste to hen eggs although only about half the size, may be used in the same way. The difference in tints has no effect on the taste.

Bantam eggs

PULLET

Another type of hen egg, laid by a hen in her first year.

Pullet egg

OTHER EGGS

PLOVER

Like quail eggs, these are considered to be a delicacy. Plover eggs are usually served lightly boiled.

TURKEY

Cream-coloured, speckled with brown and sometimes twice the size of a hen egg, turkey eggs are similar in flavour and may be used in place of hen eggs.

TURTLE

Sea turtle eggs are imported from South America, the Caribbean, Africa and Australia. Rarely available, this soft-shelled delicacy is prized by connoisseurs for its rich, slightly oily flavour.

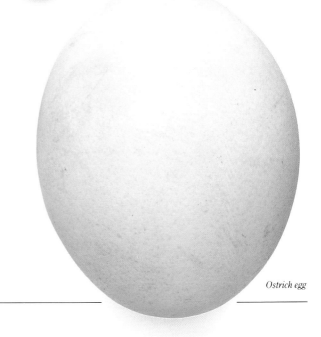

Ostrich egg

FATS AND MILK PRODUCTS

IN ADDITION TO MEAT, animals have been the main source of fat and dairy products since they were first domesticated. While westerners rely mainly on cattle, vast areas of the world use the milk of camels, sheep, goats and even yaks to produce foodstuffs.

Fats and milk products can be looked at in four categories: milks, creams, soured creams and yoghurts, and butters, margarines, cooking and baking fats.

Milk is composed of water, calcium and albumen, milk protein (casein), milk sugar (lactose), milk fat and vitamins. The final product depends on how the milk is processed and how one or more of milk's main constituents is treated.

In many countries, the milk sold has, by law, to be pasteurized – that is, freed of any bacteria which could cause milk-borne disease. Usually the milk is heated to below boiling, held at this temperature for a few seconds, then cooled immediately.

As milk cools the fat rises to the surface and this is "creamed" off to make butter or cream. The fat content of cream varies from country to country; common types in Britain include single, double, whipping and clotted cream.

Yoghurt is made by inoculating fresh milk with a lactic acid culture, of which there are several types, while fermented milks are made when both a lactic and alcoholic fermentation takes place. Soured cream is produced by introducing a lactic acid culture such as *Streptococcus lactis* into a low-fat homogenized cream.

Cream can be collected and churned into butter, which should have a fat content of 80 per cent. The cream used in butter-making can be either fresh or soured although most of the butter produced is from the former. The residue that is left after butter-making is buttermilk, although nowadays buttermilk is often made from pasteurized skimmed milk.

Margarine was originally "invented" as a low-cost alternative to butter by a French chemist. Today's margarine consists of refined, purified and hydrogenated edible oils such as sunflower, palm, soy and coconut. An expensive technological process blends together the oil and a high proportion of water to create a low-calorie polyunsaturated spread. The hard or block margarines contain saturated or animal fats. All animal fats – suet, dripping, lard – need some processing before use.

Fats and milk products in the kitchen

Milk is a versatile ingredient that can be used in many beverages and foods, including puddings, baked goods, soups and ice cream. Pasteurized milk should keep for four or five days in a refrigerator. It spoils but does not sour, so that in recipes calling for sour milk, buttermilk is usually used. Condensed milk is used to make confectionery, powdered milk in baking.

Cream can be kept for two to three days in a refrigerator, but will harden if left uncovered. It enhances many dishes and can be added to soups and sauces or used as a garnish. Overwhipped cream becomes buttery.

Margarine and butter should be kept in the refrigerator. They have good keeping qualities in temperate climates and can be deep-frozen for at least six months. Refined lard, grated suet and reduced suet can be kept for months in a refrigerator covered in a suitable container or vacuum-wrapped. Butter burns at a fairly low temperature and is unsuitable for frying unless mixed with a vegetable oil which has the effect of raising the optimum temperature. Clarifying butter by melting it so that the solids can be drawn off means that foods may be lightly fried without fear of burning. Apart from this, butter has a great number of uses in cooking, including the making of pastry, and compound butters which are mixed with fresh herbs, or other ingredients such as caviar, sardines, garlic and paprika. Some types of margarine are interchangeable with butter in baking, but, like butter, margarine is not suitable for deep-frying.

In many countries yoghurt is regarded as a guard against disease and varieties are used as a refreshing drink, also in cooking. In India, yoghurt is mixed with fruits and vegetables and served as *raita*. Soured creams give sauces a slightly acid taste. They should be added at the end of cooking time and either off the heat or on a low heat, otherwise they will curdle.

WHOLE MILK

Milk is the basis of all dairy products. Pasteurized milk (shown here) has been subjected to heat treatment to destroy bacteria. It should keep for four or five days in the refrigerator. None of the fat is removed from whole milk, and it is not homogenized, so has a cream line. It is used in drinks, puddings and baking.

BUTTERMILK

Originally the sour milk left over from butter-making, today buttermilk is usually made from pasteurized skimmed milk with an added culture to thicken its consistency. It is used as a drink, in baking and confectionery, and is a good sour milk substitute.

POWDERED MILK

A useful fresh milk substitute, powdered milk consists of pasteurized, air-dried milk particles, which should be reconstituted with water before use, although it can be included with the dry ingredients in baking.

CREAM

Cream is the fatty part of fresh milk which rises to the surface when milk is left to stand. Cream is used in a number of dishes, and as the basis for many sauces. There are several varieties: the one shown, single cream, is used in coffee and with desserts.

CLOTTED CREAM

Cream skimmed from scalded milk, warmed over a low heat, and then cooled, clotted cream is a speciality of south-west England.

WHIPPING CREAM

This type of cream is halfway between single and double cream as regards fat content. It is used exclusively for whipping.

GHEE

A type of clarified butter used in India, which is made by heating ordinary butter to rid it of impurities. It has a higher burning point than most other oils, which makes it perfect for frying and sautéing. It can be used as a sauce for lobster, and also to make *beurre noire* (French butter sauce).

YOGHURT

A product made from curdled milk with the addition of a lactic starter, *yogurt* is its Turkish name. It is eaten plain but often has fruit or honey added for extra flavour; commercial varieties use evaporated milk and often contain fruit. Yoghurt can be added to savoury dishes and is also used as a dressing for salads, particularly cucumber.

BUTTER

A natural dairy product made from cream, butter can be unsalted or salted. The salted type shown here has better keeping qualities. It can be used for light sautéing or softened and flavoured with herbs or other ingredients.

Ghee

Milk

Yoghurt

Powdered milk

Clotted cream

Cream

Buttermilk

Whipping cream

Salted butter

Dripping

Lard

Margarine

Suet

DRIPPING

Fat that has separated from meat during cooking, is strained or clarified and used as a cooking fat.

LARD

Melted, clarified and purified pork fat, this is used for deep-frying, roasting meats, and making pastry.

MARGARINE

A butter substitute made from animal or vegetable fats, or a combination of both, margarine can be bought in blocks or tubs.

SUET

The fat surrounding the kidneys of beef or sheep, suet is sold fresh for grating or already shredded and ready for use as shown. It is often used in puddings.

OTHER MILK AND BUTTER SUBSTITUTES

SOFT MARGARINE
This variety is made from refined and purified vegetable oils only and contains polyunsaturates and emulsifiers. Not as fattening as butter, it is easier to spread than margarine block.

SOY MILK
This is made from soy beans. Easily digested, it can be used as a substitute for dairy milk.

TOFU
Tofu, or soy bean curd, is soft and cheese-like with a bland taste. Available in soft, firm and silken forms, it is the staple of Japanese cooking. It may be eaten on its own or used in soups, sauces and dressings. Fermented or stinking tofu is a favourite Chinese snack, eaten deep fried and seasoned.

OTHER MILKS AND MILK PRODUCTS

CONDENSED MILK
Canned milk from which half of the water content has been removed and sugar added. It can be poured over fruit salads, and is useful for reconstituting and confectionery-making.

DOUBLE CREAM
This contains a minimum of 48 per cent fat. Sugars and flavourings are sometimes added, as in *crème chantilly*, used in cakes and desserts.

EVAPORATED MILK
This is canned milk with a large percentage of its water removed. It is similar to condensed milk but, because it has no added sugar, does not keep as well. Once opened, it should be stored and treated like fresh milk.

FERMENTED MILK or YOGHURT DRINKS
There are a number of sour milk drinks from different parts of Asia and the Middle East. These include dough from Iran, kaelder milk from Norway, kefir from eastern Europe, kumiss from the USSR, laban and lassi from the Middle East, mazoum from Armenia and skyr from Iceland.

FORTIFIED SKIMMED MILK
This has less than 1 per cent milk fat yet contains the fat-soluble vitamins, added after the milk is skimmed.

HOMOGENIZED MILK
This is whole milk processed so that the cream does not separate. It can be used in drinks, puddings, soups and baking.

LONG-LIFE MILK
Milk that is ultra-heat treated and vacuum-packed to render it sterile for long keeping.

SKIMMED MILK
This is milk with less than 1 per cent milk fat but all the protein and minerals of whole milk, with the exception of the fat-soluble vitamins.

SOURED CREAM
Cream inoculated with a lactic acid culture, this is added to salad dressings and sauces to give a slightly acid flavour.

STERILIZED CREAM
This has a minimum of 23 per cent fat. Homogenized, heated and cooled, it is sold in tins.

CHEESES

IT IS IMPOSSIBLE TO say where and when cheese was first produced, but the farmers, in Mesopotamia, who first domesticated sheep and goats about 10,000 years ago, and wild cattle 2000 years later, certainly made cheese from milk, or enjoyed cheese which was accidentally precipitated. During the Middle Ages, monks furthered the development of cheese as a necessary meat substitute. Cheese-making differed from family to family and the methods passed from one generation to another. There are now, in fact, fewer cheese types than in former times, when cheeses were strictly local and every farmhouse produced its own supply.

The dairy cow provides the bulk of the world's milk and cheese, but a significant amount of goat's and sheep's milk cheeses are made throughout Europe and the Middle East. In addition, cheese is made from the milk of reindeer in Lapland, the yak and zebu in China and Tibet, the buffalo in the Philippines, India and Italy, and from the camel and, it is said, horses and donkeys, in Afghanistan and Iran.

Categorizing cheese

A cheese type is distinguished by its flavour and texture. Fresh cheese is unripened curd eaten shortly after it is made, while soft cheese is briefly ripened and easy to spread, and contains a high percentage of moisture and fat. Semi-hard cheese, matured with less moisture, is easy to cut. Hard cheese is long-matured with a low moisture content but may contain up to 50 per cent fat. It is a good grating cheese but difficult to cut.

Cheese may be identified partly by the formation of the rind. Rinds protect the cheeses' interiors and allow them to ripen properly. Apart from those with a manufactured wax coating, there are those with a dry or natural rind, or with a natural rind which is then dyed. Some cheeses are bathed in a brine solution. This hardens the rind and improves the flavour of the paste or body. White rind cheeses have a mould flora (usually *Penicillium candidum*). Washed rind cheeses, where the cheese is regularly wiped, washed or sprayed with water to encourage the growth of bacteria moulds, have a sharper, richer taste. Some cheese is distinguished by the absence of any rind, as with most fresh cheeses.

The paste further categorizes cheeses. In the early stages of cheese-making, the curd is a white flavourless mass. If the cheese-maker desires a soft cheese, the curd may simply be left to drain. With a firmer cheese, the curd is cooked, then pressed into moulds. Some cheeses have a semi-hard body containing many holes of various sizes, caused by gas-producing bacteria during ripening. Blue-veined cheeses are those where the blueing is either induced by the application or inoculation of a bacteria culture, or occurs naturally.

There are several basic techniques in cheese-making recipes, where the consistency and flavour of the paste is determined by the cooking and treatment of the curd. Cheddar is heated to 29.5°C (86°F), cut, stirred and heated again to 38.5°C (104°F), the curd stacked to promote cohesion and acid formation, finely milled, salted and pressed. Gouda curds are cooked to 35°C (95°F), cut, stirred, moulded and pressed, after which the cheeses are steeped in a brine bath. The curd of Caciocavallo cheese is toughened by immersion in hot whey and water; it is then kneaded and shaped. All these techniques are basic to cheese-making, but equally important are the infinite variety of traditional recipes, which may demand the addition of certain mould cultures or herbs, or the wrapping of cheeses in chestnut or vine leaves.

Finally, cheese is also categorized by the type of animal that produced the milk and by the shape of the finished product. Cheeses come in various shapes: wheels, loaves, pyramids, hearts, cylinders and squares.

Cheese in the kitchen

Cheese can be used in soups, soufflés, pastry, sandwiches, salads, pies, pizzas, tarts, on toast, as a garnish and for many other applications. The choice of the cheese may depend on the nationality of the dish, but also on the cheese's behaviour during cooking. Some cheeses, such as Emmental, are inclined to draw threads and become stringy, whereas Gruyère and Sbrinz cheeses do not. On the other hand, this stringiness is desirable in some dishes, such as Swiss fondue. Cheese is also chosen for its melting and spreading qualities: Cheddar or Dunlop cheese for Welsh and Scotch rarebit; or Gruyère for *fonduta*; firm or crumbly cheese, such as Greek Feta, Cheshire, and Roquefort, for salads and dressings. One of the most useful combinations for versatility is a mixture of grated Parmesan and Gruyère, the former giving the strong piquant flavour, the latter the smooth, binding qualities suitable for cheese sauces and for the base for soufflés and quiches.

Storing cheese

Storage can be a problem, if you need to keep your cheese for any length of time. A cool room or cellar is ideal, but the cheese should be wrapped in aluminium foil or waxed paper to prevent it from drying out. One good method is to wrap each piece in foil or paper, then in a plastic bag for storage in a temperate part of the refrigerator – the salad compartment, for instance. Remove the cheese to adjust to room temperature about 1 hour before serving, depending on the type of cheese and the size of the piece. Parmesan should be freshly grated and used at once. Grated cheese should be wrapped and stored as described above.

Fresh and Soft Cheeses

CREAM CHEESE

This is prepared in much the same way as cottage cheese, but with full-cream cow's milk. There are several types: double cream cheese and single cream cheese are two. American cream cheese is made with a hot cream/milk mix. French petit-suisse cheeses are small, paper-wrapped products; Demisel is salted, as its name suggests. There are, in addition, many other versions throughout the world. The Kesong Puti of the Philippines, and Surati Panir of India are both made with buffalo milk. Sheep's and goat's milk cheeses are made throughout the Middle East, and are sold as Jupneh (Saudi Arabia) and variously as Lebbeneh or Labneh, while Latin America has its *queso blanco* cheeses, made from cow's or goat's milk.

CURD CHEESE

"Curd" is the general name given to all unripened cheeses made from the separated curds of cow's or goat's milk. Curd cheese has a slightly acid taste, and is used in cheesecakes and sweet and savoury fillings. It is also a popular base for dips and spreads. It is sold in most countries.

Curd cheese

COTTAGE CHEESE

A lumpy, mild-tasting curd cheese, often containing cream, this has a moist texture, and is usually sold in tubs. It is available in most countries, and is used in cheesecakes and salads. Pressed into solid curd and cut in cubes, it is eaten in India's *mattar pannir*.

Cottage cheese

Cream cheese

BRIE

Made by Briard farmers since the eighth century, Brie was served to Charlemagne in 774. It is a soft French cheese made from cow's milk, with a creamy, fruity taste that is delicious in snacks and as a filling for brioche. It is made in large, flat wheel shapes and there are many varieties. The thin crust, made in the same way as Camembert, is edible. Brie is ripened on straw mats for about four weeks at a controlled temperature.

Brie

Camembert

CAMEMBERT

This world-famous French cheese is made from cow's milk and there are several varieties. It has a distinctive taste which varies from mild to pungent as it ages. An excellent dessert and snack cheese, it is made in small cylinder or half-moon shapes, which means that it can be bought as an individual cheese. The cheese is sprayed with *Penicillium candidum*, and acquires a white crust of mould flora. It is brine-dipped and ripened for about three weeks.

COULOMMIERS

A French cheese made from cow's milk, this, like Brie and Camembert, has a white rind and a soft interior. It has a rich and creamy taste and is usually made in small wheel shapes. It is good for desserts and snacks.

BOURSIN AUX FINES HERBES

A soft French triple cream cheese (with a 75 per cent fat content), the variety shown contains rosemary, fennel and chives. It is most often served with biscuits.

Coulommiers

Boursin aux fines herbes

MUNSTER

A French cheese from the Vosges, Munster is made from cow's milk in wheel shapes of varying sizes (Petit Munster is shown here). It has an orange-red rind, a very soft paste and distinctive flavour that has made it popular and much imitated. The Germans make Munsters, so do the Swiss and Americans.

Neufchatel

NEUFCHATEL

A mild-flavoured French cheese made from cow's milk. Although it is eaten when ripened in Europe (when it has a white mould flora rind), in America it is often eaten as a fresh, unripened cheese. It is made in a variety of shapes and sizes and is good for desserts and snacks.

Munster

TOMME AU RAISIN

A soft French cheese made from cow's milk and covered with grape pulp, skin and pips. The word "tomme" is simply a dialect word for cheese from the Savoie region of France and there are many varieties, produced in small drum shapes. They usually have a fairly pronounced flavour and make excellent dessert cheeses.

Boursin au poivre

BOURSIN AU POIVRE

A variety of Boursin coated with crushed black peppercorns which give the cheese a spicy taste, complementing its creamy interior. Like the herb variety, it is packaged in small drum shapes as an individual cheese.

Tomme au raisin

MOZZARELLA

An Italian unripened curd cheese originally made from buffalo's milk, but now usually obtained from cow's milk. Made in various shapes, such as rounds and slabs, it is also packed shredded. It is a soft cheese with a rather moist texture. It has a mild, creamy taste and is widely used as a cooking cheese – in pizzas, lasagne and toasted sandwiches.

RICOTTA

An Italian fresh, unripened cheese made from the whey of cow's milk in Ricotta Piedmontese and Ricotta Vaccina, and sheep's milk in the regional types Ricotta Romana, Sarda and Siciliana. There is also a Maltese version, Rkotta, made from a mixture of cow's milk and sea water. It is smooth and milky-tasting and is used in a variety of sweet and savoury dishes, including pizzas, and as a stuffing for ravioli, cannelloni and pancakes. It is packaged in various shapes and sizes.

Ricotta

Mozzarella

Caboc

COLWICK

A traditional cow's milk cheese from England. Usually made in cylinder shapes, the variety shown here has a dished centre, which can be filled with cream and fruit. This cheese is usually sold unsalted to be served as a dessert, but can be salted and used as a savoury cheese.

CABOC

A Scottish double cream cheese (with a 60 per cent fat content) made from cow's milk and rolled in oatmeal. It has a fairly sweet flavour and goes well with fresh fruit. It is made in small log or cylinder shapes.

FETA

A Greek cheese made variously with goat's and sheep's milk, or a mixture. Its roughly cut pressed curd is ripened in its own whey, salted beforehand. Feta is used in many Greek recipes; Greece has the distinction of being the world's leading consumer of cheese – some 15kg (38lb) per head.

Colwick

Feta

OTHER FRESH AND SOFT CHEESES

BARBEREY
A French cheese, Barberey or Fromage de Troyes is salted, moulded and ripened for about three weeks. Sometimes it is sold unripened as a fresh cheese. Ripened cheeses resemble Camembert.

BEL PAESE
This is a relatively modern Italian cheese invented in 1929; its name means "beautiful country". It is a dessert type with a short ripening period. Bel Paese is a flat, round cheese with a slightly red rind flora.

BELI SIR
Both farmhouse and factory versions exist of this sourish Yugoslavian cheese, which is brine-ripened for about a month, and pressed in rectangular moulds.

BRENZA
A soft and buttery cheese, Brenza or Bryndza is sometimes used as a basis for Liptauer spread. It is made in Hungary, Romania and the Carpathians from goat's or sheep's milk.

CHABICHOU
A goat's milk cheese from Poitou, France, this is made in the form of a cone or cylinder, with a natural dry rind.

CHAOURCE
This is an aromatic and slightly sour French cheese with a white mould flora rind. The cheeses are cylindrical and about 6.5cm (2½in) high.

CHAUMES
A mild, tender cheese from the Atlantic Pyrenees region of France, this is factory-made from cow's milk and contains 50 per cent fat; Saint Albrey is similar. Circular and with a washed rind, it weighs 2kg (4½lb), and makes an excellent dessert cheese or may be used in Welsh rarebit.

EPOISSES
A small, cylindrical French cheese, this is a speciality of the Burgundy region, and the washed rind develops the orange smear of coryne bacteria. It may be spiced during manufacture, or dipped in marc de Bourgogne before sale.

LEIDERKRANZ
A Limburger-type rectangular American cheese with a very soft paste and mild flavour. The washed rind has the red smear of coryne bacteria.

LIPTAUER
A Hungarian cheese spread made from sheep's and cow's milk, Liptauer is a factory product based on a sheep's milk cheese, either Brenza or Liptó. Variations exist where butter, capers, onions, mustard and spices may be added.

LIVAROT
A strong, rectangular cheese from Normandy, France, with a red mould rind.

MASCARPONE
An Italian dessert cheese made from fresh cream and sold unripened, this may be flavoured with liqueurs, and is sometimes sold mixed with candied fruits.

QUARK
This is a sharp, acidic skimmed milk cheese, usually found as a solid-packed mass. There are a variety of quark cheeses, which are widely employed in cooking, and to accompany other dishes. Quark is used in pastry, and in such recipes as *quarksahnetorte, quark-schnitten* and quark soufflé.

ROULE
A soft French cheese flavoured with herbs, this is rolled up like a Swiss roll.

SCAMORZA
An old Italian cow's milk cheese related to Mozzarella, Scamorza was originally made from buffalo's milk. It is a drawn curd cheese of an oval shape, yellow in colour with a firm but supple texture. It is used in pizzas.

STRACCHINO
There are several versions and types of this Italian cheese, originating in Lombardy. Taleggio and Robiolo are very soft, delicate cheeses, with a red-orange rind flora that results from their having been brined during ripening. They are uncut, unpressed cheeses. Stracchino Cresenza develops no rind flora.

Semi-Hard Cheeses

PORT SALUT

A mild French cheese with a firm paste and a washed rind. The small, round cheeses are made by Trappist monks from an ancient recipe. They are named "Port of Salvation" after the abbey, which itself was rechristened when the monks returned from exile after the French Revolution.

Port Salut

Colby

MANCHEGO

Spain's most famous cheese, this is made from sheep's milk and has a creamy, firmish-textured interior, which sometimes has holes. Strong-tasting and ideal for snacks, Manchego is made in cylinder shapes.

Manchego

COLBY

A popular American Cheddar-type cheese from Colby, Wisconsin. It is a washed-curd cheese (if the curds are washed thoroughly in cold water, the moisture content of the cheese is increased, making it mature more quickly). Made in various shapes, it is a mild cheese with a natural rind and slightly granular texture, which is popular in snacks and salads.

CANTAL

A cow's milk cheese from the Auvergne, it is often referred to as French Cheddar. It possesses a fine flavour and aroma and can be used in place of Cheddar for many recipes since it melts easily and does not tend to draw threads. Made in cylinder shapes, it is used in several regional dishes and is a good all-purpose table cheese.

Cantal

SAINT PAULIN

A rinded French cheese made from cow's milk, it can be bland or tangy, depending on its degree of ripeness, and is similar in taste to Port Salut. It is a good snack and dessert cheese and is made in small wheel shapes.

Saint Paulin

Gjetost

Monterey Jack

MONTEREY JACK

Monterey is a Cheddar-type cheese originating in Monterey, California, but now also made in other parts of America. It is derived from an old monastery recipe, and was first marketed in 1916. Made from cow's milk, it has a rather bland taste with a smooth, open texture, numerous holes and a natural rind. It is made in block shapes or large wheels and is used in snacks, sandwiches and in recipes. Monterey Jack, shown here, has an unmilled, lightly pressed curd with a high moisture content. There is also a grating-type Monterey, which is very useful for cooking.

GJETOST

A Norwegian whey cheese that can be made from either cow's milk (when it is also called Mysost) or goat's milk. Rather fudge-like in taste and appearance, it is made in cubes or rectangular blocks and is usually foil-wrapped. It is used in sauces, desserts and snacks.

FONTINA

A cow's milk cheese from the Piedmont region of Italy, it has a delicate nutty, slightly smoky taste and is much used for *fonduta*, a fondue of truffles, eggs and cheese. It is made in flat wheel shapes and has a natural rind.

CABRALES

Traditionally a goat's milk cheese (though there are now sheep's milk varieties) this is from the mountain regions of northern Spain. Made in cylinder shapes, it has a strong, pronounced taste and makes a good snack cheese.

Fontina

RACLETTE

A cow's milk cheese from Switzerland with a mild, nutty taste. Made in wheel shapes, it gives its name to a traditional melted cheese dish. There are several varieties, including Gomser, Bagnes and Orsières, all with a firm, spicy paste.

Cabrales

Raclette

Cheshire

Double Gloucester

Dunlop

DUNLOP

A Scottish cheese made from cow's milk, this is a Cheddar-type cheese with a rather bland, buttery taste. It is a natural rind cheese said to have originated from an Irish recipe. In Scotland it is often eaten with buttered oatcakes; it makes a good snack cheese and is ideal for toasting. It is made in cylinder shapes.

DOUBLE GLOUCESTER

This cow's milk cheese has a full flavour and is considered one of the great English cheeses. It is good for desserts and snacks and is made in cylinder shapes which weigh between 4.5 and 15kg (10 and 34lb).

CHESHIRE

A famous English cow's milk cheese from the county of Cheshire, dating back to the twelfth century, this has a crumbly texture and slightly salty tang. Usually fast-ripening, there are two types: red (shown), which is coloured with annatto dye, and white. It is a good snack cheese.

LEICESTER

A firm-bodied English cow's milk cheese with a mild flavour, this is distinguished by its bright orange colour, due to the addition of annatto dye. It is used like Lancashire as a melting and toasting cheese, and also makes a good snack cheese. It is made in cylinder shapes.

EMMENTAL

This world-famous Swiss cheese made from cow's milk has a fairly sweet, nutty taste and can be used as a basis for fondues and toasted snacks. Its name means "valley of Emme", the river which runs through central Switzerland. The 100kg (250lb) cartwheel, when cut open, reveals the large holes or "eyes" throughout the paste. The cheese has a natural rind and is softer and blander than Gruyère, and draws threads when cooked.

Leicester

Emmental

Wensleydale

Lancashire

Cheddar

WENSLEYDALE

An English cheese from Yorkshire, this was once made from sheep's or goat's milk by Cistercian monks, but is now factory-made using cow's milk. White Wensleydale is a lightly pressed, salted type with a buttermilk flavour and a natural rind. There is also a blue-veined variety. White Wensleydale is a traditional accompaniment to apple pie and is made in cylinder and block shapes.

GRUYERE

Gruyère is a Swiss cheese, but variations are produced in France. France and Switzerland argued over the right to the name, which was finally granted to both by the Convention of Stresa in 1951. Made from cow's milk, Swiss Gruyère has a smooth, uniform paste with only a very few pea-sized holes, and a dark-brown natural rind. It is similar to Emmental in appearance and nut-like taste. Apart from being a good table cheese it is much used in fondues, sauces and quiches, since it does not draw threads. It is made in large wheel shapes.

LANCASHIRE

A mild-tasting cow's milk cheese from England, this is similar to white Cheshire. It melts well and thus lends itself well to cooking (particularly toasting). It is made in cylinder or block shapes and can be sold as wedges.

CHEDDAR

England's most famous cheese, this is made from cow's milk and varies from mild to very sharp. Cheddar cheeses are now made throughout the world, usually in a large, cylinder shape with a natural rind. A very versatile cooking cheese, since it doesn't draw threads, Cheddar can be used in sauces, soufflés, salads and pizzas. It is also good eaten on its own, or in a ploughman's lunch.

CAERPHILLY

This is a cow's milk cheese from Wales with a mild, slightly sour taste. Usually made in cylinder shapes it is a good snack and dessert cheese. It hardly ripens at all.

Caerphilly

Gruyère

LEYDEN

A semi-hard Dutch cheese covered with a dark yellow rind and then with red wax. It is made from whole or skimmed cow's milk and contains caraway and cumin seeds. Made in cylinder shapes, Leyden or Leiden goes well with gin and cocktails and makes a good snack cheese.

EDAM

A mild, bland, buttery Dutch cheese with a thin natural rind and red wax coating, it is usually matured for three to four months. Made from cow's milk, it is a slightly harder cheese than Gouda due to its low fat content. Edam is sometimes spiced with cumin seed, and more mature versions are available. It is sold in ball shapes.

JARLSBERG

A Norwegian cheese originating in Oslo in 1959, this ranges from white to light yellow with large holes scattered throughout. It is made from cow's milk and has a firm, buttery interior and a mild, nutty taste. It is covered with a thick rind and then with a yellow wax. A good all-purpose cheese, it is used in the Norwegian *landgang*. Jarlsberg is made in wheel shapes.

Leyden   *Gouda*

GOUDA

An excellent, mild Dutch cheese with a soft, buttery paste. Allowed to mature for over a year, Gouda develops an excellent flavour to become one of the world's great cheeses; it can also be eaten fresh. After brining, the cheese develops a natural rind. It is made in wheel shapes.

TILSIT

A firm-textured cow's milk cheese, first made by Dutch cheese-makers living in Tilsit, East Germany, but now produced all over Europe. It has a tangy taste, and is a good cheese for desserts and sandwiches. It can be made in wheel or block shapes.

Edam

Tilsit

Jarlsberg

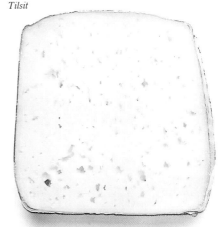

OTHER SEMI-HARD CHEESES

APPENZELLER
A Swiss cheese, cylindrical in form; its name originally derives from the Latin for "abbot's cell". These cheeses ripen in three to six months, during which time they are regularly turned, and washed with a mixture of white wine, water, and herbs.

BELLELAVE
A Swiss cylindrical cheese with a red rind flora. Also called Tête de Moine.

BRICK
A native American cheese first made in Wisconsin in the 1870s and named for its shape. It is a surface-moulded cheese with a reddish-brown rind which can be waxed. The interior contains small holes and is yellow-white. It is a mild, tangy cheese most often used in sandwiches and in toasting.

CHEVRE
Literally, the name means "goat" cheese, and there are many variations.

COON
An American Cheddar-type cheese, this is made by a patent process which includes scalding.

DERBY
An English cheese from Derbyshire. It has a natural rind, firm paste, mild flavour, and comes in cartwheel shapes weighing about 14kg (35lb). Used as a toasting cheese, it is sometimes flavoured with fresh sage leaves, which give green streaks to the cheese. Manufactured in this way, it is known as Sage Derby.

ESROM
A Danish cheese based on the French Port Salut, with a washed red flora rind. It is used in *smorgasbord* recipes.

GAMMELOST
A rapidly ripening Norwegian cheese that develops a unique mould growth on the rind. This is regularly pressed into the paste, and gives the cheese its characteristic sharp and tangy flavour. The paste is soft and dark brown in colour.

HAVARTI
A Tilsit-type Danish cheese with an open, lace-like paste and a natural or washed rind – the dry rind gives Havarti a slightly sour taste, the flora on the washed rind makes it taste sharper. Havarti was the name of the farm of the cheese's developer, Mrs Hanne Nielson.

LIMBURGER
Once Belgian but now made in Germany, Limburger is a piquant, sometimes pungent, cheese. The rind is washed with coryne bacteria and the cheese is ripened for a period of about three to four weeks.

PONT L'EVEQUE
A square-shaped, soft cheese, this is one of the oldest from Normandy in France, with a fairly strong taste and aroma. Pont l'Evêque cheeses have a washed rind and are packed in small chipwood boxes in the manner of Camembert.

REBLOCHON
A French cheese from the Haute-Savoie, a mountainous region where the cheese is ripened in caves. Reblochon is a rich, creamy cheese with a mild flavour and washed rind. Its name means "second milking", because the French herdsmen who originally made it used milk from a second, illegal, milking.

SAMSO
Originally a Danish copy of the Swiss Emmental, this was named Samso from the island on which it was made. Related cheeses have the suffix "bo" added to the name of the island or town of manufacture: Danbo is a square-shaped cheese with a natural rind, and sometimes contains caraway seeds; Fynbo is similar to Samso, but smaller in size, and the paste has smaller holes; Elbo has a more regular, firm paste with few holes and a natural rind; Tybo is a smaller, quite solid cheese with the same fat content; Molbo shares characteristics with Dutch Edam, being shaped like a ball with a red rind; similarly, Maribo is like Dutch Gouda, but contains tiny holes and has a red wax rind.

SAUERMILCHKASE
A family of German cheeses made from low-fat milk, soured by a lactic acid starter, and without use of rennet. They vary considerably in shape, but all have a rind flora which gives them a colour ranging from pale yellow to red-brown. The taste is sourish and sharp, and some cheeses have the addition of spices. Varieties include such cheeses as Mainzer, Harzer, Handkäse, Spitkäse and Strangenkäse.

Hard, Blue and Smoked Cheeses

PROVOLONE

Now made from cow's milk, but originally from buffalo's milk, this is a drawn curd cheese made in Italy, America and Australia. It is found in a variety of shapes such as pear, cone or cylinder and is hung by cords to mature and harden. All Provolones are smoked. The younger ones are milder and softer, and are used as table cheeses; the older, more robust and harder cheeses are used in cooking. Provolone is often used in cannelloni and ravioli.

Provolone

PECORINO

A variety of hard *grana* cheese made from sheep's milk in central and southern Italy. Pecorino Romano is made by heating the milk, curdling with rennet, finely cutting the curd and pressing. The cheese matures in about eight months. Pecorino Sardo is made on the island of Sardinia, while Pecorino Pepato, made in Sicily, has added peppercorns. They are used both as table cheeses, and for grating.

Pecorino

PARMESAN

Parmesan cheese or, more correctly, Parmigiano Reggiano, is the noblest of a group of Italian cheeses known collectively as *formaggi di grana*, meaning hard cheeses with a grainy texture. The wheel-shaped, golden-coloured cow's milk cheeses are made of finely cut, carefully separated curd, which is then stirred and scalded to 58°C (137°F) before being pressed. The cheeses are salted over a period of weeks, after which they mature for two to three years, or even longer – they are categorized as *vecchio* (old), *stravecchio* (extra old), *tipico* (four or five years old), or *giovane* (less mature table cheese). Other *grana* cheeses include Grana Padano, made in considerable quantity throughout Lombardy, Grana Lodigiano, a low-fat cheese with an "eyed" paste of small holes, and Grana Lombardo from around Milan. Grana cheeses are widely used as a grating type for typically Italian recipes, such as minestrone, or pasta, and they may be incorporated in sauces.

Parmesan

SAPSAGO

A Swiss cheese made from soured skimmed milk and whole milk, Sapsago is also known as green cheese because of its pale green colour, due to the presence of clover which is added to the curd. It is a hard cheese which is normally grated before use, and makes a good all-purpose cooking cheese.

CACIOCAVALLO

An Italian cheese made from cow's milk, Caciocavallo is, like Provolone, one of the *pasta filata*, or "drawn curd" cheeses (in which the curds are softened by hot water, which means that they can be easily shaped by hand). Made by nomads, Caciocavallo means "cheese on horseback" since it is said to resemble saddle bags. It is an ancient Roman cheese. Made in gourd-like shapes, the young cheeses are used for snacks or desserts; older cheeses become hard and granular and are then used for grating and cooking.

Caciocavallo

SBRINZ

A Swiss grating cheese, this is made from cow's milk by finely cutting the curd and scalding at temperatures above 55°C (130°F). The cheese is pressed to form a flat disc or wheel, then brined and "sweated" at 20°C (68°F) for about four months, after which it is racked and left to mature for about two years. Sbrinz is a piquant, aromatic cheese, used as a table variety, and also for cooking, since it grates well, and is used for sauces and soufflés.

Sbrinz

Sapsago

*Smoked
Emmental*

GORGONZOLA

With Roquefort and Stilton, Gorgonzola is one of the three premier blue cheeses. In the manufacture of Gorgonzola, Italy's most famous blue cheese, the mould culture *Penicillium gorgonzola* is added to the curds with the starter. The curds are cut and packed into moulds, then the unripe cheese is salted, pricked with needles and left for three months to develop the veining. It is used for stuffing pears, in *mousse au fromage*, and in salads. The cheese is pleasantly sharp in flavour, with a softish, white paste and greenish veins. It is fatter in texture than Roquefort and moister than Stilton.

ROQUEFORT

Considered by many to be the king of cheeses, Roquefort is a sheep's milk cheese from the Causes area of France. It is made in cylinder shapes and has a rich, strong taste. The success of Roquefort is due to the unique, very humid environment in the complex of local caves. The unripe Roqueforts are left to mature in the caves of Combalou mountain, where the moisture-laden air freely circulates spores of *Penicillium glaucum*, var. *roqueforti*, and in about six weeks the cheeses start to "blue". Roquefort is used for *tartelettes au Roquefort*, as a table cheese, and in salad dressing.

SMOKED EMMENTAL

Traditionally made in long sausage shapes, this is used mainly as a snack cheese. The most commonly used cheeses are Emmental and Cheddar, but other cheeses may also be smoked and found in this form.

Mycella

Gorgonzola

Roquefort

MYCELLA

A Danish cheese made from cow's milk, Mycella has blue-green veins. It is usually made in tall, cylinder shapes, though smaller

pieces are often sold foil-wrapped. It is used mainly as a table cheese, but can also be used to add a certain sharpness of taste to both salads and salad dressings.

OTHER HARD CHEESES

ASIAGO

An Italian cow's milk cheese from the province of Vicenza in the north-west. There are two types: the Asiago d'Allevio made from a mixture of skimmed and whole milk, producing a fairly piquant, grating cheese, and the Asiago Grasso di Monte, with a smoother paste and a mellower flavour. Asiago is used in many recipes that

require a grating cheese, such as soups, pasta and meat dishes.

BERGKASE

This is a large, cartwheel-shaped Austrian cheese with a smooth, uniform paste and mild flavour, made from cow's milk. The curds are finely cut and the cheese hard-pressed until a natural rind develops.

KEFALOTYRI

A popular hard Greek cheese, meaning "head cheese", made by finely cutting and stirring the cow's milk curds, which are then heated before being pressed into moulds – resulting shapes often resemble skulls or hats. They are then dry-salted, and left to mature for several months. The cheese is used as a grating type in several national dishes.

Blue Cheeses

BLUE CASTELLO

A Danish double cream soft-textured cheese made from cow's milk.

Blue Castello

DANISH BLUE

Lacking a national blue cheese, Danish cheese-makers in the early nineteenth century began experiments with mould cultures and came up with a selection of excellent blue cheeses, of which Danish Blue or Danablu is the most renowned. Made from homogenized cow's milk, it is soft-textured and creamy with a fairly strong taste, and makes a good dessert cheese. It is made in wheel shapes. Blucreme, another Danish blue cheese type, is an internal-mould cheese with added cream that is smoother and creamier than Danish Blue. It is made in 4kg (10lb) loaves.

Bleu de Bresse

PIPO CREM'

A popular French blue-veined cow's milk cheese made in long cylinder shapes. Pipo Crem' is larger and creamier than Bleu de Bresse and comes from Ain in the same region.

Pipo Crem'

Danish Blue

BLEU DE BRESSE

A creamy French blue-veined cheese made from cow's milk, this is soft-textured and has a rich taste. It has a slightly higher fat content (50 per cent) than most blue cheeses, and weighs about 2kg (4.5lb). Made in small cylinder shapes and often foil-wrapped, it is a good dessert cheese and is also used in *fromage cardinal* – a blend of cheese and paprika.

FOURME D'AMBERT

This is a strongly flavoured, closely veined blue cow's milk cheese from the Haute-Savoie region of France. It is made in tall cylinder shapes.

Fourme d'Ambert

DOLCELATTE

Literally "sweet milk", this is an Italian blue cheese, made from cow's milk, with a very soft paste, creamy texture, and greenish-coloured veining throughout. It is a factory-made version of the famous Gorgonzola. It is made in cylinder shapes.

Dolcelatte

Bavarian Blue

BLUE CHESHIRE

A worthy rival to Stilton, Blue Cheshire is a large, cylindrical blue version of the dyed Cheshire cheese, and one of the finest of all blues. Made from cow's milk, cheese ripens and "blues" only accidentally, although cheese-makers try and encourage the mould by pricking the cheese with needles and maturing it in a favourable atmosphere. It has a rich taste and is best served as a dessert cheese.

Blue Cheshire

BAVARIAN BLUE

A double cream, soft-textured blue-veined cheese with a mildly sour taste from West Germany, this is very rich and high in fat (70 per cent). Made from cow's milk, it has a creamy texture and spreads well, making it good for sandwiches. It has a moulded surface and is made in small wheel shapes.

Stilton

BLUE SHROPSHIRE

A new arrival among blue cheeses, this is made not, as its name would suggest, in the English county of Shropshire, but in Scotland. It comes in cylinder shapes.

STILTON

Stilton is a relative newcomer to the great blue cheeses. Gorgonzola and Roquefort cheeses have been made for a thousand years or more, but Stilton first drew public attention in the early eighteenth century. Tradition has it that the cheese was first produced in Leicestershire, England, by a Mrs Paulet, and supplied to the Bell Inn at Stilton.

Stilton is a rich cow's milk cheese. White Stilton is sold when fairly young, but the Blue (shown here) requires about six months to develop. Steel needles are driven into the cheese, and it is left to ripen. It develops a natural rind, brown and crinkly. It is sold in tall cylinders which help to distinguish it from Gorgonzola and Roquefort.

Blue Shropshire

OTHER BLUE CHEESES

BLEU D'AUVERGNE
A small 2kg (4–5lb) cheese from the French Auvergne region, made by inoculating the curd, or sprinkling the surface, with *Penicillium glaucum* mould. The cheese is first washed, then dry-salt rubbed and pierced with needles to encourage the formation of mould.

BLEU DE CORSE
A white sheep's milk cheese produced on the Corsican plains, it develops interior mould to become "blue". Other cheeses of this type are sent to mature in the Roquefort caves.

BLEU DE GEX
A cheese from the Jura mountains with a firm paste, mild flavour and delicate blue veining; there is a very similar cheese from neighbouring Septmoncel, the Bleu de Septmoncel. Both weigh 5–6kg (12–15lb). Bleu de Sassenage, from the Isère, is also similar, but firmer in texture and much smaller.

BLEU DE LAQUEUILLE
This is a fairly modern French cheese from Puy-de-Dome, introduced in 1850. Like most French blue cheeses it is quite small, 2–2.5kg (5–6lb), has a dry rind and mellow flavour.

BLEU DE L'AVEYRON
A French cheese matured in the natural caves of the Massif Central, a feature which it shares with Bleu de Causses and the famous Roquefort. This small, local blue cheese has a fine, delicate flavour and soft paste.

LYMESWOLD
This creamy, mild, blue-veined cheese was created in 1982 as an English rival to blue Brie. There are several varieties, all made in small wheel shapes. It is eaten on its own as a snack or dessert cheese.

FISH AND SEAFOOD

MARINE AND FRESHWATER fish were an important part of man's diet long before prehistoric societies learned to cultivate vegetables and domesticate animals. Fish provided protein and vitamins, and were easy to catch and prepare – it is even likely that a large proportion was eaten raw.

In Egypt, fish were abundant and cheap – cheaper than bread. Fish such as carp, barbel, bleak and loach were supplied by rivers and lakes, grey mullet and tuna by the sea. Even in early history the people of the Iberian peninsula were catching anchovies, sardines and cod, salting them, and exporting the resulting *bacalao* as far away as Asia Minor.

In Europe, pike provided both sport and feast, while in Scotland salmon was so common in the seventeenth century that a law was passed forbidding employers to give it to their servants more than three times a week. Carp – freshwater fish that often attained formidable proportions – were reared in ponds and lakes throughout Europe, the Middle East, and in China and Japan, where they provided inspiration for poets and cooks alike.

The most valuable fish of all time is the herring, which still supplies one-third of the world's catch – some 20 million tons. Today, cod, mackerel and tuna follow closely behind.

Fish in the kitchen
Fish are a good source of high-grade protein and most are low in fat. They can be cooked in various ways, including frying, sautéeing, baking, grilling, steaming and poaching.

Dover sole is chosen as the basis for a remarkable number of classic French dishes, such as *filets de sole Joinville*, and Escoffier's *timbale*, but is perhaps best when simply grilled, or prepared *à la meunière*. Turbot should be poached or steamed, and served with an appropriate sauce, while the drier halibut may be braised, grilled and served with melted butter, baked in the oven, or poached in white wine, as *à la dieppoise*, garnished with shrimps and mussels. Brill can be treated the same way. Other flatfish, such as dab, lemon sole and flounder, plaice and megrim, should be eaten grilled, or served *à la meunière*.

Choosing fish
Fresh fish have bulging eyes, firmly adhering scales and firm flesh; fish should never have an offensive odour. Some fish are skinned before sale – the dogfish, for example – others, such as the monkfish, are skinned and decapitated. Fish should be cooked as soon as possible as they decompose very quickly. They can be kept refrigerated for no more than a day and should be frozen if they are not to be cooked within that time. Only freeze fish if you caught it yourself. *Never* freeze fish bought from a fishmonger as it may not be freshly caught, and may have been frozen before it reached the fishmonger.

Types of fish
There are more than 20,000 species of fish in the seas of the world, yet we exploit a mere fraction of this huge potential harvest. Admittedly, at least 50 per cent are commercially unacceptable, but of the remainder only about a dozen different fish regularly appear in the marketplace. The Portuguese and Japanese are exceptions. In the Tokyo market over 60 species are sold each day, and Japanese fishing boats scour the oceans to bring home the national daily average – about 7000 tons of fish – most of which will be eaten raw, as *sashimi*.

Elsewhere in the world tastes are more conservative. The bulk of the European catch consists mainly of cod, hake, herring, mackerel, pilchard and anchovy, if only because they are so abundant; about a dozen species, out of a possible 160 types of fish inhabiting the Mediterranean and Atlantic, are regularly in demand. Americans are fortunate in having a large number of saltwater fish available all year round. They include salmon, flounder, cod, halibut, trout, perch and bass.

It is not possible within the scope of this book to give a detailed list of the many fish eaten, but a selection of the most prominent ones are illustrated and described in the following pages. For a fully comprehensive list of fish and their uses, refer to the *Multilingual Dictionary of Fish and Fish Products* (United Nations).

SEAFOOD

Seafood consists largely of "shellfish" – the term includes edible freshwater and marine animals without backbones, the crustaceans and molluscs. Crustaceans, such as lobsters, prawns and crabs, have a hard, jointed exoskeleton or "crust" which they periodically shed and replace as they grow. Molluscs inhabit shells that are either hinged, like oysters and clams, or single, like the scallop, whelk, and winkle. For culinary purposes, other molluscs (such as land snails and the shell-less marine animals squid, cuttlefish and octopus), and edible frogs, have traditionally been considered as seafood.

Shellfish are prized for their tender, fine-textured flesh which can be prepared simply in a variety of decorative and delicious ways, but they are notorious for rapid spoilage. It is essential that they be extremely fresh or, if frozen, be consumed immediately on thawing, and come from unpolluted waters.

Fresh shellfish are available all year round, but their availability reflects seasonal and regional demands which, for most shellfish, reach a peak during the salad days of summer. Oysters are traditionally eaten in colder months when they are fatter and tastier.

Choosing seafood

To ensure freshness and the best flavour, it is preferable to choose live specimens and cook them yourself. Freshwater crayfish, lobsters, crawfish (or langouste) and crabs should be very active and a crawfish's or lobster's tail should curl up under its body when picked up. Fresh shrimps and prawns, usually only available in fish markets near the sea, should be crisp and dry; stale ones are limp and dry.

Live mussel, clam, and oyster shells should be tightly closed. Any open ones which do not clamp shut when tapped sharply are stale or dead and should be discarded. Scallops may be alive when their shells are open – touch the inner membrane and it will move. Like snails, whelks and other gastropods will recede into their shell when touched. Once cooked, mussel, clam and oyster shells should open. If any do not, discard them. Some people think that bivalves, especially oysters, are best eaten raw when the shells have just been opened by hand (and the aid of a sharp oyster knife). It is sometimes possible to buy them like this on the half-shell or to buy them shelled in containers.

Crustaceans are often sold cooked and they should smell fresh and pleasant. A freshly boiled lobster or crawfish should have a dry, bright shell with no cracks or holes in it and the tail will be tight and springy if the animal was alive when it was cooked. A stale-bodied lobster or crawfish has a limp tail and legs which smell unpleasant. The same generally applies to crabs, which may also have a bleached appearance. Select a cooked crustacean that is heavy for its size.

When molluscs are not sold fresh, they are usually pickled in vinegar or brine, or canned. When pickled, they are often eaten raw with beer or other beverages, but if used in salads or similar preparations they should be rinsed first with cold water. Canned molluscs and crustaceans are already cooked. Commercially frozen ones may require cooking.

Preparing shellfish

A lobster or crawfish should be prepared for grilling by being laid on its back and having a heavy, sharp knife inserted between the body and tail shell to sever the spinal column and kill the animal. The shell is split lengthways and the inedible bits removed. Lobster claws should be cracked. Lobster and crawfish should be placed meat side up under the grill (about 10cm – 4in – away from heat), cooked for 10 to 12 minutes, and basted frequently with melted butter. Crabs should be put into warm water, around 21°C (70°F) for 30 minutes before boiling – a crab dropped straight into boiling water will shed its claws – covered tightly, simmered for 8 minutes per 450g (1lb) and left to cool in the water.

Raw or cooked shrimps, prawns, and freshwater crayfish are prepared by having the head, upper shell (carapace), legs, tail section and dark intestinal vein running down the back removed. If raw, they are put in to boiling water, steamed for 3 to 4 minutes or dipped in butter and deep-fried for 2 to 3 minutes or until golden. Every part of a lobster, crawfish, and crab can be eaten except the greyish gill, aptly named "dead men's fingers", the hard stomach behind the eyes and, in the lobster, the black intestinal vein running through the body. The lobster's tan-coloured liver or "tomally" (which turns green on cooking) can be left in the animal or removed and added to sauces.

The male lobster and crawfish are slightly larger and have more meat than the female, but a female may contain the "berry" (coral or eggs), which is not only delicious to eat when cooked in the animal, but can also be used as a garnish for other dishes. Female crabs similarly have smaller claws than males and may contain brown eggs, also called berry.

All molluscs should be washed well and be left in several changes of fresh water (clams overnight) to help rid them of saltiness and sand before cooking. Scallops should have the membrane or mantle around the white meat discarded, but both the meat and red roe can be eaten. Oysters and scallops are shelled before cooking – oysters only need heating through, which takes about 1 minute; scallops are boiled, steamed or sautéed for 1 to 2 minutes, depending on size. Mussels should have the "beards" removed and may also need thorough scrubbing. Mussels and other molluscs are usually steamed or boiled in their shells for 1 to 2 minutes.

Freezing shellfish
Shellfish may be frozen if freshly caught, but they must be absolutely fresh and kept frozen for up to one month only. To freeze, scrub and remove the molluscs from their shells, wash them in salted cold water, drain, pack in rigid containers with the strained juices (leaving room for expansion), cover, label and seal. Once thawed, they are best used in soups and sauces, added towards the end of cooking. Shrimps, prawns, and freshwater crayfish may be frozen with their heads removed, either raw or lightly boiled and cooled, sealed in plastic bags, and labelled. Lobster and crawfish should be cooked, cooled and frozen the same day they are caught. Crabs should be cooked and cooled, and the meat removed from the shell and packed in containers.

Preparing squid, cuttlefish and octopus
Fresh squid (calamari) and cuttlefish are prepared by having their tentacles and head pulled from the tail, or body, section. Any intact ink sac is removed from the head and may be reserved for use in cooking. The head and inner organs are discarded. The thin cuttlebone is pulled from the tail section, the bone discarded and then the animal washed and rubbed under cool running water so that its reddish-violet membrane is removed.

Once prepared, squid with tail sections less than 7.5cm (3in) long can be poached, grilled, or sliced into rounds, leaving the tentacles in one piece, battered, and fried quickly in oil. Larger squid and cuttlefish are usually sliced and stewed as they need longer, slower cooking to become tender, but they, like octopus, can also be stuffed with a mixture of chopped tentacles, beaten eggs and herbs and braised with wine. For octopus, the beak-like mouth and anal portion are cut away. The ink sac can be used in the stew. The body is turned inside out and the internal organs, suckers and tips of the tentacles are removed. After cleaning, unless the octopus is young (under 1kg – 2lb), the flesh should be softened by pounding and stewed for 2½ to 3 hours, until it is easily pierced with a knife.

Preparing snails and frogs' legs
Snails are widely available already prepared and frozen or, more usually, canned, but they can be prepared at home using either the common garden snail (*Helix aspersia*) or the more succulent variety used in France (*H. pomatia*). Before the creatures can be prepared, however, they must be starved for two days, then fed on lettuce for two weeks to purge them of any poisons they might have ingested. Their shells are then scrubbed and rinsed in several changes of water mixed with vinegar and salt. Snails whose heads do not come out should be discarded; the remainder dropped in boiling water and cooked for 5 minutes. Once drained and cooled, the snails are removed from their shells, their intestinal sacs discarded, and simmered in a *court bouillon* until tender. The shells are boiled briefly in water and bicarbonate of soda, drained, scrubbed, and rinsed.

Farms have been established in many countries to provide frogs' legs. Skinned and immersed in several changes of water to make the flesh swell and become whiter, the legs are prepared for speciality shops or for commercial canning and freezing.

Freshwater Fish

CARP

There are several varieties of this fish, native to eastern Asia but now found in ponds, lakes and rivers in most parts of the world. It is popular in America, France and England and, although available all year round, is at its best in winter. It tends to have a muddy taste and should be scaled, cleaned and soaked in mildly salted water for 3 to 4 hours before cooking. It can be bought fresh, frozen or smoked; whole or in steaks and fillets. It can be baked, poached, fried, steamed or braised. In China, carp are often cooked with a sweet and sour sauce; in Europe they can be stuffed and jellied. Other members of the carp family include roach, dace, chub, tench, gudgeon, barbel and bream.

Carp

Pike

PIKE

Readily available in the northern hemisphere, pike can be bought fresh or frozen, whole (if small) or in fillets (if large). It can be baked, braised, poached, sautéed or grilled and is available all year round. It is particularly popular in central European cooking, where traditionally it is stuffed and baked with oysters, anchovies, butter and herbs.

EEL

This fish, which is spawned in the Sargasso Sea and travels to fresh water to mature, is particularly popular in Europe and Japan. There are several varieties. It can be boiled, fried or grilled and made into soups and stews or jellied. Available all year round, it can be bought fresh, frozen or smoked.

Eel

SALMON

Found in cooler waters throughout the northern hemisphere, salmon is one of the world's finest food fish. Delicate and tasty, its firm, oily flesh can vary in colour from pink to dark red, Pacific varieties tending to be darker. Most salmon mature at sea but return to coastal streams to spawn for several weeks any time between December and August (exactly when depends on the variety), when the fish is generally available fresh. Canned salmon, frozen salmon steaks and smoked salmon are available all year round. Pickled salmon is excellent as an hors d'oeuvre, while marinated salmon or gravadlax is a mainstay of Scandinavian cuisine. There are many fine recipes for fresh salmon; it can be grilled or poached in *court-bouillon*, and served, hot or cold, with an appropriate sauce, or cold in aspic.

Salmon trout

SALMON TROUT

Also called sea trout, this north Atlantic, Baltic, and North Sea fish is often confused with salmon as it returns from the sea to spawn in European coastal rivers. At its best during the summer months, its pale pink and delicate-tasting flesh is particularly good poached and served cold or used to prepare dishes such as salmon trout in aspic. Too delicate for smoking, all other methods of preparing trout or salmon are applicable to salmon trout. It is quite often served as a salmon substitute.

Salmon

TROUT

Native to Europe and now found worldwide, there are many varieties of trout: brook, cut-throat, lake, rainbow or steelhead, brown, salmon (see opposite), and arctic char. The type shown is a rainbow trout. It is usually cooked whole and can be bought fresh, frozen, canned or smoked. Available all year round, trout can be prepared *au bleu, à la meunière, en papillote*, in aspic, baked, poached, sautéed, grilled and potted.

Trout

OTHER FRESHWATER FISH

CATFISH
Most varieties are freshwater and include blue, channel, yellow or goujon, spotted or fiddle and bullhead or horned pout. There are a few species of sea catfish, including wolf fish and the spotted catfish. Caught in the northern coastal waters of Europe, and also off Newfoundland, catfish is usually sold as fillets, which can be baked or fried.

GRAYLING
This is a beautiful silvery fish with a thyme-like scent, hence its Latin name *Thymallus*. It is also an excellent table fish, best prepared *au bleu*, or stuffed with herbs, and baked. It is caught in the northern hemisphere.

WHITEFISH
These are herring-like freshwater fish found in lakes throughout the northern hemisphere. Other species and sub-species include the houting, powan, vendace and northern white. They can be successfully substituted for trout.

Seawater Fish

WHITEBAIT

The name given to the fry (young) of herrings and sprats, these tiny silvery fish are found in the Mediterranean and the Atlantic. Available all year round they are at their best in spring and summer. They are sold fresh or frozen and are so small that they do not need gutting or topping and tailing, but are eaten whole. They are usually coated in flour and deep-fried until golden brown and crisp.

HERRING

A small 18–40cm (7–16in) oily fish found in the Atlantic and Pacific, the herring was once so cheap that it was dismissed as fit only for the poor. Now, however, it has become a great delicacy. Sold fresh either whole or filleted, it can be stuffed, baked, fried, casseroled, grilled or made into salads. It is also available canned. Its extreme oiliness makes it ideal for curing, as in rollmops, soured and marinated herrings, buckling, matjes, bloaters, red herrings and kippers (pages 186–7, 191). Herrings are at their best during summer. There are several herring-like fish, such as sea herring, in the Pacific. There is even a freshwater variety.

SARDINE

The many species of this strong-tasting oily fish, found in the Atlantic and the Mediterranean, can vary a great deal in size. The name "sardine" is reserved for the younger fish; older ones are called "pilchards" (3 or 4 larger fish will make a good portion). Available all year round, sardines are sold fresh, or canned in oil or tomato sauce. When fresh, they can be baked, fried or grilled.

Whitebait

Sardine

Smelt

Sprat

Herring

Mackerel

SMELT

Often confused with the sprat, the smelt is, in fact, a member of the salmon family and as such is far more delicate and less oily by nature. It is found in the Baltic and around Britain; another type is caught in the Gulf of St Lawrence. Its bones are so soft that it is often eaten whole. Smelt is available in winter, and is usually eaten deep-fried.

SPRAT

A rich, oily fish related to the herring and found on the coasts of Europe, the sprat or brisling is available fresh, canned or smoked (page 188) and can be barbecued, baked, fried or grilled. Smoked sprats packed in oil are a popular delicacy in northern and eastern Europe. Sprats are at their best in winter.

MACKEREL

Scomber is the true mackerel caught in the Atlantic and Mediterranean, although there are several related species. These include the chub or Spanish mackerel, the scad or horse mackerel and the Jack mackerel, amberjack and pompano of American and south-east Asian waters. A fatty, dark-fleshed fish, it lends itself particularly well to barbecueing, baking, smoking (page 187) or grilling. It can be cooked in white wine or eaten raw with lemon juice or a similarly acid garnish to counteract its richness. It is available all year round.

HADDOCK

Usually smoked and known worldwide as Finnan haddock or Arbroath smokies (page 187), this north Atlantic fish is also available fresh or frozen all year round as both fillets and cutlets. Its firm flesh is particularly good sautéed with almonds.

Haddock

MONKFISH

A deep-sea fish found off the Mediterranean and Atlantic coasts of Europe, Africa and America, the monkfish or anglerfish has such an ugly, heavy head that usually only the tail is sold. Its flesh, which averages 1–2kg (2–4½lb), is firm, white and succulent and is said to resemble lobster in taste. It can be poached, baked, steamed, fried or grilled and is excellent served hot with a butter sauce such as *choron* or Hollandaise, or cold with rich mayonnaise. Alternatively, it can be cubed, battered and deep-fried with tartare sauce.

COLEY

A soft-fleshed white fish related to cod and pollack, coley (or coalfish, saithe or pollock) is fished extensively all year round in the North Sea and north Atlantic. Usually sold as fresh or frozen fillets, the flesh is pinkish-grey but becomes white when cooked. Though it is not suited to grilling, it can otherwise be cooked like cod, and is generally used in soups, fish pies and casseroles. It is usually salted in Scandinavia; in Germany, where it is known as *seelachs*, it is mostly smoked, and canned in oil.

Coley

Pollack

POLLACK

Pollack is caught all year round off north Atlantic coasts from Newfoundland to northern Europe and is available fresh in many local markets. It has fairly firm white flesh and can be prepared like fresh hake or cod, though its taste is considered slightly inferior. It is good used in mixed fish soups such as the French *bourride* or *chaudré*, in stews, or poached and served with a sauce like Creole sauce. In America the Alaska or walleye pollack is salted, dried or pickled.

Monkfish

Ling

LING

Ling or sea turbot, a member of the cod family, was once so popular it is was called "beef of the sea". Today, however, its soft white flesh is usually only available salted or smoked, rarely fresh. Tusk is closely related. When ling is found fresh, it should be cooked in the same ways as hake.

GREY MULLET

No relation to the smaller, firmer-fleshed red mullet, the grey mullet has a similar taste to sea bass. Available all year round, it can be bought whole or in fillets. The smaller fish are suitable for grilling; larger ones can be stuffed and baked, and the fillets can be poached or fried.

SEA BREAM

Found in the Atlantic, Pacific and Mediterranean, the bream family contains over 200 species of red, grey and bluish varieties weighing up to 1.6kg (3½lb). All have firm, white flesh though the red bream or daurade is reputed to have the best taste. Available all year round, it is usually bought fresh and whole. The larger fish can be casseroled, baked and stuffed; the smaller ones can be grilled whole. In the Mediterranean it is often served on a bed of dried fennel stalks.

Grey mullet

Whiting

WHITING

Whiting is a European seawater fish found off coasts from the Baltic to the Mediterranean. In America, the slightly larger silver hake – measuring 30–35cm (12–14in) – is also sometimes known by this name. Available fresh, frozen, smoked and salted, it can be fried, poached or grilled. It is available all year round.

Sea bream

HAKE

Varieties of hake are found almost all over the world. Hake is a large seawater fish of the cod family with slightly firmer white flesh and is available all year round. Small pieces of hake weighing 1–1.5kg (2–3lb) can be poached whole; larger hake are cut into fillets, steaks or cutlets and sold fresh or frozen, canned or smoked. These can be sautéed, fried or grilled, but they are usually poached in seasoned fish stock or *court bouillon* and served with lemon or herb butter. They are also poached, chilled and served with mayonnaise. Hake is an excellent fish to use in stews, casseroles and soups, and it can be used in any recipe that calls for cod or haddock. Salted hake is prepared and used in the same manner as salt cod.

Hake

Cod

COD

One of the world's most important food fishes, cod is found in the cold northern waters of the Atlantic, mainly off the coasts of New England, Newfoundland, Iceland and Norway. It has soft white flesh and can grow to a weight of 36kg (80lb). Codlings weighing under 1kg (2½lb) are sometimes called "scrod", and their flesh is firmer and sweeter. Available all year round, cod is sold whole when fresh and small (when it is particularly suited to poaching and baking), and in fresh or frozen fillets and steaks (which can be fried or grilled). It is also available salted, smoked and dried (page 185), in which form it is an important ingredient in Mediterranean and Caribbean cooking. Cod's roe is also sold fresh, canned and smoked (page 189).

SEA BASS

One of a large group of seawater fish which includes groupers, the sea bass (also called striped bass or loup de mer) is found in the north Atlantic and Mediterranean. Freshwater bass such as the large mouth, smallmouth, rock, white (or silver) and yellow bass are also available. Sea bass is a firm, white fish which can weigh up to 4.5kg (10lb) – although sea bass caught off the Pacific coast can weigh twice this – but the ones sold for cooking purposes are usually a good deal smaller. Usually bought fresh, sea bass is available whole or in steaks and fillets, all of which are suitable for poaching, stuffing with fresh or dried herbs and baking, or grilling.

Sea bass

RED MULLET

This 0.5–1kg (1–2lb) fish is native to the Atlantic, and now also found in the coastal waters of the Mediterranean. Available all year round, but at its best during the summer months, it has firm, tasty white flesh and is suitable for frying, baking or grilling. Many people prefer to leave the liver inside during cooking. It is also known as the sea woodcock, since, like the game bird, it is usually cooked and eaten whole and ungutted.

Red mullet

RED SNAPPER

This Gulf of Mexico fish can weigh up to 14kg (31lb) and has choice white creamy flesh. Those under 2.5kg (5lb) are usually baked whole and stuffed. Larger fish are cut into fillets or steaks and can be prepared in a variety of ways: grilled with lemon-butter, deep-fried and served with *rémoulade* sauce, sautéed, poached, or used in soups. Available all year round, it is usually sold fresh, although it can be bought frozen in America. Species such as grey snapper are also available, but they are smaller and inferior in taste.

Red snapper

OTHER SEAWATER FISH

ARGENTINE
There are several varieties, including the lesser argentine or silver smelt, the larger argentine or great silver smelt and the eastern, deep-sea argentine of Japan. All these small, silvery fish may be grilled or fried. They are found in the north Atlantic, Pacific and Mediterranean.

BLUE FISH
This is found on the Atlantic coast of America and in the Mediterranean. It can be grilled, fried, or baked with tomatoes, onions and herbs.

BONITO
Caught in Atlantic, Pacific and Mediterranean waters, bonito is of the tuna family, and is generally marketed cut into steaks. It is also salted.

CONGER EEL
Although it can be stuffed and baked, conger eel is best used for soups and stews. It is caught off the Atlantic coast of Europe, Africa and in the Mediterranean.

CROAKER
Caught off the eastern coast of North America, this fish is cooked in the same way as bass.

DOLPHIN FISH
This large golden fish, caught in warm waters, is also known as lampuga or dorado. It is usually bought as fillets or steaks, which can be grilled, baked or fried.

GARFISH
The slightly oily flesh of this fish (also called the garpike or sea eel) is sometimes compared to mackerel. It can be fried or grilled.

GROUPER
This is a common Mediterranean fish, especially

along the north African coast. The steaks are grilled or baked.

GULF HAKE
There are two varieties of gulf hake: the lesser or tadpole fish and the greater or forkbeard. The lesser is black-skinned; the greater resembles a small pollack. Both are cooked in the same ways as hake.

GURNARD
Also called the sea robin, this is an armour-plated, spiny fish, including the red gurnard and the ray gurnard. There are also several Mediterranean species. Gurnard can be baked or braised.

MEAGRE
The meagre is found in the Atlantic and Mediterranean. It can be prepared as for bass.

NEEDLEFISH
The needlefish, skipper or saury closely resembles the garfish, but is plumper. It can be fried or grilled.

OCEAN PERCH
This is caught in the Atlantic and the Mediterranean, though there is also a freshwater European variety. Other related species are the Norway haddock and the blue mouth. All are rather coarse, and best used in soups and chowders.

OPAH
Also known as kingfish, sunfish or moonfish, this is a large, beautifully coloured fish, with a plump oval body. It can be fried, and in Japan is eaten raw. It is available worldwide.

ROCKLING
There are several types of rockling found among the coasts of Europe and off Newfoundland. They should be cooked as for whiting.

SHAD
Shad are a larger, plumper type of herring found in the Atlantic, Mediterranean and Pacific, but mostly caught in rivers, where they come to spawn. Shad can be treated like herring, and are also smoked or canned in brine or oil.

STURGEON
The fish is famous for its roe, made into caviar (page 189), but less known for its flesh, which is also of good quality. It is caught in the Caspian, Black Sea and Danube.

SWORDFISH
Caught in warmer seas, the swordfish is usually sold as steaks, occasionally smoked. It may be baked or grilled.

TILEFISH
A large, deep-water fish which can weigh up to 14kg (31lb), this is best cooked like cod.

TUNA
Familiar to most people canned, tuna – which has several names including tunny and longfin – is also sold fresh, when it can be grilled, baked, or braised with wine, tomatoes and herbs. Tuna also features in *salade Niçoise*.

WEAVER
Caught in European shallow coastal waters, the spines and venom sacs of both the greater and lesser weaver have to be removed before cooking. They are used in *bouillabaisse*, grilled or deep-fried.

Flat Seawater Fish

BRILL
Found in the North Sea, the Mediterranean, the Black Sea and the Atlantic, it is available all year. It can be cut in halves, slices or fillets and lends itself to baking.

DAB
A small flatfish, the dab is caught in north Atlantic waters off the coast of Europe. The American sand dab is of finer quality. Sold whole or in fillets, it can be grilled or fried. The best season is April to November.

FLOUNDER
Similar to plaice, the flounder is caught in the Baltic and European Atlantic waters, and there are sub-species in the Mediterranean. (In America the word applies to several types of flatfish: blackback, fluke, grey and American lemon sole from Atlantic and south Pacific waters.) Available all year, it is sold fresh, frozen, and smoked. It can be fried or steamed, whole or in fillets.

Brill

Flounder

Dab

PLAICE
From the North Sea and north Atlantic, plaice is sold fresh and frozen, whole or in fillets. It can be fried or grilled and is available all year round.

Plaice

Skate

OTHER FLAT SEAWATER FISH
JOHN DORY
This is suited to recipes for turbot or sole and flourishes along the coasts of Europe and Africa. Related species can be found elsewhere.

SKATE
Many varieties are available in the Mediterranean, the north Atlantic and the Arctic. Sold fresh, only the "wings" are eaten. The principal season is from October to April. Skate can be poached and served with capers and a black butter sauce (a classic French recipe), fried or grilled.

Dover sole

TURBOT

These large inhabitants of the Atlantic coast of Europe, North Sea, Black Sea and Mediterranean are available all year. Sold whole or as steaks or fillets, turbot may be poached or baked; steaks may also be fried or grilled.

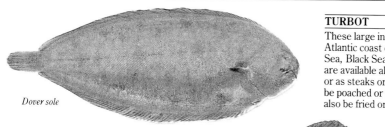

Turbot

DOVER SOLE

Dover sole is caught in European waters from southern Norway to the coast of North Africa, and in the Mediterranean, and is exported all over the world. Available fresh or frozen, it can be fried whole or divided into fillets. One of the finest of the smaller flatfish, it is available all year.

LEMON SOLE

A fish that is at its best from December to March. Although less tasty than the Dover sole, it is found in the same waters and can be cooked in the same way. Lemon sole is available fresh or frozen, whole or in fillets.

HALIBUT

The largest of the flatfish, varieties include the Greenland halibut, and sub-species. Halibut is caught in the north Atlantic from Newfoundland to Norway, in the Barents Sea and the north Pacific. Sold fresh, frozen, canned and smoked, it may be poached or baked.

Lemon sole

Halibut

Crustaceans

CRAYFISH

This freshwater crustacean is found mainly in France (where it is called *écrevisse*) in lakes and lowland streams. Fairly rare, but theoretically available all year round, it can be bought alive or cooked (as shown). When alive it is pale pink. It is especially popular in Scandinavia. It can be fried or boiled and is the main ingredient of Nantua sauce and the French *bisque d'écrevisse*.

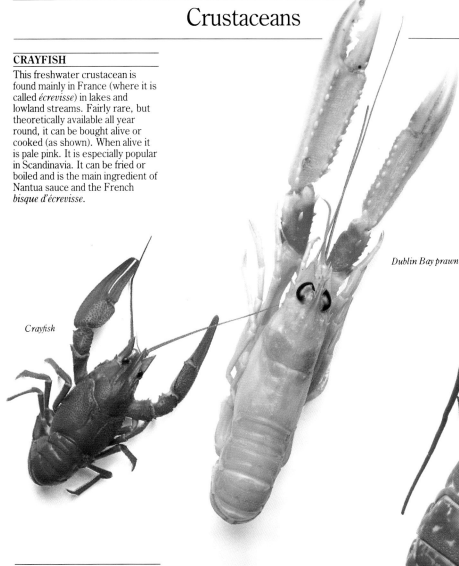

Dublin Bay prawn

Crayfish

DUBLIN BAY PRAWN

Known as Norway lobster in Atlantic countries and saltwater crayfish in America, these small crustaceans with claws were often found in the nets of fishing boats looking for other catch and were sold locally in Dublin markets. Today, they are scarce and much prized, and the early name has stuck; the Italians who fish them from the Adriatic call them scampi, and the French langoustine. They are sold fresh or frozen, alive or cooked (as shown), and with or without the shell. Their tails, prepared like shrimps, are usually served in rice dishes or salads, deep-fried or grilled. Prawns or monkfish can be substituted in most recipes that call for Dublin Bay prawns.

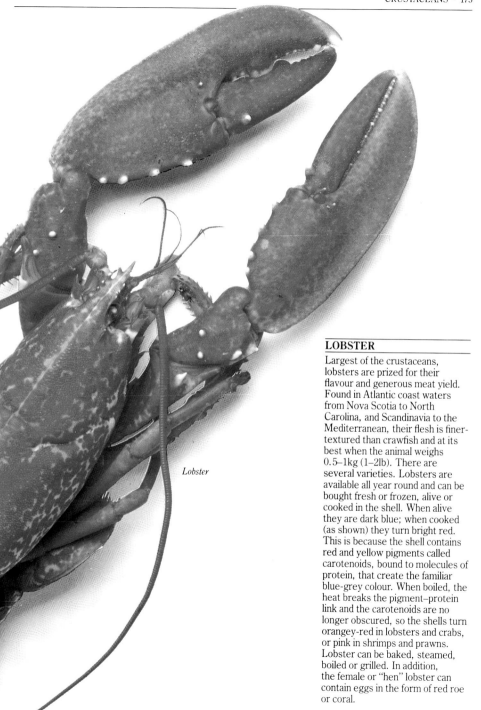

Lobster

LOBSTER

Largest of the crustaceans, lobsters are prized for their flavour and generous meat yield. Found in Atlantic coast waters from Nova Scotia to North Carolina, and Scandinavia to the Mediterranean, their flesh is finer-textured than crawfish and at its best when the animal weighs 0.5–1kg (1–2lb). There are several varieties. Lobsters are available all year round and can be bought fresh or frozen, alive or cooked in the shell. When alive they are dark blue; when cooked (as shown) they turn bright red. This is because the shell contains red and yellow pigments called carotenoids, bound to molecules of protein, that create the familiar blue-grey colour. When boiled, the heat breaks the pigment–protein link and the carotenoids are no longer obscured, so the shells turn orangey-red in lobsters and crabs, or pink in shrimps and prawns. Lobster can be baked, steamed, boiled or grilled. In addition, the female or "hen" lobster can contain eggs in the form of red roe or coral.

PRAWNS

The terms for these small clawless crustaceans vary from country to country, but in Europe "prawn" usually refers to those around 3–5cm (1½–2in) in length while in America "shrimp" is generally used for all sizes. There are several varieties of prawn, a crustacean indigenous to the Mediterranean but now also found in the Atlantic. It can be steamed, stewed or grilled, and is often used in salads. Available fresh or frozen, it is usually bought cooked, though it can also be bought uncooked, shelled or unshelled.

Cooked prawn

Uncooked prawn

Shrimps

SHRIMPS

There are several varieties of this tiny crustacean, which reaches a maximum of 7.5cm (3in) in length. They are often boiled on board ship or on reaching port as a precaution against spoilage. Pale pink when raw, shrimps are available fresh, frozen or canned.

CRAWFISH

Found worldwide in most temperate coastal waters, the crawfish, or langouste, has no claws and weighs 1.5–4kg (3–8½lb). Most of the flesh is contained in the tails and it can be used in any recipes calling for lobster. Available fresh or frozen, crawfish can be steamed or boiled. Unlike other crustaceans, it does not turn bright red when cooked.

Crawfish

Crabs

Many species of this crustacean are found in American and European coastal waters. Atlantic coast favourites are the blue, Jonah, rock and stone crabs, while the Dungeness and king crabs are renowned on the Pacific coast, especially towards Alaska. Popular European varieties are the blue, edible or common crab, the shore or green crab, and the spider crab.

Crabs shed their shells many times before reaching maturity and in some places, from mid-spring to mid-autumn, they are in demand fresh as young "peelers" or "soft-shells", when they have just emerged from their latest shell. At this point they are smaller, with more flavour, and so tender that almost every part of the crab can be eaten. Crab is also sold canned and frozen.

Spider crab

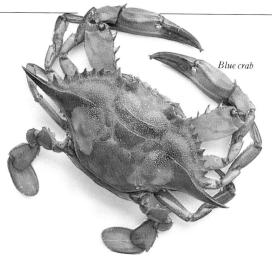

Blue crab

BLUE CRAB

Native to the east coast of America, where it is still popular, the blue crab is also found in the north and south Atlantic and the eastern Mediterranean. Available all year round, it can be bought as a soft-shelled crab in the summer. Otherwise it is sold alive, uncooked in the shell (as shown), cooked (with or without the shell), fresh, frozen and canned. Blue crab can be baked, steamed or boiled; when cooked it turns red.

Edible crab

SPIDER CRAB

Found in the south Atlantic and the Mediterranean, the spider crab is available all year round. It can be bought alive and uncooked in the shell or cooked. It can be baked, steamed or boiled, and turns bright red when cooked.

EDIBLE CRAB

Found in the Mediterranean and the Atlantic, this large crustacean has powerful claws – larger in the male than the female – which, as in other crabs, contain white meat (the shell contains dark meat). It can be bought alive, uncooked in the shell (as shown), cooked (with or without the shell), fresh and canned, and is also sometimes bought "dressed" (prepared ready for eating). Available all year round, it can be baked, steamed or boiled. When cooked it turns bright red.

Frogs' Legs and Molluscs

FROGS' LEGS

Prized for their delicate texture, the flesh tastes something like chicken. Only the hind legs of certain frogs (usually *Rana esculenta*) are used. Available canned, frozen or fresh, they are mostly sold ready-prepared. The tender white meat goes well with a variety of flavours, and is usually battered and deep-fried, or sautéed and served with sauce. Frogs' legs can also be stewed or grilled, and are often served with garlic butter. About 4 pairs should be allowed per person.

OCTOPUS

An eight-legged cephalopod mollusc found in all temperate waters, and prepared like squid, the flesh of the octopus should be beaten with a blunt object until no longer springy, and the suckers and ends of the legs removed before cooking. When longer than 20cm (8in), the head is usually discarded, but it can be cleaned, stuffed with the chopped legs, and stewed. Smaller ones can be coated in batter and fried whole.

Frogs' legs

CUTTLEFISH

Found in the Mediterranean, Adriatic and temperate oriental coastal waters, this is prepared like calamari and does not require beating. Those under 20cm (8in) can be sautéed whole in oil, or stuffed and poached. In the case of longer cuttlefish, the body can be cut away and discarded, the 10 legs blanched (with the outer skin peeled away) and stewed.

Octopus

Snail

Squid

Cuttlefish

SNAILS

The edible snail or escargot is a gastropod mollusc, gourmet fare since ancient Greece. Widely available canned or frozen, they are sometimes sold fresh. Slightly resilient in texture, they are usually served with garlic butter in reusable shells or dishes. Allow 6–8 per person.

SQUID

Found worldwide in temperate waters, the squid or calamari is a cephalopod mollusc. It is available fresh or frozen. Its ink sacs (only found in fresh animals) contain a dark brown liquid, often used as a basis for a sauce in which to cook it. Smaller squid can be sautéed, poached, boiled or grilled; larger ones are often stewed.

OTHER SEAFOOD

SEA URCHINS
Not a mollusc but an echino-derm, sea urchins are found off the coasts of America and Europe attached to coral. Salty-tasting, they have a texture like raw egg and a hard, spiny shell that must be cut open. They can be eaten raw or used to flavour omelettes and sauces.

Molluscs

CLAMS

Found the world over in the wet sand of freshwater streams and sea coasts, clams are often cultivated alongside oysters. In Europe clams are cultivated mostly in France and Portugal. They are, however, more popular in America where there are soft-shelled, which include round and long "razor" clams; and hard-shelled round ones – some types of hard-shells are shown. Larger, stronger-tasting hard-shells are usually reserved for chowders, while some of the smaller cherrystone varieties are eaten raw; the larger littleneck clams may be steamed open and served with melted butter.

MUSSELS

Closely related to the clam, mussels are found the world over on sea shores and estuaries. Varieties are usually specific to a certain area, but the blue mussel (*Mytilus edulis*) is found along the Atlantic coasts of both America and Europe where it is also bred commercially. Mussels are generally sold fresh in their shells and may be eaten raw, steamed in the famous dish *moules marinière*, or used in salads, soups and pâtés.

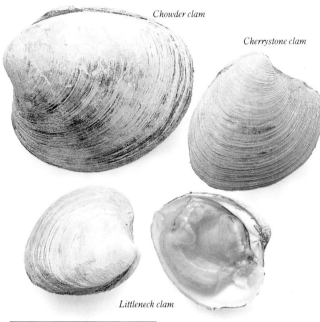

Chowder clam

Cherrystone clam

Littleneck clam

SCALLOP

Named for the fluted shape of their shells, scallops are commonly found along the European and American Atlantic coasts. There are many species but two basic types: the delicately flavoured small bay scallops and the larger deep sea scallops. Scallops can be grilled, floured and deep-fried, or poached and served in the shell with cream sauce, as *Coquilles Saint-Jacques*. In America only the white muscle is eaten; in Europe, as in Britain, the roe is eaten too.

Mussel

Scallop

COCKLES

About 2.5cm (1in) long, cockles are round marine molluscs mostly consumed in Europe. They are found in the Mediterranean, Baltic and north-west Atlantic. Unless by the sea, when they are fresh and may be eaten raw, cockles are sold ready-cooked, shelled and packed in ice, or canned, pickled in vinegar. They are good in salads, soups, and can be used in pasta dishes.

OYSTERS

There are many varieties of this mollusc, which is found in Mediterranean, Atlantic and Pacific waters, all of them varying in size and shade of brown. The recommended way of eating oysters is raw, straight from the half-shell complete with juices. If served hot, they should be only lightly cooked. The giant American Pacific oyster can be more than double the size of the European varieties. They are usually not sold in the summer months when spawning makes them thin and less succulent.

WINKLES

A darkish brown shell is most common. Although available on both sides of the Atlantic, it is much more popular in Britain than America. Winkles are usually cooked in boiling salted water and may be served with a sauce.

WHELKS

Generally with a brownish or greyish shell, this is found on both sides of the Atlantic Ocean, although the North American variety is inclined to be much larger. Whelks are usually cooked in a covered pot in a little water but some are sold canned and precooked or pickled.

OTHER MOLLUSCS

CONCH

A pink-shelled, warm-water mollusc eaten mostly in Florida and the Caribbean islands. It has a similar flavour and texture to scallops. Usually marinated and tenderized before cooking, it is used in salads and chowders.

LIMPETS

Marine molluscs with a single tent-like shell, limpets cling to rocks around the world at low tide. Usually 2.5–5cm (1–2in) across, they can be eaten raw, or cooked and used in soups and oyster dishes.

Cockle

Winkle

Whelk

Portuguese oyster

European oyster

PRESERVED FISH

THE PROCESS OF CURING foods, and thus preserving them, by methods of drying, smoking and salting, was a discovery of major importance and was, no doubt, the result of observing natural phenomena – for example, fish trapped in coastal salt deposits by the tidal flow would have been found to be preserved.

Methods of preserving
Unsalted fish are cleaned, headed and gutted, tied in pairs, and dried for about six weeks in a current of air. Heavy salt-cured fish are headed and gutted and their backbones removed. The split fish are piled in layers with a mixture of coarse and fine salt between each layer, about 15kg (33lb) of salt to every 50kg (110lb) of fish. They are then hung in a current of air, or machine-dried. Light-cured fish are headed, gutted, washed and split, and about one-third of the fish is salted with dry salt, using 4–5kg (9–11lb) of salt to every 50kg (110lb) of fish. The fish are laid in tubs until the juices dissolve the salt and form brine, in which the fish remain for two to three days. They are then taken out of the brine solution and sun- or machine-dried.

Pickled-cured fish are cleaned, eviscerated, packed with plenty of salt into wooden barrels and left for ten days to allow shrinkage to take place. The juices and salt form a brownish liquid called "blood pickle", which is drawn off and then poured back to top up the barrel. The lid is then sealed and the barrel of fish ready for storage.

Anchovies are cleaned, dry-salted, pressed to remove fat, and sprayed with their own brine for several months at room temperature. Sardines are headed and gutted, then immersed in brine for about 15 minutes before being tunnel-dried.

There are two main types of smoke cure: cold-smoking, below 30°C (85°F), and hot-smoking, at 120°C (250°F), which also cooks the fish. Smoke is generated in kilns by sawdust, which is regularly recharged to give uniformity to the product. In both cases, fish are normally given a preliminary brine bath before smoking.

Fish roes
The ova or eggs of the female fish are called "roe", and that of the male fish "milt". Both are normally eaten smoked. The best roes come from the sturgeon and salmon but others commonly available include those of the carp, cod, pike-perch, grey mullet and herring. The roe of the sturgeon, caviar, is the most highly prized and, consequently, the most expensive.

Preserved fish in the kitchen
Dried fish, such as lutefisk and salt cod, require a preliminary soaking in water for a day, to soften the fish and remove some of the salt. Salt cod, or *bacalao*, common in the Mediterranean where it is sold on market stalls straight from the barrel, is transformed into such dishes as the French *brandade de morue*. In Spain and Portugal it is generally served braised, stewed or fried. It can also be eaten raw in salads.

Smoked fish may be pounded to make a savoury paste or butter or used in pâtés. It also makes a pleasing addition to soufflés. Smoked fish have limited keeping properties that vary according to type. As a general guide, they will keep for up to five days at normal temperatures and up to fourteen days at temperatures below normal.

Pickled and canned fish, once opened, should be refrigerated if they are not to be consumed at once. Anchovies are used in salads and sauces, in pizza, and the Provençal *pissaladière*, in anchovy butter and paste. In Scandinavia, pickled fish are commonly used in everyday cooking and form an integral part of the traditional *smorgasbord*.

Dried Fish

BOMBAY DUCK

Despite its name, this is really an unsalted, sun-dried fish. In its fresh state it is from a long, silvery species called "bummalao", which is native to India, where it is often eaten fresh. Once dried, Bombay duck or bombil loses its fishy taste and adopts instead a curious flavour, rather like burnt oil or fat. It is used to flavour curries, or may be fried or pickled.

BACALAO

This is salted and dried cod. The fresh fish is caught in the north Atlantic, and then imported by European countries (often already dried). It can be bought either whole, as shown, or cut up in pieces, and is much used in Iberian cookery for stews and casseroles, one of the most famous of which is *bacalao a la vizcaina*. It needs overnight soaking before use.

Bombay duck

SHARK'S FIN

The dried cartilage of a shark's fin, this is much used in oriental cookery, where it is considered a delicacy. It requires overnight soaking before use and is best known as the basic ingredient for shark's fin soup.

Shark's fin

Bacalao

OTHER DRIED FISH

KATSUOBOSHI
A Japanese dried fish which can also be smoked.

LUTEFISK
The reconstituted unsalted cod from Norway known as stockfish or stockfisk. It is usually prepared in the early spring. In Sweden there is a smaller version made with dried ling.

MIGAKI-NISHIN
From Japan, this is a mixture of dried fish fillets and abalone.

Smoked Fish

KIPPERS

The most common smoked
herring, kippers should be plump,
juicy and properly smoked, not
dyed to disguise inadequate
treatment, as is often the case.
Kippers are sold whole – usually in
pairs – or as fillets, which are often
available frozen. They can be used
to make pâté, and otherwise can
be grilled. They are part of the
traditional English breakfast.

Kipper

Smoked trout

Buckling

SMOKED TROUT

Both the rainbow and the brown
trout can be smoked, but the
rainbow trout is normally used.
The fish are gutted with the head
left on, brined, speared on rods,
cold-smoked and then hot-smoked
(at a temperature of over 26°C
– 80°F). Smoked trout requires no
cooking and is usually served as
an appetizer with thinly sliced
brown bread and butter and
lemon wedges.

SMOKED SALMON

The unrivalled king of all smoked
fish, this is usually served as an
appetizer, in paper-thin slices
accompanied by wedges of lemon.
The fish are headed, gutted and
filleted, and string is passed
through the lug bones to facilitate
hanging. The skin is scored with a
sharp knife, and the fillets dry-
salted with fine salt. Some curers
use traditional mixtures such as
brown sugar, saltpetre and rum.
The salmon is washed in cold
water before being hung to dry
for a day, then cold-smoked.

BUCKLING

Of the many versions of smoked
herring, this is undoubtedly the
best. Originally from Schleswig-
Holstein in Germany, it is also
prepared in Britain, the
Netherlands and Norway. It is
brined and hot-smoked, requires
no cooking, and is eaten cold in
the same way as smoked trout.

Smoked mackerel

Smoked salmon

FINNAN HADDIE

Originally from the village of Finnan in Aberdeenshire, Scotland, from which it takes its name (it is also called findon haddie or smoked haddock), this haddock is traditionally cured over peat smoke. The fish is headed, gutted, split down the backbone and immersed in brine. Dyes are not added. After this, it is threaded onto spears, the protein gloss is allowed to develop, and then it is smoked. It can be eaten as it is, served with a rich egg sauce, or flaked and used as an omelette filling. It is also an ingredient of kedgeree, the classic English breakfast dish of smoked fish, eggs and rice.

Finnan haddie

Arbroath smokie

SMOKED EEL

A good smoked eel is a succulent delicacy, so smooth and buttery in texture that it becomes virtually spreadable. Dutch smoked eels are acknowledged to be among the best. The eel is gutted, headed and brined, and dry-salted. It is then washed, dipped in boiling water, and hung up to smoke.

ARBROATH SMOKIE

Another version of smoked haddock from the east coast of Scotland, this is usually headed and gutted but otherwise left whole. Whiting may also be used. The fish are headed and gutted, but not split, and tied in pairs. Arbroath smokies are usually served as an appetizer.

Smoked eel

SMOKED MACKEREL

Smoking intensifies the already rich, strong taste of the mackerel. It is ready for eating and is usually used for hors d'oeuvres, served with lemon wedges.

OTHER SMOKED FISH

BLOATER

First developed at Yarmouth England, in 1835, bloaters, which are prepared whole, are said to owe their special flavour to the activity of gut enzymes. The fish are dry-salted for about 12 hours, washed to remove surplus salt, threaded on metal "speats", and stacked in the kiln to smoke.

GLASGOW PALE

These are called "pales" because they are lightly smoked and undyed. They are first split and gutted, then brined and smoked.

RED HERRING

This is named for the colour its skin turns after smoking. The whole fish is dry-salted or heavily brined, and smoked intermittently.

Smoked Fish and Roes

Smoked sturgeon

SMOKED STURGEON

This is a delicacy regarded as a sort of *objet d'art* of the gourmet world – very expensive and yet worth every effort to track down! It should be thinly sliced and served as an appetizer.

SMOKED HALIBUT

Usually it is the Greenland halibut which is smoked; it is quite a fatty fish and smoking seems to suit it. Serving suggestions include slices of the fish on open sandwiches, accompanied by lemon wedges.

SMOKED SPRAT

A German variety of sprat is smoked whole and eaten in the traditional German way with a dark rye bread and butter. The most famous are the Kieler Sprotten from the port of Kiel in Germany. The fish are washed and brined.

Smoked halibut

Smoked sprat

SOFT HERRING ROE

Sperm of the male fish, herring roe has a creamy smooth texture. It is often fried in butter and served with lemon slices. A hard variety is also available, though it is quite scarce.

Soft herring roe

SEVRUGA CAVIAR

Caviar is called after the species of sturgeon providing it. This one is the smallest-grained from the small Caspian sturgeon, and is sold fresh and pressed. Pressed caviar is made from damaged eggs, salted and crushed together.

BELUGA CAVIAR

The largest-grained caviar, and the most expensive, comes from the large Caspian sturgeon, which have been known to live for over 70 years, and reach a length of 4m (12ft). It is available fresh, pasteurized and pressed.

COD'S ROE

Also available uncooked and boiled, it is here shown smoked and in this form can be used to make a variety of *taramasalata*, the Greek dip. Boiled roe can be fried or grilled.

Pressed sevruga caviar

Fresh sevruga caviar

Fresh beluga caviar

Pressed beluga caviar

Pasteurized beluga caviar

LUMPFISH ROE

Lumpfish roe is usually from Iceland and Denmark and there are both orange and black varieties. The black variety is dyed artificially to resemble the superior and more expensive Beluga caviar.

Black lumpfish roe

Cod's roe

Orange lumpfish roe

SALMON ROE

Eaten in the same way as caviar, this is sometimes referred to as caviar, though the word should really apply only to sturgeon roe.

Salmon roe

OTHER ROES

BOTARGO CAVIAR
This Sardinian delicacy is made from compressed and salted mullet roe.

OSETR CAVIAR
A caviar taken from the Danube sturgeon, a fish also found in the Caspian Sea.

ROES
Japanese preserved roes include: hontarako, a salted and dried cod's roe; karasumi, made from the roe of the grey mullet or tuna, salted, pressed and dried; and tarako or momojiko, the salted roe of the Alaskan pollack.

Seaweeds and Canned and Pickled Fish

JELLYFISH SEAWEED

Although sold as a seaweed and usually thought of as such, these are, in fact, strips of jellyfish which have been dried and salted. It is used in China, Japan and south-east Asia.

Jellyfish seaweed

DULSE

A coarse northern seaweed which, when fresh, is red, dulse is harvested along the coasts of the British Isles, Iceland and parts of Canada. Usually sold dried, it can be cooked, like spinach, used to flavour soups, or chewed like chewing gum.

Dulse

CANNED ANCHOVY

A tiny, very fatty fish with a powerful flavour, it is cured by having most of its fat content removed by pressure and fermentation. Anchovies are usually filleted, brined and then preserved in oil, though they are also available salted in jars. Very strong-tasting, they are used in canapés, pastes, pizza toppings, *salade Niçoise*, patum peperium (page 69) and anchovy butter.

Canned anchovy

KOMBU

A type of dried kelp which is particularly popular in Japan, where it is used to make the soup stock *dashi* and infused to make a tisane. It should be washed before use.

Kombu

MEKABU

A Japanese lobe-leaf seaweed similar to wakame (the traditional Japanese seaweed), this is available in the form of curled, dried strands. Used mainly in soups and salads and as a garnish, it should be soaked before use.

LAVER

This seaweed has been gathered along the coasts of Britain and Eire for centuries. One type, sea lettuce, is used in salads, sauces and soups. A fine, silky plant, it is mashed and boiled and then sold as laverbread. The Japanese laver *Porphyra tenera* is pressed and dried to a thin, flexible, dark-brown sheet called nori, shown here. It is used in sauces, soups, sandwiches and *sushi*, a dish of rice and fish, and also as a garnish for other dishes.

CARRAGEEN MOSS

This seaweed, also known as Irish moss, is hand-raked on the coasts of northern Europe and New England. A gum similar to agar-agar is extracted from it, and it is also cooked and eaten as a vegetable which is very like spinach. In Scotland it is made into a type of milk jelly.

Carrageen moss

Mekabu

Laver

Canned tuna

CANNED TUNA

Tuna is usually preserved in oil, brine or water. Its firm flesh makes it useful in sandwiches, cold dishes and casseroles.

Canned sardine

CANNED SARDINE

These small fish of the herring family (page 164) are usually canned whole, in oil (as shown) or tomato sauce. The scales are left on, but the fish is thoroughly gutted before processing. The preserving process softens the bones, which means that they can be eaten as they are. Their main use is in appetizers and sandwiches, and they may be fried in peanut oil or steamed.

ROLLMOP HERRING

The raw herring is beheaded, gutted, boned and left in the form of double fillets. It is then spread out flat, rolled up around pieces of pickled cucumber or onion and marinaded in a spiced vinegar. After several days in the marinade it is ready for eating with dark bread and butter.

Whole matjes herring

Rollmop herring

Matjes herring fillet

MATJES HERRING

This is a young Netherlands herring caught in the spring, before it becomes too fatty. It is lightly salted and barrel-stored for a few days only, just sufficient to ferment the gut enzymes. It is usually bought whole and salted from the barrel, though salted fillets are also available. Both should be soaked in water before use.

OTHER PRESERVED FISH AND FISH PRODUCTS

BAGOONG
This shrimp paste from the Philippines may also be made from small fish. These are cleaned, mixed with salt in the proportion of 1 part salt to 3 parts fish, pressed into vats and coloured with dyes. Nam pla, from Thailand, is a distant cousin.

BISMARCK HERRING
A German herring from the Baltic which is simply filleted and marinaded in vinegar with onion rings for 2–3 days.

NUOC-MAM
A clear brown liquid with a cheesy smell and salty taste, this is prepared in Vietnam from small fish such as the clupeids (herring and sprats).

The whole fish are pressed into tubs, salted and tightly sealed, and left for about 12 weeks before the liquid is drained off. Salting is heavy, and caramel, molasses, rice or boiled corn may be added as extra flavourings. Petis and nuoc-mam roc are variations.

OYSTERS
Oysters are steamed, brined, dipped in oil, then hot-smoked before being packed in oil in sterilized jars.

PRAHOC
A fish paste from Cambodia, prahoc is made with eviscerated fish which are scaled, washed and pressed under banana leaves. The fish are then mixed with coarse salt

and sun-dried in order to lose some of their moisture, before being pounded to a paste. The product is then left to ferment.

TRASSI
Also called trasi udang, this is a cured shrimp paste made in Sumatra from shrimps mixed with 10–15 per cent salt. The mixture is spread out in the sun for a few days, and it is then kneaded and dyes are added until a sticky red mass is obtained. Other ingredients may be included – potato peel, for example, and rice bran. Mature trassi keeps indefinitely and when cooked and mixed with chilli peppers becomes *sambal goreng*, a popular condiment.

POULTRY AND GAME

THE WORD "POULTRY" IS used to describe all domestic birds which are bred especially for the table, and covers chickens, turkeys, ducks, geese, guinea fowl and domestic pigeons or squabs. Over the years, poultry farming has developed enormously. Selective breeding for meat and eggs has led to automated production techniques, and today poultry meat is more popular than the meat from any other animal or bird.

Nowadays chickens are readily available both fresh and frozen. Supermarkets usually sell packaged birds by oven-ready weight, though they may be artificially injected with water, but a fresh bird bought from a butcher is likely to be sold at plucked, not drawn, weight. A larger bird generally is better value, because the proportion of meat to bone is higher. Poultry can also be bought in individual portions, and chicken and turkey are frequently smoked as gourmet items (page 214).

Cooking poultry

Chicken is a particularly delicate meat, and needs considerate cooking since it has a rapid rate of shrinkage in high heat, but much depends on the age of the bird: tender young poultry can be barbecued, fried, grilled or roasted; old birds need long, slow braising or stewing. Traditional dishes such as Scottish cock-a-leekie and French *coq au vin* are unlikely to have been prepared with cockerels, but with capons or boiling fowl. The age and type of poultry therefore determines the method and the recipe. When frying chicken, cut-up portions should be cooked in deep fat at 148–62°C (300–25°F) in a thick-bottomed pan for about 20 to 25 minutes. Grilled chicken pieces need to be cooked at a distance of 17–22cm (7–9in) from the source of heat until well-browned and tender.

To roast a chicken, brush with oil or fat and, if it is to be stuffed, pack the stuffing loosely just before roasting; tightly packed stuffing will go soggy. Never stuff in advance; a chicken that, for convenience, has been stuffed the previous day may encourage bacterial activity. Birds that are roasted in aluminium foil or in a ceramic "chicken brick" are in fact cooked by steam and not by radiant heat, and will need a final 20 to 30 minutes browning, uncovered. As a general guide, a 1kg (2–2½lb) broiler will take 1 to 1¼ hours at 200°C (400°F), Gas 6. To test whether the bird is cooked, pierce the thigh or drumstick to the bone with a sharp pointed knife or fork. If the juices run clear and free of blood, or if the joints sever easily when pulled, the chicken is ready for serving.

Turkeys are usually roasted, and a meat thermometer will be a useful aid to this: a 5.5–8kg (12–17lb) bird will take about 3 to 3¾ hours uncovered, or until a meat thermometer inserted in the leg shows 85°C (185°F). A turkey of comparable weight, covered with foil and roasted at 230°C (450°F), Gas 8, cooks in 2½ to 3 hours. To roast a duck or goose, pierce the skin in several places during cooking to allow the excess fat to run off into the pan. A 1.5–2.5kg (3–5½lb) duck takes 2½ to 3 hours, uncovered, at 170°C (325°F), Gas 3, a goose of 2–3.5kg (4½–8lb) needs 2¾ to 3½ hours at 170°C (325°F), Gas 3.

When roasting guinea fowl, choose young birds of 675g (1½lb). Older (and probably tougher) birds of 1–1.5kg (2½–3lb) are more suited to casserole cooking and braising. A 675g (1½lb) bird will need about 1½ hours at 180°C (350°F). Squab should be roasted for about 45 minutes – at 220°C (425°F), Gas 7, for the first 20 minutes and at 180°C (350°F), Gas 4, for the final 25 minutes. Guinea fowl and squab are roasted covered with strips of bacon or pork rind to stop the breasts drying out.

Storing poultry

Fresh, uncooked poultry should be used within two or three days of purchasing provided it has been kept in a refrigerator. Once cooked it should be kept in the refrigerator, loosely wrapped, and eaten within a few days. The meat can also be frozen, if separated from the stuffing and the gravy.

When thawing frozen poultry, it is best to do so gradually in a refrigerator, allowing about 15 hours for a 1.5kg (3lb) bird; alternatively it can be thawed by placing the bird in a sink and covering it with cold water (the water should be changed regularly until the bird thaws).

GAME

For culinary purposes, the word "game" is used to describe all birds and animals which are hunted for food, and although several types are now being reared domestically, they are still classified as game.

Basically, game is divided into two types: feathered and furred. Hares are decidedly game animals, but many people don't think of rabbits and pigeons as game, even though they are hunted for food. Game is further distinguished by the characteristic texture and taste of its meat, which differs from that of poultry and farmyard animals: it is generally darker, stronger-tasting and often tougher.

Wild animals, because of their diet and general lifestyle, have certain enzymes in their tissues which break down or metabolize meat proteins. These enzymes, which become active about 24 hours after the animal has been killed, soften the meat, making it gelatinous and palatable, and giving it that "gamey" flavour. While the enzymes are at work, the game carcass hosts anerobes, micro-organisms which also help to break down the protein, forming non-toxic ptomaines. Provided that there are no dangerous staphylococci present, the bacteria that affect game meat are harmless; it is curious that game and certain types of fish can be safely eaten and enjoyed at a stage of advanced putrefaction, when many white meats, notably pork, are positively dangerous. Although hanging game is traditional, it is a mistake to think that game must be mature, and there is historical evidence to suggest that it may not always have been eaten when well matured.

Choosing game

The most important factor when buying game is to know its age, since this will determine how to cook it. Although they are not infallible, there are some guidelines when buying young birds. Look for clean and soft-textured feet, pliable breastbones and rounded spurs. Young partridges have a pointed flight feather (the first large feather of the wing), while in older birds the feather is rounded. When buying game animals, bear in mind that the ears of young hares and rabbits split easily.

Hanging game

Game bought from a dealer will probably have been correctly prepared and hung, but you can, of course, order in advance and specify your requirements. Here are some approximate hanging times for freshly killed game: grouse, 3 to 4 days; pheasant, 6 to 14 days; partridge, 7 to 8 days; wood-pigeon, 2 to 3 days; snipe and woodcock, 7 to 10 days; hare and rabbit, 2 to 3 days; venison and boar, up to 3 weeks. Quail does not need to be hung at all.

Game should be hung in a cool, dry, airy place and protected from flies. Although there is no real need to hang game if you object to the taste, as a general rule, you should hang a carcass until you detect the first whiff of tainting – in birds this is around the crop or vent. Game is left intact during hanging, except venison, hares and rabbits, which may be "paunched" or gutted straight away.

In Britain, birds are usually hung by their heads, and rabbits and (particularly) hares with the head down. The blood of hares is usually collected in a receptacle as it drains off, and is used to thicken the sauce in jugged hare.

Cooking game

Game meat responds best to roasting. Young game birds, in particular, should be roasted, and it is traditional to leave them unstuffed. In practice, however, large birds such as pheasant and ptarmigan may be stuffed with seasoned ground beef, which helps to keep the flesh moist. Older, tougher game should be casseroled, braised or made into pies, pâtés and terrines. Marinading in a mixture of oil, vinegar, wine or beer, herbs and spices helps to make meat tender and enhances the taste.

The oven should be set at 200°C (400°F), Gas 6, for the first 10 minutes, then at 180°C (350°F), Gas 4, for the following times: grouse, 30 minutes; partridge, 30 minutes; pheasant, 45 minutes; pigeon, 60 minutes; ptarmigan, 45 minutes; quail, 25 minutes; snipe, 45 minutes; duck, 45 minutes; woodcock, 30 minutes. Roast a hare or a young rabbit at about 220°C (425°F), Gas 7, for about 45 minutes; venison should be roasted at 220°C (425°F), Gas 7, for 20 to 25 minutes, then at 180°C (350°F), Gas 4, according to the weight – a haunch takes about 1½ to 2 hours.

Poultry

STEWING or BOILING CHICKEN

A mature bird weighing 1–3kg (2½–6½lb), this is quite tasty but requires long, gentle cooking to soften its relatively tough flesh. The age of a bird is often determined by the state of its breastbone: in an older chicken the bone is hard and rigid. Stewing chickens are used in fricassees, in main dish pies, for ballottines and galantines and, most importantly, for soup.

Stewing or boiling chicken

Roasting chicken

ROASTING CHICKEN

A young cockerel or hen about 12 weeks old which weighs up to 3kg (6½lb). Sometimes larger birds up to 4.5kg (10lb) are available – these are older birds, of no more than 20 weeks of age. Roasting chickens are equally good cooked in an oven or on a rotisserie, and may be cut up for barbecueing.

Capon

CAPON

A young cockerel which has been castrated and specially fattened, the capon is bred for its meat. From 2.7–4.5kg (6–10lb) in weight, they are larger than most chickens. Capons are noted for their tenderness and have a large proportion of white meat to dark. They are usually roasted but can be prepared in the same ways as other chickens.

POUSSIN

This is a baby or young chicken weighing from 450–900g (1–2lb). The bird should be old enough to have a firm flesh and good taste. The term "poussin" also describes a very small chicken of the Hamburg type. Poussins are similar in appearance to Rock Cornish Game Hens, which are a cross between Cornish and White Rock chickens. Poussins have delicate flesh and can be roasted, baked, sautéed or grilled. One serving usually consists of an entire bird.

Poussin

DUCK (*Anas,* spp.)

Most of the duck eaten is the domestic variety, shown here. Ducks have a big frame and a high fat content, but not a great deal of meat. On the other hand, there is little wastage because the carcasses make an excellent soup stock and the livers are often used in pâtés. The French and Chinese are noted for their duck recipes. In the French dish *caneton à l'orange,* the acidity of the orange provides a perfect complement to the bird's richness. Ducks are available fresh or frozen and, on average, weigh around 1.8–2.7kg (4–6lb). Ducklings weigh 1.5–1.8kg (3½–4lb) and are at their best roasted.

Duck

TURKEY (*Meleagris,* spp.)

Today's domesticated bird is a descendant of the wild turkey, native to Mexico. Nowadays it is available throughout the year and considered a traditional Christmas bird, and in America is also served at Thanksgiving. Although the cock is larger than the hen, the latter is often more tender. Varieties include the traditional English Norfolk Black. Turkeys are sold whole or in pieces, and fresh or frozen. Their weight can range from 2.7 to 13.5kg (6 to 30lb), though the usual weight is from 4.5 to 6.5kg (10 to 14½lb). The younger birds are best used for roasting; older ones are usually used in stews and soups. Some birds are bred with heavy breasts and small bone structure to speed up cooking and help eliminate dryness.

Turkey

GUINEA FOWL (*Numida,* spp.)

Originally, it is believed, these birds came from Africa. Related to the pheasant, they were once considered game birds, but they have been reared domestically for centuries in many parts of the world. Like game, they are best hung for two or three days before plucking, dressing and cooking. Their flesh is tender (the hens more so than the cocks) with a gaminess that is reminiscent of pheasant, and is suitable for roasting, casseroles, braising, and, in general, any recipe suitable for pheasant.

GOOSE (*Anas,* spp.)

There are many varieties, including the Emden goose, originating in Germany and the Low Countries, the Chinese goose, the Roman and Brecon Buff, all of which are reared for Christmas and Michaelmas. The French Toulouse goose is bred for its contribution to *pâté de foie gras*, the Strasburg for *confit d'oie* (cut-up pieces of goose preserved in goose fat). The larger domestic bird is sometimes too tough and usually too fatty to eat, but the younger bird (shown here) is delicate and tender. While table geese are expensive and their meat yield low by comparison to the turkey, goose, with its slightly gamey flavour, is considered by many to be the best poultry. Available fresh or frozen, a goose usually weighs between 2.5 and 5.5kg (6 and 12lb), and is best roasted. The goose and gander are similar in appearance and size. When prepared for the oven, the word goose is applied to both.

Goose

OTHER POULTRY

SQUAB
A squab is a young pigeon especially bred for the table. It is normally about 4 weeks old, and weighs between 350 and 675g (12 and 24oz). Squab is drawn and prepared in the same way as other domesticated birds. It is tender, and can be roasted, sautéed, grilled or stewed.

Guinea fowl

Feathered Game

Woodcock

Grouse

GROUSE

Grouse is considered to be the most delicious of the game birds. The grouse family includes many varieties: the red grouse of Scotland (shown here), the blackcock or black grouse, the capercaillie or wood grouse, and the ptarmigan of northern Europe. There are no true grouse in North America, but the sage grouse, rugged grouse and prairie chicken are close relatives. Like other game birds, its availability is limited by hunting seasons. Young birds are suitable for roasting or grilling, while older birds can be casseroled or braised successfully. One bird is served per person.

WOODCOCK

Native to Europe and America, woodcock is now found worldwide, but its availability is often limited by hunting seasons. Woodcock should be well hung but the skin should remain intact on plucking. One woodcock should be served for each person. It is suitable for roasting, braising or grilling; like its relative, the snipe, if roasted, it is not drawn or decapitated, although the gizzard is removed.

Snipe

Partridge

Quail

SNIPE

This bird, native to Europe, is subject to the same availability restrictions as most other game birds. It is best roasted, although it is so small it can also be cooked under the grill. It is often cooked with its entrails, which are regarded as a delicacy. One bird should be allowed per person.

PARTRIDGE

The type shown is native to Europe, but there are many other varieties, all related to the pheasant. Its availability is restricted by hunting seasons. Partridges can be roasted, stewed, braised or casseroled. Young birds especially should be roasted and served with their own gravy as a sauce – when roasting, one bird should be allowed per person. In France, it is cooked with cabbage and other vegetables and made into a decorative mould called a *chartreuse*.

QUAIL

Native to the Middle East, the quail is a migratory game bird that, like the partridge, is related to the pheasant. Popular varieties include the Californian quail and the European quail, which is reared on quail farms and sold as a gourmet item to restaurants. Available all year round, it can be roasted, sautéed or grilled, and features in many *haute cuisine* dishes, especially when it is served in aspic. Since birds are small, allow at least one per person when serving.

Feathered and Furred Game

DUCK

Originally from the northern hemisphere, the most famous and largest of the wild ducks is the mallard (the male is shown), from which all domestic varieties are descended. There are several other types, including teal (one of the smallest wild ducks, and highly regarded by gourmets), widgeon, shoveller, pochard and scaup. It can be bought fresh (though its availability is restricted by hunting seasons), or frozen. It is excellent for roasting and one bird will serve two or three people.

Hen pheasant

Cock pheasant

Duck

PHEASANT

Native to China, but now found all over the northern hemisphere, the cock and hen pheasant are often sold together as a brace. Though the hen pheasant is considered to be more tender, it will only serve about three people, whereas the cock will serve four. Perhaps the most popular game bird, it responds well to hanging. Bought fresh (though its availability is restricted by hunting seasons) or frozen, it is excellent for roasting, stewing, braising and serving *en papillote*. Farm-reared birds are also sold, oven-ready, either fresh or frozen.

HARE

Originally from Europe, the hare is now found worldwide, but its availability is restricted by hunting seasons. Though they belong to the same family as rabbits, hares are "gamier". They are also larger, and their flesh is darker and stronger-tasting. Young hares do not need hanging and can be fresh roasted; older animals of two

Rabbit

Hare

OTHER FEATHERED AND FURRED GAME

BEAR
The European bear (*Ursus arctus*) and the American bear (*Ursus americanus*) are occasionally enjoyed for their steaks, but bear paws are considered to be the prime part. Bear is most popular in German and Russian cooking.

BOAR
The European wild boar (*Sus scrofa*), although plentiful on the Continent and in some parts of America, is still best known for its medieval associations. Only the meat of the young boar is really tender; older animals need to be hung for two or three days, and the flesh marinaded before cooking. It is usually roasted, and is popular in German and Russian cooking.

DEER
The meat of any animal from the deer or Cervidae family is called "venison". It is one of the most popular game meats, but needs to be hung and marinaded, unless the animal is very young. The best meat is taken from the buck in its second year, and the most popular cut is the haunch, although the loin and fillets also make good eating. Deer in general, and elk (*Alces alces*) in particular, are eaten for their meat and liver, while smoked elk tongue is a delicacy. Young, tender venison may be grilled or larded with pork fat and roasted (some cooks pour soured cream over the meat before roasting).

PIGEON
Pigeon is sometimes tough, and therefore best suited for stewing or braising. In North Africa, pigeons feature in *bstilla*, a delicate pie made with fine pastry, sugar and nuts.

RABBIT
Originally from Africa, wild rabbits are now found worldwide, but their availability, unlike that of domestic rabbits, is restricted by hunting seasons. The meat is generally tender, but the animals need to be drawn (gutted) and hung for four to five days. Curiously, it has never become an *haute cuisine* ingredient, but has always been a countryman's dish, and countless recipes for rabbit pie and stew testify to this trend. Usually bought whole (domestic rabbits can also be bought cut up and frozen), they are used in casseroles, stews and roasts.

years upwards should be hung and the meat made into casseroles, stews, pâtés and terrines. Its main use, of course, is in jugged hare, and it is also used in the German casserole with red wine *hasenpfeffer*, and in the French dish *lièvre à la royale*. Many classic French dishes call for the back or saddle (*râble*) or the saddle and hind legs (*train*) only.

Sausages and Preserved Meats

A N EARLY CULINARY DISCOVERY was that meat would keep for an extended period if the moisture content could be reduced by drying, salting or smoking. In this way, regular year-round supplies of meat became available and a new era began that was eventually to see hams, bacon and sausages take their place as a staple part of our diet.

Inhabitants of hot climates pounded meat to release the juices and dried the strips in the sun or over a fire. The South African biltong is an example of this technique. In North America, the Red Indians invented pemmican – dried, lean buffalo meat, pounded and mixed with fat, vegetables and fruit (usually cranberries), then packed in hide skins and sealed with tallow. Meat is still sealed with fat in the preparation of pâtés and terrines.

In Mexico and Central America, buffalo meat was cut into strips and sun-dried. This charqui was later made by the pioneers, who knew it as "jerky" or "jerked beef". The peasants of Europe, and in particular those of Britain, lived for centuries on a diet of bread and beer, supplemented with bacon. Most of the beef that came to the table was powdered with dry salt. Ships' victuallers bought it by the ton for the British fleet.

Cooking techniques were devised to offset the saltiness; these included adding cereals such as barley to absorb the salt, or a variety of vegetables: the *pot-au-feu* of France and the boiled beef dinners of New England were dishes born of expediency. Spices, especially ginger and pepper, played an important role in enhancing the taste of salt meat and, during one period in the seventeenth century, piles of oranges were kept in the kitchens of wealthy households, so that the juice could be added to cooked meat dishes.

Although salt beef and sun-dried buffalo meat certainly played an important role regionally, much of the tradition of preserved meats actually rests firmly on the pig. French butchers in particular have a long history of charcuterie – the hams of Gaul were so famous that they were even exported to Rome.

An ancestor of the sausage (the word comes from the Latin *salsus* meaning "salted") was made by primitive peoples, using the paunch of an animal to contain other parts of the viscera, which would then have been cooked over a fire; Scotland's haggis is a probable descendant. The Greeks and Romans encouraged sausage-making and it is believed that the Germans, who claim to have invented the sausage, learned their skills from the Romans, but it was left to the French to develop the idea so imaginatively – the range and variety they have devised over the years is staggering. Following France, the most varied contributions to sausage-making come from Germany and Italy, with several other European countries also providing a significant number.

The European ways with hams and sausages spread to America – the French inspired the Creole-Acadian boudins and andouilles, the Italians the bologna and salami of New York, the Germans the frankfurters and knackwursts of Milwaukee, and Spain and Portugal originated the chorizos of Latin America. The American diet of the nineteenth century consisted largely of salt pork. Utility and poverty saw that every scrap of the animal was used, preferably salted and smoked, so that the products could last the months following pig-killing time – usually November. The tradition of using every part of the animal is still maintained: sausages, liver sausages and blood puddings use the inexpensive cuts, while the choicer portions – the belly, loin and legs – are reserved for the smoking and curing processes, to produce bacon and ham.

Processing

The word "cure" simply means that meat is cured of its propensity to putrefaction. In the past, dry-salting was often unsatisfactory because salt was coarse and unrefined, and could produce uneven results. Sugar, which helps soften the meat and adds flavour, was used only by the few who could afford it. Meat was thus dry, hard and very salty, but in the late eighteenth century some attempt was made to refine curing techniques.

Types of sausages and hams vary because local tastes, ingredients and techniques vary.

Hungarians add paprika to their sausages; Germans utilize the wild juniper that flavours Westphalian hams. Brine recipes vary too, and so do smoking techniques. The following are the most commonly used.

Brine cure: This is also known as "pickle" and, if sugar is added, it becomes a "sweet pickle". Most pickles are sweet – an exception is that used for Bayonne ham. Some brines are spiced and may contain juniper, coriander, ginger, and other flavourings. Saltpetre is added because it keeps the meat attractively pink – bacteria in the meat convert the salt to a nitrite (or nitrite is added to the brine). Nitrites stabilize the red pigment myoglobin in the blood, retaining the characteristic colour of the meat.

Dry cure: Dry salt is rubbed into the meat, special attention being paid to the area around the bone, if any. The salt is moisture-absorbing and draws out the juices to form a brine which then penetrates the meat.

Smoking: Wood smoke contains several antiseptic tar products, and meat is usually smoked over hardwood logs and sawdust. Duration of smoking varies considerably, according to the product and the recipe.

Corning: In the sixteenth century the word "corn" was synonymous with "grain", and meat rubbed with grains of salt was thus corned. In New England saltpetre was omitted from the cure and the resulting grey colour of the meat is still preferred. In Britain, corned beef refers to a product of cured, boiled, pressed and then canned beef.

Hams, bacons and other cured meats

Ham is the cured and smoked hind leg of pork, while bacon is usually the cured belly of pork, which accounts for its high fat content. Back bacon, however, is cut from the loin of the animal and is consequently much meatier.

There are perhaps a hundred or more different hams, each country contributing to the selection, but most are cured in more or less the same manner – dry-salted or brined, smoked and matured. Bacon is available smoked and unsmoked in two forms, either sliced or as unsliced slab bacon. Other meats such as mutton and beef are sometimes cured.

Sausages

Sausages are made from the minced meat of pork, veal, beef, chicken, mutton, rabbit, even horseflesh and armadillo. Some countries add a certain amount of cereal to the mixture, notably Britain, while other countries, like Germany, forbid it. A rich variety of ingredients is used in sausage-making: eggs, cream, beer, wine, pigs' blood, tripe, bread-crumbs, oatmeal, potato flour, onion, garlic, herbs, spices, salt and pepper. Some sausages are precooked, others fresh, others cured, air-dried or smoked.

Sausage skins, or casings, are made of the intestines of sheep and pigs and there are also artificial casings. Those sausages to be smoked are first air-dried, then smoked over hardwood chips or sawdust, either cold-smoked or hot-smoked depending on the product.

There are literally thousands of sausages – Germany alone boasts nearly 1500 varieties, not to mention the legion of Italian salamis. Germany categorizes sausages into bratwurst (lightly smoked and scalded fresh sausages, to be cooked by the purchaser), rohwurst (salami-type sausages, raw, air-dried and smoked), and kochwurst (ready-cooked, used for spreading, or slicing and eating cold). French types are divided into large saucissons, which may be smoked (saucissons fumées), fresh saucisses and saucisses fumées, and the boiling sausages (cervelat). The most diverse and varied of all sausage types must certainly be the Italian salami. The characteristic of this type of sausage is that it is brine-pickled, smoked, or both, and is made of raw ingredients.

Fresh Sausages

LINK SAUSAGES

A general term covering fresh sausages, which may contain pork, pork and beef, or venison and seasonings. There are many varieties from different countries available under many names. All the above contain chopped or emulsified meat and seasonings. Occasionally herbs are added. The casings are usually made out of synthetic edible materials.

Pork   *Beef*   *Venison*

Pork and beef

SKINLESS SAUSAGE

Sausage meat is also sold without a casing. The meat may also be shaped in patties.

CHIPOLATA

Made in small-sized casings, chipolatas or breakfast sausages are often used as a garnish. The one on the left contains pork; the one on the right is a pork and beef mixture.

BRATWURST

Made in longish links, this rather pale German bratwurst sausage contains pork and/or veal, bacon, milk and chopped onions. It is quite highly seasoned with salt, pepper and mace, and can be grilled or fried.

CUMBERLAND SAUSAGE

This is a coarse-textured English sausage consisting of roughly chopped pork and black pepper stuffed in to a long casing.

LUGANEGHE

A pure pork Italian sausage, which, like the English Cumberland, is not twisted into links. It is particularly associated with northern Italy. Luganeghe can be boiled or grilled.

Skinless sausage

Bratwurst

Chipolatas

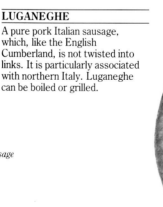

Cumberland sausage

Luganeghe

MERGUEZ

A spiced sausage from north Africa made from goat or mutton and flavoured with *hrisa*, a mixture of hot pepper and cumin. It is usually grilled.

Merguez

LAP CHEONG

A Chinese sausage of chopped pork, cereal, soy sauce and paprika. (*Lap* means "wax" and *cheong* means "intestine".)

SALSICCIE CASALINGA

The name simply means "home-made sausage". They are usually made of pure pork and flavoured with garlic and peppercorns, and may be poached, grilled or fried.

SALAMELLE

This is the Italian name for a variety of spiced sausage.

Salamelle

TOULOUSE SAUSAGE

A sausage from Toulouse in France made of pork and pork fat, coarsely chopped and flavoured with pepper and a little sugar. These sausages feature in several French recipes, especially the regional dish *cassoulet*.

Toulouse

Lap cheong

Spiced French sausage

Salsiccie casalinga

Spiced English sausage

Paprika sausage

SPICED FRENCH SAUSAGE

A fairly coarse-textured sausage, highly spiced and well seasoned with garlic.

SPICED ENGLISH SAUSAGE

This is a pale pink sausage that incorporates pork and spices. Its texture is quite smooth. The Oxford sausage (shown here) is made from pork, beef suet, herbs and spices, while the Cambridge sausage contains pork, herbs and spices.

PAPRIKA SAUSAGE

A dark, fairly coarse-textured sausage, made of lamb and beef and containing paprika, coriander, fennel and a variety of seasonings.

OTHER FRESH SAUSAGES

BOCKWURST
A delicately flavoured, highly perishable German white sausage consisting of fresh pork and veal, chopped chives, parsley, eggs and milk.

HAGGIS
A Scottish sausage, served hot on festive occasions and at other times of the year. Haggis is made from the liver, lungs and heart of a sheep, chopped with onions, oatmeal, parsley and seasonings. The mixture is then stuffed into the stomach lining. It needs long cooking, but commercial ones are precooked and only require about 30 minutes.

THURINGER
A pork sausage that may also contain some beef or veal. It can be either fresh or cooked.

Fresh and Lightly Cooked Sausages

BLACK PUDDING

Traditionally, this black sausage is associated with the north of England, although it appears under different names in many areas. Main ingredients are pig's blood, groats, fat, oatmeal, onions, spices and seasonings. The German variety is called blutwurst, the Irish, drisheen, and the Italian, biroldo.

MORCILLA

The Spanish version of black pudding, morcilla is used as an ingredient of a national dish, *fabada*, which includes chorizo and bacon.

BOUDIN

Boudin noir (shown here) is a French version of black pudding, and contains pig's blood. Boudin blanc is a fresh sausage made with white meat and may also include pork, chicken or veal with eggs, cream, seasonings and spices. It is eaten hot, and may be poached or grilled.

Black pudding

Morcilla

Boudin

BUTIFARA

There are many variations of this Spanish firm-textured sausage. Generally they include pork, white wine, garlic, seasonings and spices. Butifara is preboiled and air-dried and may be eaten cold. It features in the Catalonian cooked dish *cazuela à la Catalana*.

ANDOUILLETTE

A French sausage which, like the larger andouille, is made of pork and/or tripe, chitterlings, calf mesentery, pepper and perhaps wine, onions, and spices. Sometimes smoked, it can be grilled or fried.

Greek sausage

Andouillette

Butifara

GREEK SAUSAGE

A dark, stubby sausage from Greece, this is usually quite heavily spiced.

CREPINETTE

The term "crépinette" covers many varieties of small minced meat sausages, consisting of either lamb or pork. Wrapped in caul, crépinettes are coated with melted butter and breadcrumbs.

Crepinette

COTECHINO

An Italian lean and fat pork sausage with white wine and spices. In Italy they are made fresh, but a part-cured, part-cooked type is commercially distributed and exported. The fresh sausage needs several hours cooking, the commercial one only about 30 minutes. It is often served hot with beans.

Cotechino

FRANKFURTER

The genuine frankfurter is lean pork and salted bacon fat blended into a paste and smoked, but there are now many variations in ingredients as well as in size and shape, as shown here. Often the ingredients include beef and pork trimmings, tripe and pig hearts. Vienna sausage is a small "cocktail" frankfurter. Knackwurst is a small, plump lean-meat frankfurter containing pork and beef.

Frankfurter

Cervelat

TEEWURST

This quality German rohwurst sausage is made of the best meat. A mixture of finely minced pork and beef, it is sometimes highly spiced and lightly smoked. It is a spreading sausage.

Teewurst

Saveloy

ZAMPONE

An Italian pork sausage from Modena where the meat is stuffed into a boned pig's trotter instead of a casing.

Zampone

CERVELAT

The name originated from the Latin word for brains but nowadays it generally contains a finely minced mixture of beef and pork, seasoned with garlic and smoked until golden. There are many different varieties in many parts of Europe: a Swiss version is the landjaeger – a black, wrinkly and heavily smoked sausage – while the goettinger is a German cervelat made with spiced beef and pork. A variety of German cervelat is shown on page 211.

SAVELOY

An English version of cervelat, saveloy contains pork and lights. The addition of saltpetre gives it a red tinge.

Cooked and Lightly Smoked Sausages

SCHINKEN KALBFLEISCHWURST

This mixture of minced pork, beef and veal with ham pieces usually has a touch of garlic included, and is sometimes flavoured with peppercorns and caraway seeds. It is sliced and eaten cold.

ZUNGENWURST

Often quite spicy, this large German smoked sausage is made of pork fat, large pieces of pork tongue, and sometimes liver and blood.

METTWURST

A German spreading sausage of pork and beef, this often contains paprika. There is a coarse version, shown here, and a smoother, pinker one. Both are available ready-to-eat, either as a spread or in slices.

Schinken kalbfleischwurst

Zungenwurst

Mortadella with pistachio nuts

Mettwurst

Bierschinken

Schinkensulzwurst

Bierwurst

MORTADELLA

One of the largest types of sausage, the ingredients vary but usually consist of pork, garlic and seasonings. This bland sausage from Bologna is available plain or sometimes with pistachio nuts or coriander seeds. It should be thinly sliced.

SCHINKENSULZWURST

Pieces of ham and mushroom slices are set in jelly.

BIERWURST

A German pork or pork-and-beef sausage flecked with fat and smoked. It is usually spicy.

BIERSCHINKEN

Pistachio nuts and peppercorns are often included with the lean and fat pork and ham pieces in this German sausage.

EXTRAWURST

A pale pink mixture of beef and pork or bacon fat, this German sausage is smooth in texture and slices easily. It is lightly smoked and may be poached or grilled.

KNOBLAUCHWURST

The strong, distinctive taste of garlic characterizes this German sausage, which contains fat and lean pork and is also flavoured with salt, pepper and spice. It can be grilled or poached.

JAGDWURST

There are various types of this "hunter's" sausage, some large and round, others narrow and flat. They contain pork and spices and are smoked. Schinkenjagdwurst, shown here, contains finely minced pork with diced pork fat and pieces of ham.

Extrawurst

Knoblauchwurst

Schinkenjagdwurst

Plain mortadella

OTHER COOKED AND SMOKED SAUSAGES

BERLINER
A pork and beef sausage mildly flavoured with salt and sugar.

LINGUIC
This Portuguese pork sausage is cured in brine, seasoned with garlic, and spiced with cinnamon and cumin.

STRASSBURGER
A liver and veal sausage containing pistachio nuts.

WEISSWURST
This is a mildly spiced German sausage made of pork and veal.

Smoked Sausages

PEPERONI

A dry Italian sausage that consists of a mixture of coarsely chopped beef and pork and is lightly seasoned with ground red pepper and other spices. It is commonly served on pizzas.

Kabanos

KABANOS

A Polish sausage, kabanos is made of minced pork.

CHORIZO

A Spanish (and Latin-American) spicy sausage made with pork and cayenne, pimento or other hot pepper, usually in narrow casings. Some chorizos are fresh, but most are dried and smoked. Longaniza is a Portuguese version.

Chorizo

Peperoni

Katenrauchwurst

KATENRAUCHWURST

This dark-skinned sausage is firm in texture and contains coarsely cut smoked pork. Originally it was produced in *katen* or peasant huts, hence its name. It was hung in the chimneys of the huts and left there for long periods to be smoked.

BIRNENFORMIGE SALAMI

The name means "pear-shaped"; a perfect description of this German salami before slicing.

Birnenformige salami

NETZ SALAMI

A German salami that takes its name from the string in which it is hung.

Netz salami

LAND SALAMI

A country-style salami usually with spices or herbs mixed into the pork.

Land salami

EDEL SALAMI

The name "edel" means "noble". It is a rich salami of mixed pork and beef.

Edel salami

KIELBASA

A Polish sausage of ground pork and beef that is garlicky and well seasoned, and available fresh or smoked. The word means "sausage", as does the Russian "kolbasa", which is similar.

Kielbasa

SAUCISSON FUME

Saucissons are large and can be air-dried or smoked. The saucisson fumé is typically made from pork, with flecks of back fat or bacon, peppercorns and garlic and herbs. Saucisson fumé aux herbes, shown here, has a generous coating of dried herbs.

Saucisson fumé

OTHER SMOKED SAUSAGES

KALBWURST

Generally a German veal smoked sausage, it may also contain pork, pork fat and pistachio nuts.

SMOKIES

Smoked, cooked links of pork and beef spiced with pepper.

CERVELAT

German minced beef and pork sausage that is smoked to a golden brown. Its meat is more finely ground than Italian salami and usually less highly seasoned.

Cervelat

BLOCKWURST

A German beef or beef and pork rohwurst. There are several varieties, including the pfeffer-blockwurst shown here. It is one of the few square sausages, hence its name, and is coated with coarsely ground black pepper.

Blockwurst

Salami

There is a vast range of salami sausages available, including versions from Germany, Italy, America, Denmark, Hungary and France. All are made with uncooked meat which may be pork, beef or a mixture of the two, and variously flavoured. Some are decorated with pistachio nuts, peppercorns or coriander seeds. Kosher salami is an all-beef type flavoured with garlic, mustard, coriander and juniper. Salami may be air-dried, smoked or both. It is usually thinly sliced and eaten cold, although chopped slices find their way into many Italian cooked dishes, including pizza. Salamini are smaller versions of the usually large sausage.

DANISH SALAMI

An even-shaped salami which is useful in sandwich-making. A mixture of pork, veal, spices and sometimes garlic.

Danish salami

Milano salami

MILANO SALAMI

An Italian salami made with lean pork, beef and pork fat. It is seasoned with garlic, pepper and white wine (see Milano style).

FRENCH PEPPER SALAMI

Pork and beef are mixed with coarse fat and seasoned with whole black peppercorns. It is often used in hors d'oeuvres.

MILANO-STYLE SALAMI

Another variety of Milano salami. Both are often used for antipasto.

TOSCANA

Fiorentino is the best known of the Tuscan salamis. Larger than average, they often consist of pure pork mingled with pieces of lean meat and fat.

French pepper salami

FRENCH HERB SALAMI

A small beef and pork salami coated with herbs. Useful for picnics, it is also served in hors d'oeuvres.

Milano-style salami

Toscana

French herb salami

FELINETTI

From Parma, this is a delicate salami containing white wine, peppercorns and a little garlic.

Felinetti

GERMAN SALAMI

The German varieties generally are a finely ground beef and pork mixture and tend to be more heavily smoked than any of the Italian salamis.

German salami

NAPOLI SALAMI

A long thin salami made with pork and beef. It is seasoned well with both black and red pepper to make it quite hot.

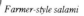

Napoli salami

GENOA SALAMI

Popular as an antipasto served with broad beans, this is seasoned with garlic, peppercorns and red wine and contains a mixture of pork and veal.

Genoa salami

FARMER-STYLE SALAMI

A salami that is usually a coarse-cut beef and pork mixture with whole peppercorns and garlic.

Farmer-style salami

Country-style salami

COUNTRY-STYLE SALAMI

The basic sausage mixture is bound with twine and left to dry and mature instead of being eaten immediately. It contains pork, pork fat, garlic, herbs and peppercorns.

HUNGARIAN SALAMI

Very fat pork is mixed with a blend of several spices in this salami. The casings are lightly smoked and the taste of this salami improves with age.

Hungarian salami

Preserved Meats and Bacons

CORNED BEEF

Also called salt beef, this is a cut of beef – usually brisket – cured in brine and spiced.

Corned beef

TONGUE

Usually beef tongue, it is salted, poached and served in cold slices with salads. It can also be smoked or corned.

Tongue

SMOKED TURKEY

The meat is soaked in pickling brine and then smoked. It should be served sliced with cold dishes.

Smoked turkey

BRESAOLA

This dried salt beef is a speciality from Lombardy, Italy. Cut thinly, it is served as an hors d'oeuvre.

Bresaola

GALANTINE

This is made from boned meat or poultry prepared in a gelatine stock and set.

Galantine

RILLETTES

From France, this is potted belly of pork, sometimes with goose or rabbit added.

Rillettes

BOLOGNA

There are now a number of versions of this famous sausage which is basically a mixture of cooked smoked pork and beef. Polony is the English version.

Bologna

PASTRAMA

Romanian cured meat taken from either goat, mutton, beef, pork or goose. The meat is dry-cured with a mixture of salt, saltpetre, black pepper, nutmeg, paprika, garlic and allspice, before smoking. The American version, pastrami (shown here), is cured, smoked plate (underside) of beef. It is usually thinly sliced and used for sandwiches, and often served hot.

Pastrama

DUCK TERRINE

Duck, lean ham and bacon fat are mixed with seasonings, spices and sometimes brandy.

Duck terrine

LIVERWURST

Originally from Germany, liver sausage is now made in many different countries. Most varieties are made of ground pork, pork or veal liver, onions and seasoning, and may also contain truffles, peppercorns or flecks of back fat. They are usually finely minced and lightly smoked and are ready to eat, as slices or a spread.

Liverwurst

PATE DE FOIE GRAS

Made from the liver of specially reared geese, mixed with spices and seasonings to a smooth texture, this pâté is a luxury item.

Pâté de foie gras

TERRINE DE PYRENEES

A semi-smooth-textured terrine which includes mushrooms.

Terrine de Pyrénées

PATE DE FORESTIER

A much coarser texture than terrine de Pyrenées, this is also a true pâté as it is surrounded by a pastry crust.

Pâté de forestier

OTHER PRESERVED MEATS AND BACONS

BAUERNSPECK
Austrian belly and flank of pork is cured in brine with juniper berries, then cold-smoked.

BRAUNSCHWEIGER
A cooked, smoked liver sausage containing eggs and milk.

BRAWN
A cooked meat speciality product containing small pieces of pig's head bound together by gelatine.

BUNDERFLEISH
This Swiss dried beef is brined, rubbed with spices, then air-dried.

DUTCH LOAF
This is a cold cut comprised of pork and beef.

FENELAR
In this Norwegian smoked mutton the leg is dry-salted with salt, saltpetre and sugar, rubbed with the mixture for several days, then brined in a

sweet pickle after which it is smoked and air-dried.

HONEY LOAF
A mixture of pork, beef, honey, spices and pickles.

SCRAPPLE
A speciality product of cooked pork and cornmeal.

SOUSE
Pieces of pork meat in a vinegar-spiked gelatine base to which dill pickles, sweet red peppers and bay leaves may be added.

SPINKGANZ
This is German smoked goose. Only the breast is used, which is dry-salted with salt, saltpetre, sugar and pepper, then smoked.

Smoked back bacon

BACK BACON
Available smoked and unsmoked, back or Canadian bacon is cut from the loin of the animal and is much meatier than other bacon cuts.

Unsmoked back bacon

STREAKY BACON
This is cut in individual slices, either unsmoked or smoked. Because of the evenness of the slices it is usually more popular than the slab bacon.

Unsmoked streaky bacon

SLAB BACON
Below left, smoked bacon with rind, below right, unsmoked bacon without rind, and right, back bacon. The first two are cut from the belly and are quite fatty.

Smoked streaky slab bacon

Back slab bacon

Unsmoked streaky slab bacon

Smoked streaky bacon

Hams

BAYONNE

Almost every region of France has its own salted and smoked ham. This one from the Basque country is one of the best known. Cured at Orthez in south-west France, this is a raw ham type – a *jambon cru*. The brine contains red wine, rosemary and olive oil. After brining, it is wrapped in straw and smoked.

PARMA

A fine-quality raw ham (*prosciutto crudo*), cured at Langhirano near Parma in Italy. Hams are rubbed with a mixture of salt, sugar, nitrates, pepper, allspice, nutmeg, coriander and mustard. They are packed together for 10 days, then the process is repeated. After maturing, the hams are pressed, steamed and rubbed with pepper.

WESTPHALIA

One of the most famous of the German hams, this is a raw ham, like Bayonne and Parma. After curing (with salt, sugar and saltpetre) and smoking, this rich, dark ham undergoes a lengthy ageing process.

Westphalia

Bayonne

Parma

SUGAR-GLAZED

A rolled boneless cooked ham with a sugar glaze; it is sold whole, in halves or sliced.

ARDENNES

A Belgian ham of great quality which is considered to rank in taste with Parma, York and Bayonne hams.

Ardennes

APPLE-GLAZED

Fully cooked boneless ham with an apple glaze usually made of apple jelly, lemon juice and cloves.

Apple-glazed

Sugar-glazed

YORK

This English ham enjoys a worldwide reputation. Firm and tender, it is noted for its delicate taste. It is often cured with dry salt instead of brine and then lightly smoked. The one shown has been coated with breadcrumbs.

Suffolk

SUFFOLK

This expensive English ham is soaked in molasses rather than salt – a process which turns its skin a distinctive black.

York

SMITHFIELDS

This ham takes its name from an American town in Virginia where its particular curing process was first developed. Virginia ham is similar. The hams are given two rubbings of salt and saltpetre, washed, and heavily smoked with hickory. They are then rubbed with pepper, and matured for up to 18 months.

Smithfields

Bradenham (slice)

Smithfields (slice)

Bradenham

BRADENHAM

This ham is from Chippenham in England. The ham is dry-cured, treated with spices and molasses (which gives it its characteristic black skin), and then hung for many months to age.

OTHER HAMS

DEVILLED
A prepared product made of finely ground ham and seasonings.

IRISH
Usually dry-cured and smoked over peat. Limerick and Belfast are two well-known types.

KENTUCKY
A dry-cured country ham, treated with the cure throughout the maturing process.

SEAGER
Ham from Suffolk, England, cured by a sweet pickle of brine and syrup. The ham is dried, smoked and matured.

OFFAL

OFFAL – THE WORD LITERALLY means the "off-fall" or off-cuts from the carcass – has been both enjoyed and condemned for centuries, condemned because certain items such as the brain and heart were thought to provoke melancholy, while the head – and especially the boar's head – has been invested with symbolic significance of victory, similar to the fox's brush after the hunt.

Many people are still reluctant to eat brains, sweetbreads and tripe, and many more are unable to actually identify or pinpoint the location of caul, mesentery and chitterlings. Some forms of offal have proved unpopular for social, economic and religious reasons; others have always been in considerable demand, especially liver and kidneys – and particularly those of the calf. A tour around the anatomy of an animal will reveal some less familiar cuts.

Offal in the kitchen

All offal cuts should be purchased as fresh as possible. If they are stale, they are usually dark in colour with a dry appearance.

Brains, sweetbreads and tongues need a preliminary soaking. Brains should be soaked in cold water until all the blood is leached away and the arteries and fibres should then be removed. Sweetbreads require soaking for an hour or more, then blanching (parboiling) in acidulated water (about 7 minutes for lambs'; 10 for calves'). Tongues should be soaked in acidulated water for an hour if fresh, or in plain water overnight if salted. Small tongues should be blanched for 10 minutes, larger ones for 30

minutes, and they should then be plunged in cold water before removing the skin.

Beef and pork kidneys can be soaked in acidulated water for about 30 minutes. Other items, such as liver, tripe, trotters and calves' feet, hearts and heads are usually prepared by the butcher.

Calves' and sheeps' heads may be boned or left whole. They may also be served whole – but more often than not divided into pieces – with appropriate sauces, the garnish being the sliced tongue and the brain. Pig's head is used mainly for charcuterie, in brawn and sausages. Pigs' and calves' ears can be grilled or stuffed. Calves' feet and pigs' trotters are highly gelatinous, and used to thicken stocks. They are also boned, stuffed, fried, and used in brawn. Tails can be braised or boiled; sheeps' tails are made into a pie. Oxtail, which is rich in gelatine and has plenty of flavour, responds to long, moist cooking in casseroles and soups.

Many offal cuts come from the inside of the animal. Examples are the spleen (the pig's is used as a sausage ingredient, while that of the ox and calf can be stuffed) and intestines (pigs' intestines are used as casings for sausages, and chitterlings or "chitlins" are famous in the southern states of America served with collard greens). Calf's mesentery (part of the peritoneum) is also a sausage ingredient, but may be fried or prepared in the manner of tripe, while the lungs or "lights" are for stewing. Pig's caul (the lace-like membrane around the paunch) is the binding for *crépinettes* (small sausages – page 207).

BRAINS

Lamb brains and veal brains (the most popular) are pale pink and delicate in texture. They are often sautéed or chopped and fried or creamed. Veal brains are sometimes served with black butter sauce or fried and cooked in batter.

Lamb brains   *Veal brains*

Pork lights

Lamb lights

LIGHTS
These are the lungs of an animal, which in Britain and America are generally reserved for pet foods, but they are cooked for the table in other countries. Not very substantial in themselves, they are either served with a nutritious sauce, added to stews or used by pork butchers as an ingredient in *pâté de foie*.

MILT
This is the spleen of animals (a pig's milt is shown). Although cooked for the table they are often sold in western society for pet food. Generally not highly regarded by gourmets, they are used either in sausage-making or, with the heart and lungs, are incorporated into stews. Ox and calves' milts can be stuffed.

SWEETBREADS
Delicate in taste and pale in appearance, sweetbreads – or, in France, *ris de veau* – are the pancreas (stomach sweetbreads) and thymus glands (throat sweetbreads) of young animals. The former are plump and rounded, the latter elongated (veal throat sweetbreads are shown). A certain amount of preparation is needed before cooking – they should be thoroughly washed and soaked. They can then be braised, fried or sautéed, and are often eaten with black butter sauce. Recipes for veal and lamb sweetbreads are more or less interchangeable.

TRIPE
Tripe comes from the two stomachs of oxen and cows. Plain tripe comes from the first stomach or rumen, and honeycomb tripe (generally more tender) from the second stomach or reticulum. All tripe is sold cleaned, washed and blanched, and sometimes it is fully cooked. When bought raw, however, it needs long, slow cooking – the classic dish is a white stew with onions. Perhaps the most famous recipe is the French *tripe à la mode de Caen*.

Milt

Sweetbreads

Tripe

EYEBALLS

Eyeballs (particularly sheeps' eyeballs, as shown) are considered a great delicacy in the Middle East. They are usually removed from the head after it has been roasted or boiled and are eaten straight away, with or without extra sauce or seasonings.

Sheeps' eyeballs

HEART

Hearts are nutritious and contain very little waste. Lamb and veal hearts have the finest taste and are suitable for stuffing, pork hearts are larger and slightly coarser, and beef hearts are the least tender of all. All require long, slow cooking.

MARROWBONE

The shoulder or thigh bones of oxen or calves contain large quantities of marrow, a soft, fatty substance which is extracted from the bones after they have been cooked. Marrow is used in sauces, soups, stews and risottos; it is also eaten hot as a spread for an hors d'oeuvre.

TAIL

Tasty, nourishing and relatively inexpensive, tails are usually sold skinned and jointed for use in soups and stews. Oxtails should have creamy white fat and deep red meat, with an equal proportion of meat to bone. Rich in gelatine and with plenty of flavour, they respond to long, moist cooking in casseroles and soups. Sheeps' tails may be made into a pie.

Ox marrowbone

Oxtail

Pork heart

Lamb heart

Chicken heart

Beef heart

Pig's tail

TONGUE

In some markets, tongue is sold ready to serve, but it is more usual to buy it fresh, smoked or corned for cooking and eating hot or cold, with or without sauce. Salted tongue is used cooked, pressed and sliced cold (page 214), while fresh tongue may be braised with wine, or boiled and served with various garnishes. Beef and veal tongues are the commonest, lamb tongues the most tender.

Lamb tongue

Veal tongue

Beef tongue (pickled)

Beef tongue

Pigs' trotters

TROTTERS and FEET

Pigs' trotters and calves' feet are bought whole or split in half and are used for making strong, gelantinous stock, consommés and aspic. They may also be grilled and eaten hot with sauce, added to brawn and stews for extra richness, jellied for eating cold, or boned, stuffed and fried.

Calves' feet

OTHER OFFAL

CHITTERLINGS
Pigs' intestines which are often used in sausage-making, they are particularly popular in America and France. They can be grilled or fried.

EARS
Pigs' and calves' ears can be grilled or stuffed. In China, pigs' ears are cooked with spices.

HEAD
Pig's head is used mainly in charcuterie, in brawn and sausages. It is also often boiled – with the tongue and brains removed – or marinated. Calves' and sheeps' heads may be boned or left whole, and are usually prepared by the butcher. They may also be served whole, but are usually divided into pieces and served with a sauce. Bath chaps, the smoked cheeks of the pig, are mainly boiled and eaten cold like ham.

MESENTERY
This is a membrane which forms part of the peritoneum. Calf's mesentery is a sausage ingredient, but may be fried or prepared in the same way as tripe.

TESTICLES
Also known as fries or animelles, lambs' and calves' testicles can be fried in batter, sautéed or cooked in a *court-bouillon* and served with vinaigrette.

LIVER

A rich source of iron, liver is probably the most popular of offal meats eaten in western countries. Several varieties are shown, of which the finest in quality and flavour, and therefore the most expensive, is calf's liver. Although all types can be fried or grilled (with the exception of ox liver, which is usually used in stews and casseroles), sautéeing is the best cooking method to retain its moistness. Lamb's liver is more strongly flavoured and often less tender than calf's liver. It is spit-roasted in the Middle East. Ox liver is inexpensive, with a strong flavour, but usually tough, while pig's liver is also strongly flavoured and largely used in charcuterie, where it is one of the ingredients in pâtés. Chicken and goose livers are also most often used to make pâtés.

Calf's liver

Beef liver

Goose liver

Pork liver

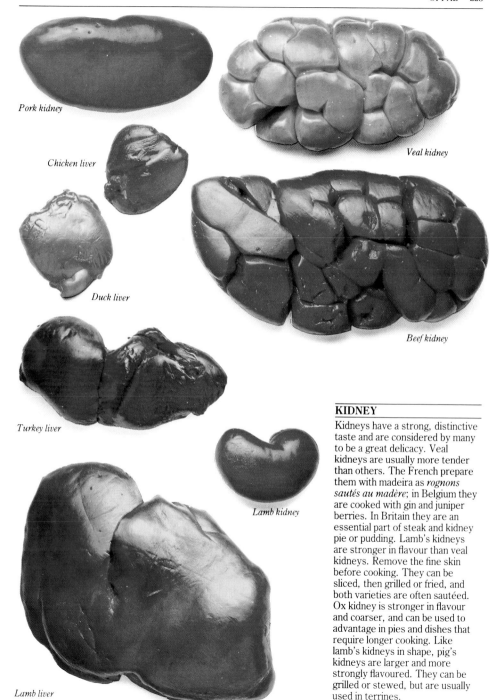

Pork kidney

Veal kidney

Chicken liver

Duck liver

Beef kidney

Turkey liver

Lamb kidney

Lamb liver

KIDNEY

Kidneys have a strong, distinctive taste and are considered by many to be a great delicacy. Veal kidneys are usually more tender than others. The French prepare them with madeira as *rognons sautés au madère*; in Belgium they are cooked with gin and juniper berries. In Britain they are an essential part of steak and kidney pie or pudding. Lamb's kidneys are stronger in flavour than veal kidneys. Remove the fine skin before cooking. They can be sliced, then grilled or fried, and both varieties are often sautéed. Ox kidney is stronger in flavour and coarser, and can be used to advantage in pies and dishes that require longer cooking. Like lamb's kidneys in shape, pig's kidneys are larger and more strongly flavoured. They can be grilled or stewed, but are usually used in terrines.

MEAT

FROM THE EARLIEST TIMES, man has been a carnivorous animal. Though today there is a reappraisal of the importance of meat in the diet – whether its drawbacks, like cholesterol and high prices as well as ethical considerations, outweigh its value as a protein-provider – meat is still the most expensive item in the budget and a great deal of thought should be put into choosing and using it wisely.

The meat used in the bulk of recipes comes from the three main types of domestic farm animals – cattle, sheep and pigs, giving us beef and veal, mutton and lamb, and pork. While regional preferences, religion and climate may have certain influences, these meats feature in the majority of national cuisines, and may be supplemented by other domestic types, such as horsemeat, goat and reindeer.

Butcher's meat today is largely a product of selective breeding and feeding techniques, whereby animals are carefully reared to reach high standards and specific needs: the present-day demand is for lean and tender meat, and modern cattle, sheep and pigs are well-fleshed yet compact creatures compared to their forebears of a century ago. The most tender and lean meat is found along the backbone and the rump.

Cuts of meat

The consumer's requirements (affected by social and economic trends), religious custom and the animal's anatomy influence the way in which the butcher cuts his carcasses. Regional climates, family occupations and the use of local ingredients, such as herbs, fruits and vegetables, influence cooking methods and therefore demands for cuts. Butchering techniques vary considerably, not only between countries, but even within cities and towns. The names given to the cuts vary too, except in America, where regional variations were standardized in the 1970s. In Britain, names may vary to such an extent that one cut in particular, the thick flank of beef, has as many as 27 local names, including bedpiece, pope's eye, rump, mouse, crown, broil, top piece, and soft side. Meat from specific parts of an animal may be cut and cooked according to local custom and, more strictly, by religious observance – especially in Jewish kosher and Muslim halal butchery.

Choosing meat

Meat is a natural, and therefore not a uniform, product, varying in quality from carcass to carcass, while flavour, texture and appearance are determined by the type of animal and the way it has been fed. There is no reason to think that flavour is only obtained in meat which possesses a proportion of fat, although it does give a characteristic flavour to meat and helps to keep it moist during roasting. The colour of meat is also no guide to quality. Consumers are inclined to choose light-coloured meat – bright red beef, for example – because they think that it will be fresher than an alternative dark red piece. Freshly butchered beef is bright red because the pigment in the tissues, myoglobin, has been chemically affected by the oxygen in the air. After several hours, the colour changes to dark red or brown as the pigment is further oxidized to become metamyaglobin. The colour of fat can vary from almost pure white in lamb to bright yellow in beef. Colour depends on the feed, on the breed and, to a certain extent, on the time of the year.

The most useful guide to tenderness and quality is a knowledge of the cuts of meat and their location on the carcass. The various cuts are described under their respective headings, but in principle the leanest and tenderest cuts, the "prime" cuts, come from the hindquarters. The "coarse" cuts, or meat from the neck, legs and forequarters, those parts of the animal that have had plenty of muscular exercise and where fibres have become hardened, provide meat for braising and stewing. Many consider these cuts to have more flavour, although they require slow cooking to make them tender.

The meat from young animals is generally more tender and, since tenderness is a prime factor, animals may be injected before slaughter with an enzyme, such as papain, which softens the fibres and muscles. But this merely speeds up a natural and more satisfactory process: meat contains its own proteolytic enzymes which gradually break down the protein cell walls as the carcass ages. That is why meat is usually hung from 10 to 20 days in controlled conditions of temperature and humidity before being offered for sale. Meat which is aged for longer becomes more expensive – the cost of refrigeration is high and the meat itself shrinks as a result of evaporation and the trimming of the outside hardened edges.

Meat in the kitchen

Meat is an extremely versatile product that can be cooked in a multitude of ways, and matched with practically any vegetable, fruit and herb. The cut (shin, steak, brisket), the method of heating (roasting, braising, grilling) and the time and temperature all affect the way the meat will taste. Raw meat is difficult to chew because the muscle fibre contains an elastic protein (collagen) which is only softened by mincing – as in steak tartare – or by cooking. When you cook meat, the protein gradually coagulates as the internal temperature increases. At 77°C (171°F) coagulation is complete, the protein begins to harden, and further cooking makes the meat tougher.

Since tenderness combined with flavour is the aim in meat cookery, much depends on the ratio of time and temperature. In principle, slow cooking retains the juices and produces a more tender result than fast cooking at high temperatures. There are, of course, occasions when high temperatures are essential: you need to grill a steak under a hot flame for a very limited time in order to obtain a crisp, brown surface and a pink, juicy interior – using a low temperature would not give you the desired result. But in potentially tough cuts, such as breast, or where there is a quantity of connective tissue, as with neck of lamb, a slow rate of cooking converts the tissues to gelatine and helps to make the meat more tender.

Meat containing bone will take longer to cook because bone is a poor conductor of heat. Tough or coarse cuts of meat should be cooked by braising, pot-roasting or stewing. Marinading in wine or wine vinegar helps to tenderize the meat, and imparts an additional flavour. Searing meat in hot fat, or in a hot oven before roasting or stewing, helps to produce a crisp exterior by coagulating the protein but does not, as is widely supposed,

seal in the juices. However, if the external temperature is too high and cooking prolonged, rapid evaporation and contraction of the meat will cause considerable loss of juices and fat. Salt sprinkled on meat before cooking will also hasten loss of moisture since salt is hygroscopic and absorbs water.

Meat bones are useful for giving flavour to soup and stock, especially beef ones with plenty of marrow. Veal bones are gelatinous and help to enrich and thicken soups and sauces. Fat can be rendered down for frying, or else used as an ingredient when suet or lard is called for.

Cooking meat

Briefly, meat cookery can be broadly divided into the following categories: quick cooking at moderate to high temperatures, as when grilling, barbecuing and frying (suitable for such prime tender cuts as steaks, chops, veal scallops and kebabs); slow to moderate cooking, as when roasting or using a rotisserie (suitable for prime tender joints such as beef sirloin, leg of lamb, cuts of pork and veal); and slow cooking in a liquid, as when stewing, braising or pot-roasting (suitable for coarse cuts such as thick flank, leg, shin and neck cuts). One big advantage to braising and stewing meat is that any quantities left over can be easily re-heated. In fact, many dishes are improved by allowing them to "mature" and then re-heating. Roasts, on the other hand, are less adaptable, and cold roast meat is not suitable re-heated, since it lacks the essential moisture. Re-heated meat must be heated through thoroughly, and then only once, to avoid risk of food poisoning.

When you are preparing meat for cooking, never wash it, simply wipe the surface with a damp cloth. Use a meat thermometer when roasting; many are graded with temperature scales and also scaled according to the type of meat and the cut. They record the internal temperature of the meat. Meat that requires carving should rest for 15 minutes so that it loses its springiness and is easier to carve, and juices do not escape so readily. Always carve on a non-slip surface, and one where the juices can be collected. Use a sharp knife, otherwise the meat will simply tear along the grain, and a guarded carving fork.

Beef and Veal

Domestic cattle, from which we derive our beef, have been gradually developed over thousands of years. Their ancestors were the wild aurochs, *Bos primigenius*, first domesticated in Anatolia and Greece in about 6000 BC. The lineage of this ancient breed was so enduring that the last known specimen of aurochs was recorded in Poland in 1627. The Greeks and Romans prepared their beef dishes with an abundance of pepper and other spices, not because the meat was not fresh or lacked flavour, but because spices were an expensive item, and so was beef. Such fine ingredients were used on special occasions, and denoted the wealth of the household.

Beef in Europe

Beef has always been an expensive meat. During the Middle Ages, the infrequent fare of the common man was salt pork and mutton, and beef the privilege of the wealthy. In Britain, farmers maintained herds of cattle and sheep, only slaughtering a part of their stock as winter approached and grazing ended. Beef would then be eaten fresh, the remainder salted for the coming months. Yet by the eighteenth century the English had a reputation as a nation of beef-eaters. Massive roasts were cooked on spits before the open fire. This might imply that butchering was rather primitive, and smaller cuts unknown or ignored. But in London an event took place that was, in some respects, a culinary revolution – the introduction of the beefsteak.

In France, the *bifteck* had been noted by the epicure Brillat-Savarin. Here, as in London, butchering techniques were gradually improving, yet only city butchers could be relied upon to cut a steak for the grill: "It would seem", wrote one steak fancier, "that country butchers have not learned the secrets of proper cuts".

Beef in America

Beef has always been the most sought-after meat in America and steak was established as the favourite by the mid-nineteenth century. It was often served to travellers at coach stops or "porterhouses", as they were called.

The early American desire for beef was met by the successful transplantation of Spanish cattle to Texas. Bred to withstand the heat and lack of water in Andalusia, the Texas Longhorns overcame the rigours of being herded to the railroad centres for shipment. And if the cattle supplied Americans with their favourite meat, the cowboys who herded them popularized a favourite way of cooking it – the barbecue. Although the Texas Longhorns, the staple of the American meat economy, have long been displaced by meatier breeds from Britain, today it is America, and not Britain, that has become a nation of beef-eaters – Americans eat and import more beef than any other country in the world, consuming some 29kg (65lb) per head of the population every year, in the form of barbecued sirloin steaks, hamburgers and grilled T-bone and porterhouse steaks.

Choosing and using beef

The cuts of beef vary considerably, from the very tender fillet steak to the tough brisket or the shin, and there is a greater variety of cuts in beef than in any other type of meat. While their names may vary, there are fourteen primary cuts from a side of beef, each one composed of muscle, fat, bone and connective tissue. The least developed muscles, usually from the inner areas, can be roasted or grilled, while leaner and more sinewy meat is cut from more highly developed external muscles. Exceptions are rib and loin cuts which come from external but basically immobile muscles.

Knowing where the cuts come from helps to designate the cooking method. A forequarter, which normally weighs 70–86.5kg (155–190lb) produces eight main sections: the neck, clod, shin, chuck and blade, fore-rib, top (thick) rib, flat (thin) rib and brisket. The neck, clod, and shin sections come from one of the most mobile areas of the animal. Cuts from these sections are likely to be sinewy with a large amount of connective tissue and need slow, moist cooking such as braising, stewing, or pot-roasting to give the best, most tender result. The chuck and blade section – found behind the neck – can be cut into two joints, into several smaller joints, or into slices. While less coarse than the neck, the chuck and blade section is also cooked by moist methods. The fore-rib is an immobile section from the centre of the back and is the only prime grade meat found in the fore-quarter. It can be roasted whole as a joint or boned and rolled, or cut into rib steaks to grill or fry. Beneath the chuck and blade and fore-rib sections, just above the brisket, there is the top rib section and behind it the flat rib section. Both are best boned or cut into steaks and slow-roasted or braised. The brisket is also a very mobile section which requires slow, moist cooking; however, curing, as for corned beef, or salting and boiling can also produce tender meat.

The hindquarter, which normally weighs 68–82kg (145–180lb), is made up of seven main sections: leg, topside, silverside, top rump, rump, sirloin and flank. Meat from the leg section is best stewed or braised, while the flank, which also has a good deal of connective tissue, is usually sold as mince. Cuts from the other hindquarter sections are prime meat which can be roasted or cut into steaks to grill or fry. Porterhouse, Châteaubriand and fillet steaks come from the sirloin section.

VEAL

Veal is the meat from dairy calves usually slaughtered at three months of age. Today this meat is in short supply – due to more efficient dairy production from fewer animals – and expensive: young animals have a coddled upbringing and many are completely milk-fed. The association of milk and veal goes back at least to Norman times, when chefs prepared *blancmange* – veal cooked with milk and almonds – and taught English cooks to make *veel bukkenade* with veal, eggs, milk and spices, a medieval *blanquette de veau*.

One particular veal dish, the breaded scallop, has had a curious, military history. It probably originated in Spain, and was introduced to Milan when the city was a part of the Spanish Empire in the sixteenth century. They called it the *scallopine Milanese*, perhaps after the scallop shell, the emblem of Spain's patron saint, St James, and it featured in Milan homes as a delicacy. When Milan was later occupied by Austrian soldiers under Marshal Radetsky,

the Marshal introduced the dish to the kitchens of Emperor Franz Josef, where it became the famed *Wiener schnitzel*.

French dishes include the provincial *blanquette de veau*, and the grand *selle de veau Orloff*. Italy, already replete with *scallopine*, is known for its cold veal with a sauce of tuna fish (*vitello tonnato*); the Tuscan stew *stufatino* and the famous *ossobuco*, where pieces of veal knuckle are gently stewed with tomatoes. Romanians mince veal and make a casserole, while the Bulgarians stew it with horseradish.

Choosing and using veal

Unlike beef, veal may be judged by the colour of the meat. The whiter it is, the greater proportion of the calf's diet has been milk and the more likely the meat is to be tender with a delicate flavour. More mature veal is pink or rosy pink, with creamy white fat. A dry, brown, or mottled appearance indicates staleness. Veal is inclined to dryness as it has little internal fat and for this reason it is often larded with pork fat if roasted, pot-roasted or braised to make it moist.

A veal carcass is divided into the forequarter and the hindquarter. The forequarter has five primary cuts or sections – the scrag, middle neck, shoulder, best end of neck, and breast. The scrag is usually sold in one piece but is sometimes chopped. The middle neck is sold as cutlets or boned for pie veal. Both these sections require slow, moist cooking such as stewing or braising. The shoulder is usually roasted and is sold as a whole joint or boned to stuff and roll. The best end of neck is sold as cutlets to grill or fry, as a joint, or a boned, stuffed and rolled cut to roast. Veal breast is cut into strips for braising and stewing or boned to stuff, roll and roast. The hindquarter provides the majority of better cuts from its three sections – the leg, loin and flank. The leg is usually divided into the hock and the fillet ends. The hock is sold both as a joint and as slices to braise or stew (*ossobuco*), or it is boned and diced for casseroles. The fillet end of leg is sold as a large roasting joint, or thin scallops are cut from the top of the leg to grill or fry (as for *Wiener schnitzel*) and the rest of the joint boned and rolled into smaller cuts for roasting. The flank is usually rolled as a roasting joint or used for sausages.

Topside

TOPSIDE

A lean tender cut from the hindquarters, it is suitable for braising or pot-roasting.

SILVERSIDE

Taken from the hindquarters, it is a cut from the round. It can be pot-roasted, or used for traditional boiled beef.

Silverside

TOP RUMP

Taken from the round, top rump or thick flank is available boned and rolled. It can be pot-roasted or braised.

Top rump

Rump

RUMP

A good-quality cut, though it is less tender than fillet. It is suitable for grilling or frying.

Brisket

TOP RIB

Sometimes called "leg-of-mutton cut" because of its shape, it is usually boned and rolled. It may be pot-roasted or braised.

Top rib

T-bone steak

ENTRECOTE STEAK

A boneless steak which is cut from the ribs or sirloin. Less tender than rump, it is suitable for grilling or frying.

Entrecote steak

SIRLOIN

A lean and tender joint taken from the back. It is available boned and unboned, and is suitable for roasting.

Sirloin

BRISKET

A cut from the fore end of the animal, below the shoulder. Quite a fatty joint, it is sold on or off the bone or salted. It is suitable for slow roasting or braising.

Rib; Fore-rib

RIB OR FORE-RIB

Sold on the bone or boned and rolled, it is suitable for roasting.

T-BONE STEAK

Taken from the fillet end of the sirloin, this cut is suitable for frying or grilling.

Minute steak

MINUTE STEAK

This is usually a slice of flank or entrecôte, cut thin and beaten. It is suitable for grilling.

FILLET STEAK

A lean steak cut across the fillet, this is the most tender steak for grilling or frying.

Fillet

Fillet steak

FLANK

A boneless cut from the belly of the animal, this is suitable for boiling, braising or stewing.

Flank

OTHER BEEF CUTS

CHATEAUBRIAND
A thick steak taken from the middle of the fillet; suitable for grilling or frying.

FILLET
Taken from the back of the animal, this is the tenderest part, cut from the centre of the

sirloin. If not cut into steaks, it may be roasted.

ROLLED RIBS
Taken from the underside, fore end. It is sold on the bone or boned and rolled, and is suitable for roasting or pot-roasting.

SKIRT
A boneless rather gristly cut. It is usually stewed or made into mince.

BEST END OF VEAL NECK
A cut that is suitable for roasting, braising or stewing.

Best end of neck

Cutlets

VEAL CUTLETS
Cut from the best end of neck, these can be grilled or fried.

VEAL CHOPS
These are taken from the loin and have the bone in them. They may be grilled or fried.

Chops

KNUCKLE OF VEAL
This is the end of the leg. It is a bony cut and is used for boiling and stewing, and in *ossobuco*.

Knuckle

Leg

LEG OF VEAL
A prime cut which is usually roasted on the bone.

Boned and rolled shoulder

SHOULDER OF VEAL
This can be boned and rolled for roasting but is usually cut up for stews and pies.

Loin

Boned and rolled loin

LOIN OF VEAL
A cut from the back of the animal that is suitable for roasting on the bone or boned and rolled.

VEAL FILLET
A boneless cut from the hindquarters, this is sometimes sold for roasting but more often cut into fillet steaks or escalopes.

Fillet

Escalope

PIE VEAL
Trimmings cut from the shoulder, breast, neck or knuckle, they are suitable for pies and stews.

Pie veal

BREAST OF VEAL
Although usually boned and stuffed for roasting, breast of veal may alternatively be cut into riblets.

Breast

Lamb and Mutton

Sheep and goats have an ancestry that certainly predates that of cattle and pigs, going back to around 9000 BC. Like cattle, which yield both milk and meat, sheep have a two-fold purpose to provide wool and meat, and of the two, meat is today by far the most important.

Lamb is the meat from a sheep under a year old; above that age the animal is called a hogget, and its meat becomes mutton. Lamb provides smaller cuts of more tender meat; mutton needs to be well ripened by long hanging before cooking and, as it is usually fatty, needs a good deal of trimming as well.

The best domestic lamb is marketed when it is between five and seven months old, and is known as "spring", "summer" or early lamb. Much of the flavour of lamb has now been sacrificed to productivity – a deep-frozen leg of lamb bears no comparison with a leg of fresh spring lamb but the latter is in short supply and is expensive. Very little mutton is now marketed. New Zealand and Australia, the world's main producers of lamb, export significant quantities to Britain, Russia, the Middle East, and to Japan.

Lamb in the kitchen

Lamb is a popular meat in many parts of the world, and different countries have their own lamb dishes. In Middle Eastern and North African cooking, lamb features as the whole, spitted and roasted carcass called *mechoui*, or as *shish kebab*, which in fact means "skewered lamb". Minced lamb with cracked wheat is widely eaten, either raw or cooked. In Iran, mutton is stewed; in Tunisia it is cooked with spices and raisins. The French are particularly fond of roasting the leg. Lamb, or originally mutton, created the immortal Irish stew and the Lancashire hotpot.

Lamb is well suited to certain fruits and adjuncts: mint sauce with lamb and caper sauce with mutton are favourites in Britain. Algerians cook it with prunes and almonds, Moroccans with lemons and olives, the Belgians with endives, the Swedes with dill. Other herbs include rosemary and juniper berries. Lamb should be cooked so that it is still pink, and carved very thinly.

Choosing and using lamb

Good-quality lamb should have a fine, white fat, with pink flesh where freshly cut; in mutton the flesh is a deeper colour. Lamb has a very thin, parchment-like covering on the carcass, known as the fell, which is usually left on roasts to help them maintain their shape during cooking. It should, however, be removed from chops. The flesh of a younger lamb is usually more tender. A good way to judge age is through weight – especially with legs of lamb: the highest quality weighs about 2.3kg (5lb) and never more than 4kg (9lb). Smaller chops are also more tender and therefore more expensive.

A lamb carcass weighs 13.5–47.5kg (30–60lb) and a mutton one 32–36.5kg (70–80lb). Both are divided into the forequarter and the hindquarter and have the same primary cuts. The forequarter contains the scrag, middle neck, shoulder, best end of neck, and breast. The scrag and middle neck sections are usually sold as joints or chops for stewing or for pot-roasts and casseroles. The shoulder can be sold whole, cut into the blade and the knuckle end, or as boneless meat for kebabs, casseroles and pies. Lamb scrag, middle neck, and shoulder sections are more tender than similar cuts from other animals as lamb is less well-developed. The best end of neck (rack) is sold whole – boned or as a joint – or as cutlets. The two best ends may be sold together as a crown roast or a guard of honour roast. The breast is sold boned and chopped or as a joint for roasting or braising.

The hindquarter contains the loin, the chump and the leg. The loin is sold as a joint, sometimes boned and rolled, or as loin chops. The chump – from the thick upper section of the leg – is usually sold as chops, though when cut with the loin it is sold as a large joint. The leg is sold whole or it can be cut in half to give the fillet end and the shank end joints.

Cuts from the scrag, middle neck and breast sections of lamb and mutton need slow, moist cooking. All other cuts can be roasted at 180°C (350°F) Gas 4 until medium or well done. Large chump and loin chops brushed with oil can be grilled or fried for 12 to 15 minutes, other chops and cutlets need 8 to 10 minutes.

Shank end

Fillet end

Noisettes

Shoulder

NOISETTES

These are small round slices, about 50mm (2in) thick, cut from the loin or best end of lamb. They are usually roasted or pan-fried.

CHUMP CHOP

Cut from between leg and loin, it is grilled or fried.

SHOULDER

Sold on the bone, it has quite a lot of fat. It can be roasted on the bone, or boned, stuffed and rolled, or cut up for kebabs or casseroles.

Chump chop

Riblets

Leg

LEG

A tender cut often divided into fillet and shank. It is sold on the bone for roasting, or boned and rolled for casseroles.

CUTLETS

These are cut from the best end of neck divided between the bones. They can be grilled or sautéed.

BEST END OF NECK

A small joint sold on the bone. It is suitable for roasting.

RIBLETS

Breast meat on the bone that has been separated between the ribs. It is usually cooked in liquid.

Best end of neck

Loin

Cutlets

LOIN

A tender cut from the back sold on the bone or boned. It is suitable for roasting.

SCRAG END OF NECK

Bony and fatty, it is usually used for stews and soups.

LOIN CHOP

This cut from the loin contains part of the backbone and is suitable for grilling, frying or braising.

Scrag end of neck

Breast

BREAST

A cut that contains quite a lot of fat. It is usually sold boned for stuffing and slow roasting.

Loin chops

Pork

The first people to taste roast pork were probably the Chinese, and Neolithic sites excavated in China show that pigs, used as food, were the only domestic animals. In the eighteenth century an Asian variety, *Sus scrofa vittatus*, was introduced. Most modern pig strains are descended from this Asian stock.

One of the most controversial aspects of pork is the fact that it is taboo in certain religions. It has been variously proposed that pork is basically unhygienic, and in hot climates presents a health hazard. Another view is that the pig was once a tribal emblem (a totem), and thus is sacrosanct.

Be that as it may, pork is greatly esteemed by many nations as a prime and tender meat. The pig's later associations with man have been very close. For centuries the diet of the European peasantry was supplemented by salt or pickled pork from their own pig; navies rationed it to their seamen who grew to despise it, and so did the aristocracy, who viewed pork as the food of the poor. Pigs were a feature of every homestead, however humble; pigs went with the settlers to the New World, and became so prolific that pork was a main item in American cooking long before beef took command, so that pork dishes feature among America's earliest recipes. The pigs were left to fatten in the woods and then, as today, they were utilized to the last ounce, including the head, entrails and trotters (see pages 202–17, and 218–23).

Pigs will eat almost anything – they are nature's vacuum cleaners, omnivorous and greedy – but pig farmers have to control their animals' diet to produce the right combination of fatness, weight, and carcass quality. Pigs cannot eat grass alone, and are fed cereals, proteins, minerals and compound vitamins; diet influences the flavour of the meat, and it is likely that the free-ranging, ancestral pigs, though probably tougher and fattier than today's breeds, had a more natural flavour.

Pork in the kitchen

The pig's hardy, omnivorous, scavenging nature is the quality which has made it so enduring in a wide variety of climates and conditions. Perhaps because of its long association with salt, pork is often cooked or served with fruit: England and many other European countries serve it with apple sauce, Danish cooks stuff pork with prunes, so do the Germans, who also stew pork in beer, serve it with sausages and potatoes, or with sauerkraut. In Russia, Italy, Greece and Poland suckling pigs are spitted whole and spit-roasted – suckling pig is an essential part of the Polish Easter festivities. But it is the Chinese who really excel with a wide variety of pork dishes – pork is shredded and stir-fried, spiced with star anise and ginger or braised with mushrooms.

Choosing and using pork

Pork should be pale pink with firm, white fat. Nearly all cuts of pork are prime, that is, they can be grilled or roasted because porkers are slaughtered at a young age and the meat is therefore tender throughout. The majority of cookery books recommend that pork be well done to the point of dryness to minimize the danger of the parasite trichina; however, scientists have now recommended a new safe internal temperature for pork – 77°C (170°F) – so that the meat remains moist and tender.

Fresh pork is divided into seven primary cuts. Pig's jowl is sold to processors to become sausage meat and the trotters are sold as offal (page 221). The five consumer cuts are the leg, loin, belly, neck end and the hand and spring. The leg is sold whole, boned, or as two joints – the knuckle (shank) end and the fillet of leg. The hind loin can be cut into large bony chump chops but is usually left as a roasting joint or boned and cut as pork steak. The rest of the loin is cut into more fatty joints and chops. The belly can be cut into a fairly lean joint around the ribs and a less bony but fatter joint towards the leg. The neck end is usually cut into a blade joint and a spare rib joint (where spare rib chops are cut). The hand and spring is usually cut into a joint and several steaks.

All cuts of pork should be roasted to an internal temperature of 77°C (170°F). Grill or fry chops and steaks, brushed with a little oil, for 15 to 20 minutes.

TENDERLOIN

A boneless cut of lean meat from the inside of the loin, the tenderloin or pork fillet is good for roasting, braising, grilling or frying.

Fillet; Tenderloin

LOIN

A lean joint which sometimes includes the kidney. It is suitable for roasting.

Loin

LOIN CHOP

Taken from the fore or middle loin, it is suitable for grilling or frying.

Loin chops

BELLY

This generally yields bacon but is sometimes sold fresh and used in sausage-making; otherwise it is grilled or baked.

Belly

Leg

LEG

The hind leg – a lean, tender joint sold on the bone or boned and rolled. It is suitable for roasting.

CHUMP

Available on or off the bone from the hind loin, this is suitable for roasting. It can also be cut into large, meaty chump chops.

Chump

AMERICAN SPARE RIBS

These rib bones are taken from the belly of the animal, they are usually used for barbecueing.

American spare ribs

Hock

HOCK

A small bony cut from the hand. It is stewed or used for soups.

SPARE RIB

Taken from the fore end of the animal, it is sold whole or as spare rib chops. It is suitable for roasting, grilling or frying.

Spare rib

Rib chop

BLADEBONE

A tender fore end cut that is available boned or on the bone, bladebone or shoulder is used for casseroles and kebabs.

Blade; Shoulder

HAND AND SPRING

A cut from the fore end of the animal, it may be sold whole on the bone, or divided into hand and shank, and is suitable for roasting or braising.

Hand and spring

INDEX

Page numbers set in italic refer to illustrations

· C ·

· D ·

· S ·

· T ·

ACKNOWLEDGMENTS

Designers: Christine Wood, Hilary Krag
Editor: Sydney Francis
Photographer: Philip Dowell, except pp 10/11, 12/13, 14/15, 16/17, 20/21, 36/37, 40/41, 42/43, 88, 114/115, photographer: Stephen Oliver
Home economist: Mandy Wagstaff
Illustrator: John Woodcock
Studio: Lorraine Abraham, Beverley Waldron
Typesetter: Bournetype, Bournemouth
Reproduction: Colourscan, Singapore

Dorling Kindersley
Managing editor: Jemima Dunne
Managing art editor: Derek Coombes
Editorial assistance: Candida Ross-Macdonald, Julia Harris-Voss
Design assistance: Mark Regardsoe
Production: Jeanette Graham